Childism

CHILDISM

Confronting Prejudice
Against Children

Elisabeth Young-Bruehl

Yale
UNIVERSITY PRESS

New Haven and London

Yale University Press books may be purchased in quantity for educational,
business, or promotional use. For information, please e-mail sales.press@yale
.edu (U.S. office) or sales@yaleup.co.uk (U.K. office).

Set in Fairfield Medium Roman type by Integrated Publishing Solutions,
Grand Rapids, Michigan.
Printed in the United States of America.

Library of Congress Cataloging-in-Publication Data
Young-Bruehl, Elisabeth.
    Childism : confronting prejudice against children / Elisabeth Young-Bruehl.
        p. cm.
    Includes bibliographical references and index.
    ISBN 978-0-300-17311-6 (alk. paper)
    1. Children.   2. Age discrimination.   I. Title.
HQ767.9.Y667 2011
305.23—dc23   2011028318

A catalogue record for this book is available from the British Library.

This paper meets the requirements of ANSI/NISO Z39.48-1992 (Permanence
of Paper).

10   9   8   7   6   5   4   3   2   1

For Ava, Daphne, and Walt, the under-fives in our family, and their contemporaries everywhere; may we all act in their best interests, and may they, in turn, being well cared for, act in the best interests of the world they share

Contents

Childism

Introduction
What's in a Word?

THERE WILL ALWAYS BE INDIVIDUALS AND SOCIETIES that turn against their children, breaking the natural order Aristotle described two and half millennia ago in his *Nicomachean Ethics* (8.11.2): "The parent gives the child the greatest gifts, its existence, but also cherishment and education [*kai trophes kai paideias*]; . . . and because the child receives, it owes the parent honor and helpfulness." People as individuals and in societies mistreat children in order to fulfill certain needs through them, to project internal conflicts and self-hatreds outward, or to assert themselves when they feel their authority has been questioned. But regardless of their individual motivations, they all rely upon a societal prejudice against children to justify themselves and legitimate their behavior.

We are accustomed to thinking in terms of prejudice against women, against people of color, against other groups that are "targets of prejudice," as we call them, in Western society, and we accept the idea that struggles against sexism and racism have been going on since the eighteenth century and will have to keep going on if these prejudices are ever to be overcome. But prejudice against children? Who even acknowledges its existence?

Let me give you an example of American society's prejudice against children—the subject of this book—and ask you to think about it. The example is a fact, a shameful fact: America incarcerates more of its children than any country in the world. Half a million American children are currently in juvenile detention centers (juvies), where many of them are victims of abuse and neglect, as many of them were victims of abuse and neglect before they arrived. Some of the "delinquents" are there because they were arrested for a crime and are awaiting trial. They will be tried in courts that are permitted to sentence children convicted of homicide to life *without parole* in adult prisons. Until a recent Supreme Court decision, the courts could have sentenced them to death. Others were incarcerated without arrest: they were simply found on the streets, sometimes homeless, sometimes mentally ill, and judged to be out of control and dangerous "to themselves and others." No one knew what else to do with them.

America also incarcerates a higher proportion of its adult population than any other country in the world—a fact that is directly related to the one about child incarceration. Many children who have spent years of their lives in and out of juvie will join the adult prison population, which has increased sevenfold since 1970, and has now reached over two million inmates. Prison-building is one of the nation's fastest-growing industries.

Although a movement is now afoot to do something about the escalating child-incarceration rate, it is not framed as a struggle to overcome prejudice against children. Far from it. In 2010, for example, a Juvenile Justice Department task force recommended that the State of New York support community-based "alternatives-to-detention programs" that might decrease the number of young people who were, in effect, being sentenced to life imprisonment. The governor ignored this recommendation when creating his budget. An editorial in the *New York Times* (Feb. 19, 2010) criticizing the governor summarized the report, emphasizing that "the report also found that judges often sent children to [detention] facilities—often hundreds of miles away from home—because local communities lacked the means to help them with mental problems or family issues. These are costly decisions, both in the emotional toll they take on children and the financial toll they take on taxpayers. To institutionalize one child for a single year, the state can spend as much as $200,000."

The *Times* was certainly right to stress that means should be found to support local therapeutic programs and prevent the "costly decisions" being made by judges. But what about the motive and rationale for building those detention homes in the first place? Why was it ever considered a good idea to put a child in a prisonlike facility? Why was it not considered abusive to imprison a child? And wouldn't the effect of such abuse take more than an "emotional toll" on the child? Yet the United States tolerated and even encouraged such policies toward children even as the rest of the world—192 countries—ratified the 1989 U.N. Convention on the Rights of the Child, in which child imprisonment is forbidden. (Somalia, which has not had a legitimate government since 1989, is the only other country that hasn't signed.)

It is the questions about adult motives and justifications that were *not* raised by the *Times* that point to American society's prejudice against children: in this case, the idea that troubled children and youths should be removed from sight. The beliefs that children are dangerous and burdensome to society and that childhood is a time when discipline is the paramount adult responsibility reflect this prejudice. A view is anti-child that considers adult authority over children absolute, to the point of life and death. But we have no generally accepted term for such a prejudice, nothing comparable to *racism,* another societal prejudice, and one that helps explain why African Americans, particularly young males, make up a disproportionate percentage of the population of juvenile detention centers and adult prisons.

My first task in this book, then, is to make that word, the term whose definition is "prejudice against children," a part of our vocabulary and to provide a nuanced, comprehensive definition of it. My aim is to enable us, Americans and others, to move beyond editorializing over how much the care for "antisocial" children costs, and to start thinking about the huge range of anti-child social policies and individual behaviors directed against all children daily. The word I propose is *childism,* and its definition is the subject of this book.

I anticipate your skepticism: why do we need another word, another "ism"? The initial task for anyone who wishes to make *childism* part of our lexicon is to take your doubts seriously. We do not need more useless social science verbiage. Nor do we need to identify new social problems; we have plenty already. So a definition of childism must also anticipate a reaction against the very idea of prejudice against children. That reaction was the standard response when the word *childism* was coined in 1970. Isn't it obvious, skeptics argued then, that adults love their children and want to make the world better for them? Even if they come up with mistaken policies for dealing with children, adults are not *against children.* Not children *as a group.*

When childism pervades a society, however, even people who genuinely want to make the world better for children may find it hard to realize that it exists. Many in the eighteenth century found the idea difficult to imagine when the word *misopedia*, "hatred of children," was coined (on the model of other Greek-derived group-hatred words—*misanthropy, misandry, misogyny*—most of which are still used). *Misopedia* fell out of use in the nineteenth century, even though writers like Charles Dickens were describing in graphic terms the persecution suffered by real-life Oliver Twists and David Copperfields throughout Britain. There was no need for *misopedia,* harrumphed skeptics, in a world that was becoming ever more child-centered. To the nineteenth-century social reformers engaged in "child-saving" through the Society for the Prevention of Cruelty to Children, only bad children were to be hated—and deservedly so. Good children were the adored and treasured possessions of good, loving adults.

But as Dickens knew, there was a flaw in the arguments of the child-savers: children were being seen as possessions that served adult needs the way gadgets and animals do, the way slaves and servants do, the way any group construed as "naturally" subservient does. Treating a child as a possession was not philopedic. In today's society, the word *childism* might do what *misopedia* could not: highlight the fact that prejudice is built into the very way children are imagined. Unlike *misopedia, childism* does not reference the older "mis-" words of group *hate*; rather, it invokes contemporary words for prejudices—*racism, anti-Semitism, sexism*—each of which refers specifically to the idea of treating a group of people as a possession and *legitimating* their servitude with an idea, an "ism." People do not always hate those they subordinate; but those they subordinate with an "ism," a prejudicial *political* ideology, they cannot love.

But childism differs crucially from other ism prejudices named in the late nineteenth and early twentieth centuries because, although many features of the phenomenon have been explored, it has not been studied thoroughly *as a prejudice.* The word is not in our political discourse or our dictionaries, and no subfield of Prejudice Studies has been dedicated to childism. Nor is there a discipline dedicated to childism within the relatively new field of Children's Studies, which dates only from 1990. But such a focus could guide experts' explorations of how and why adults fail to meet children's needs or respect their rights; why children deemed antisocial are imprisoned (and how such designations are determined); why children remain in poverty; why adults feel justified in attacking children; and, in general, why American society fails to support the development and well-being of its children. Because we do not look for an underlying social cause when adults fail to cherish their children or meet their developmental needs, little effort has been made to combat what I argue is a prejudice that rationalizes and legitimates the maltreatment of children.

Since the mid-twentieth century, social scientists have been exploring the many reasons why individual adults harm individual children, but they have not looked at the wider picture of how harm to children is rationalized, normalized. Prejudice against children is not the sole or the immediate cause of child maltreatment, but it is the conditio sine qua non, and we need to understand its various features if we wish to uncover the specific causes of maltreatment in any given instance.

Why have we refused to recognize prejudice against children as a prejudice; why have we refused to name that prejudice as we have named other prejudices—racism, sexism, ageism? Consider the word *sexism,* which dates from 1965. Its usage enabled us to understand many phenomena— sexual harassment, unequal pay for women, gender-biased language, patriarchal property and divorce codes, pseudoscientific conclusions about femaleness, domestic violence, sexual trafficking—as manifestations of a way of imagining or stereotyping women in order to justify treating them differently from men. These phenomena are all behaviors or institutions that work against women, and all have been justified as acceptable or normal or natural by sexism—that is, by attitudes and belief systems that are prejudiced against women.

The word *childism* could similarly guide us to an understanding of various behaviors and acts against children as instances of stereotyping children and childhood. We could recognize the many social and political arrangements that are detrimental to children or that fail to meet their needs—the many anti-child trends in every aspect of our society, from legal structures to cultural productions—as instances of adult behavior toward children that is rationalized or justified by a prejudice. *Childism* could help identify as related issues child imprisonment, child exploitation and abuse, substandard schooling, high infant mortality rates, fetal alcohol syndrome, the reckless prescription of antipsychotic drugs to children, child pornography, and all other behaviors or policies that are not in the best interests of children. The behavior of adults who are childist—most of whom are *parents*—harms directly or indirectly the huge human population under the age of eighteen, which is now close to a third of the population worldwide, and in some places more than half.

At the end of the nineteenth century, the word *racism* began to replace *racialism* and *colorism*. It came into use after the Emancipation Proclamation, after the Civil War, and after the Fourteenth and Fifteenth Amendments to the Constitution had enfranchised former slaves. While a political victory had been won, many African Americans recognized and decried the racism that remained, deeply entrenched, in the social and political life of the nation. It remains still. *Sexism,* too, appeared at a moment when women whose grandmothers had won the right to vote in the United States and in other nations were struggling to find the promised equality in private as well as public life. They realized that they were up against something—or something was up against them—for which they did not have a name. Something more complex than "misogyny" was relegating them to the position of "the second sex." The existing understanding of prejudice against women, they realized, was neither comprehensive nor psychologically deep; it lacked a philosophical *Kritik,* or questioning of premises, and thus had in many ways misconceptualized the phenomenon. These women's courageous rethinking of the prejudice against their sex led to Women's Studies programs and Second Wave feminist theorizing, and these, in turn, led to efforts to combat this prejudice that spread to include every realm of culture and every region of the world. These efforts continue today.

I am not proposing that we adopt the word *childism* in order to launch an inquiry into prejudice against children. In diverse areas of science and social science, social policy, and child advocacy that inquiry already exists, without the word, or with out-of-focus words like *anti-youth racism, juvenile ageism, ephebophobia* (fear of adolescents), and *adultism* (indicating a prejudice in favor of adults). But the inquiry into prejudice against children—and these terms for it—have spurred no political consciousness and had no political meaning. What is needed now is a term that will have political resonance, something that can operate as *sexism* did to raise our political consciousness. To help those who have been pursuing inquiries into anti-child behavior formulate, unify, and report the results of their studies, *childism* can act as an umbrella concept, a heuristic, and a synthesizer, and it can function as a guide for political action. It can help researchers connect a lot of dots.

Just as important, acceptance of childism as both a word and a social reality could help us correct existing ill-conceived inquiries and misunderstandings. The matter is urgent, for on the basis of misguided and rigid theories we have put in place institutions and policies that harm children—that are, themselves, manifestations of childism. The legal phrase "in the best interests of children" has given guidance in the courts; it is now being applied to work for reform in policies affecting children, including child-imprisonment policies. But we need a word that applies across all facets of children's lives, that reflects their experiences and what they themselves know about prejudice.

The moment is overdue for adults to rethink and reform their attitudes toward children. Giving children the vote, or encouraging them to take part in the political process, both avenues for combating prejudice against women and persons of color, will not work for children. A brief, wrong-headed, adult-led "children's liberation movement" in the early 1970s did try to position children as political actors—even as voters with voting rights. But this was sheer patronization and quickly became part of the problem of childism, not part of its solution. Unlike any other group that has been targeted with prejudice, children cannot be direct political actors, although they should be educated to become political actors, thinking and acting for themselves, individually and in concert. But while children are learning to become political participants, adults need to consult them about their needs and to represent them in the political arena.

A beginning has already been made. Two remarkable U.N. documents, drafted by adults, acknowledge that children have basic human and political rights. The first, the Declaration on the Rights of the Child, published in 1959, was reinforced in 1989 by the second, the Convention on the Rights of the Child, which was the result of thirty years of scientific and political explorations into how best to implement and enforce the Declaration. Not coincidentally, over those thirty years a reliable science of child development emerged for the first time in history. Child Development as a field can reinforce the international political work of adults who are determined to create a better world for *all* children.

The Declaration begins with the forthright announcement that children have rights and that adults and governments have obligations to children. And it implies that those who have not met their obligations to children have justified their actions on the basis of a prejudice against children—first and foremost by their prejudicial assumption that children are possessions of adults and thus do *not* have rights. The Convention, building on these statements, lays out the kinds of obligations that adults have toward children, as well as the areas where they have failed to meet those obligations. The Preamble affirms both that children are "entitled to special care and assistance" and that what is "in the best interests of the child" should be a primary consideration in all questions concerning them. Its fifty-four articles promise what U.N. educational guides for young people call the 3 Ps: Provision, Protection, and Participation.

The signatory nations—more than have ever signed a U.N. convention—committed themselves to developing programs in these "3 Ps" and reporting their progress biannually to an international oversight committee and to UNICEF. Their common goals are reducing and eventually ending child poverty and providing every child with the means and education to develop healthily and freely; protecting children from exploitation, abuse, and neglect; and promoting children's participation in familial and communal life "to the extent of their evolving abilities." The promise of the third P, participation, is truly revolutionary. And it has provoked enormous counterrevolutionary opposition, especially from adults who believe that children belong to their families, their governments, or religious institutions or corporations that act as proxies for families or governments.

The U.N. documents, though crucial first steps, are only the opening statements in a conversation that must be ongoing and that needs to address questions that neither the Declaration nor the Convention was designed to raise, for it is the answers to these questions that will help us understand what keeps parents and governments from fulfilling their acknowledged obligations to their children. We need now to turn to what motivates childism in individuals and groups and what conditions most foster, or hinder, childism in societies. We must seek the underlying motive that helps explain why many adults do deny that children have rights; why they refuse to provision, protect, or encourage the participation of their children in family and community affairs; and why they discriminate against their young—the future of their societies—in order to favor not just themselves but adults generally.

It is important to recognize that the answers to these questions will not uncover the specific cause of any individual case of child abuse, but they will help us understand what the abusing adult believed and how he or she justified the abuse. Until recently researchers in various disciplines have explored specific motivations and legitimating motivations without attempting to distinguish between the two, and this has meant that their efforts lack a coherent vision; they have not been systematized or summarized. Without such a vision, it has been difficult for researchers to present the results of their work in a way that has theoretical, practical, or educational value. But first steps toward such a vision have been taken by the Swedes, for example, who spearheaded the U.N. Global Initiative to End All Corporal Punishment of Children, based on achievements in their own country, where corporal punishment was made illegal in 1969. Swedish researchers have investigated the beneficial effects of their law and the parent-education campaign that accompanied it. Both parenting practices and parental attitudes toward children have radically improved in Sweden. But this is a rare case in which researchers both investigated the issue as a societal problem, rather than an individual one, and considered the problem from the point of view of the children.

How might we go about listening to the victims of childism as researchers looking into racism, sexism, and homophobia learned to listen to the victims of those prejudices—including themselves? By consulting children and considering their viewpoints, we can help them understand their own experiences and prepare them to participate in the struggle against childism and other prejudices. One approach is the psychoanalytic method that I use in my own practice: listening to patients tell their childhood stories in a consulting room. Combined with the science of Child Development, this methodology can help illuminate the basic forms childism takes and how those forms manifest themselves in childist actions, policies, and institutions.

The psychoanalytic tradition has contributed the key reflection on how to listen to children and theorize for their social benefit on the basis of what they say. My touchstone text is a trilogy collected under the title *In the Best Interests of the Child,* which the child psychoanalyst Anna Freud began to publish in the 1970s with her colleagues Albert Solnit of the Yale Child Study Center and Joseph Goldstein of the Yale Law School. The audience for their work was the legal profession—particularly judges in family courts—but their insights into how to see children's issues from a child's viewpoint can be applied more broadly.

In the Best Interests of the Child has had a dramatic effect on American legal work involving children and children's rights. Following several key progressive Supreme Court decisions, it helped spur the field of Child Advocacy. Yet despite these advances, since the 1970s childism has grown more intense in other arenas in America, with disastrous consequences for American children. In this book I examine that forty-year-long story as itself a case study: a case study in American childism.

By examining this period of American history as a case study, we can explore at a societal and political level the reasons behind the increase (and occasional decrease) in childist attitudes and policies. This is something that children themselves cannot usually tell us about; their insight is at the micro-level of their families and their individual experiences. Our task is to apply theoretical concepts, analysis, and history to their insights in order to broaden our inquiry to the macro-level of social attitudes, legislation, and policy. For this, we need to examine their parents, who were and are at the center of the case study. This generation of parents—my own generation, the post–World War II Baby Boomers, now in their sixties—became in the 1970s deeply conflicted in relation to their children, as well as to the future more generally, with progressive and regressive tendencies waging a constant battle. The widely used phrase "culture wars" hardly does justice to the confusion and malaise that have permeated America from those years forward.

Many of this generation came to adulthood as vocal opponents of contemporary forms of racism and sexism, and they devoted vast energy to improving the study, discussion, and policies directed at both those prejudices, with varying degrees of success and subject to varying degrees of backlash. But most of them ignored the childism that surrounded their own children, born in the 1970s, and that sometimes pervaded their own homes. Further, over time the majority of this generation (including both conservatives and liberals) became, for complex reasons, childist. The clearest sign of this was the widespread acquiescence in policies that required future generations to shoulder responsibility for present prosperity and present endeavors; that gave less attention to supporting healthy child development than to U.S. political dominance and economic growth. The young have been saddled with a world filled with violence, riddled with economic inequality, and endangered by a disastrous lack of environmental oversight; they must assume a gigantic burden of peacekeeping, legislating fairness, and halting environmental degradation.

Even as their children's future was being mortgaged, some in the Baby Boomer generation were fighting to protect it, forming child-advocacy organizations like the Children's Defense Fund (CDF). Since the 1970s, the CDF has kept statistics on the harm being done America's children. Consider the chilling numbers in the 2009 summary report that preceded the present economic crisis:

> Today, 14.1 million children in America, or 1 in 5, are poor, the majority living in working families. . . . Almost 900,000 children each year in America are abused or neglected, one every 36 seconds. Forty percent of these children get no services at all after the initial investigation. Each year, more than 800,000 children spend time in foster care. . . . On any given night, 200,000 children are homeless. . . . Using the most recent data from the Centers for Disease Control and Prevention [it can be reported that] 3,184 children and teens were killed by firearms in 2006, a 6 percent increase from

the previous year. . . . The U.S. has the sixth lowest high school graduation rate among the 30 industrialized countries that are OECD members.

But the child advocates, supporters of the 1960s Great Society initiatives to help children, could not stop or even slow the anti-child trend that began during Richard Nixon's presidency, was normalized during the Reagan years, continued during the Clinton years, and escalated dramatically during the George W. Bush administration. So strong has been the anti-child trend that every U.S. Congress since 1989 has refused to ratify the U.N. Convention on the Rights of the Child, the international community's pioneering effort to hold adults accountable for the well-being of their young.

In this American story, the first group of victims—children denigrated as they reached adolescence with the title Generation X—were cast by childist policy decisions into increasingly unequal groups: the well off and the poor, the abused and the not-abused. Such divisions, especially the less well-known one between those who were abused and those who were not, made it almost impossible for policy makers and the general public to recognize the diverse motives of child maltreatment. It also practically closed off any consideration of what maltreatment feels like to children, who experience it as running on a continuum from they-love-me to they-love-me-not. From the children's point of view, it is their parents' and caretakers' *attitudes* toward them that matter most. When childism is prevalent in a society *all* children are hurt, not just those classified as "the abused."

Both these groupings had terrible effects on children as well as on the understanding of children (including inquiry into childism). Many within the growing ranks of child advocates, teachers, family lawyers, and pediatricians who cared for children outside their homes could see these ill effects accumulating. And since the early 1970s, they have studied some American children as victims of "child abuse and neglect," and they have made efforts to protect this group. These children—"the abused"—became the concern of a new field of study, Child Abuse and Neglect (CAN), which emerged at this time. But abused and neglected children have been ill served by the way they were classified, studied, and interpreted historically, and by the influence such studies have had on legislation, policies, and programs, including child-protective services. Although analysts, who work with children psychotherapeutically, have begun to recognize not only that childism exists but that the keys to understanding and preventing it might lie in the knowledge children have of the motivations and circumstances of adults—if you want to know about sexism, ask a woman; if you want to know about childism, ask a child who has been granted a safe and supportive setting in which to talk—most child advocates have focused narrowly and wrongly on protecting individual children from child abuse. This focus narrows the idea of children's basic rights to simply Protection and so does little or nothing to help the nation's children as a group. Indeed, by every measure of Provision, Protection, and Participation promised in the 1989 Convention on the Rights of the Child, the condition of America's children as a group has deteriorated over the past forty years, particularly among the poor and the abused. On UNICEF's measures of child well-being, recent reports rank the United States lowest among first-world nations. America has the highest rates of child abuse in the world.

The situation is not likely to improve as America deals with a new economic crisis. Further escalation in childism is likely unless the new leadership generation acknowledges that prejudice against children is a social reality as well as a feature of individual psychology and pathology. This new generation includes women and men who were inspired by the many nonviolent youth-led revolutions that have taken place around the world since the Berlin Wall was pulled down and the Soviet Union collapsed. The revolutionary young are now of an age to recognize that they have participation rights (and have always had those rights), and that only participation will help them prepare to exercise their rights as citizens.

The new leadership generation must be able to grasp the meaning of these post-1989 revolutions as well as heed the hopes for a new beginning that are coming from their own children and their children's advocates. Around the world, the young themselves are speaking up. They see the connection between political oppression and their hopes for the future. They see the connection between their own endangered future and that of the planet we all live on.

This book is intended as a working paper for all who are fighting the oppression of children, both those who recognize it as a result of prejudice and those who don't. It is my hope that through conceptual analysis, philology, history, literary analysis, political theory, and psychoanalytically informed therapy it can offer a manifesto on why we must—and how we can—combat this newest ism. The struggle against childism is one of the most important battles we will ever wage, for it is a fight for the future.

CHAPTER ONE

Anatomy of a Prejudice

IT SEEMS A VERY SIMPLE MATTER INTELLECTUALLY TO distinguish between acts that harm children or fail to meet their basic needs and the attitudes, ideas, or prejudices that rationalize such acts. Yet child-advocacy groups, Children's Studies, and the field of Child Abuse and Neglect (CAN) alike focus almost exclusively on the harmful actions, ignoring the even more harmful attitudes. Similarly, the lessons learned from studies of other victim groups that have helped analyze previously unacknowledged victim groups (as the racism model helped researchers understand sexism) have not been applied to children; the scientific field where these studies are gathered—today called Prejudice Studies—has no sub-field for children or the prejudice against them that can be named childism.

But we cannot understand the acts that harm children unless we understand the prejudices that underlie and, in the actors' minds, legitimate them. Before we turn to cases of children who have been the victims of harmful acts and rationalizing prejudice, then, we need to explore why Prejudice Studies, the home of research into racism, sexism, anti-

Semitism, and other isms, has no room in its house for childism. Many factors are involved, but key among them is the way childism differs from other prejudices.

Modern Prejudice Studies began after World War II as a field in which white people analyzed prejudice against blacks and men analyzed discrimination against women, marginalizing the voices of the victims. It evolved into a discipline in which the victims told their own stories, analyzed their own experiences, and created their own names to help them understand those experiences: racism, sexism, homophobia. Child advocates, working to protect children and formulate policies that protect children's rights, have not joined their work or children's voices to Prejudice Studies. Children and their advocates have not had the concept of childism to coordinate their thinking with the approaches developed within Prejudice Studies.

A key realization to understanding childism has been missing: the idea that children worldwide are a *target group*. A target group is one whose members share characteristics and conditions that those prejudiced against them seize on and distort for their own purposes. As a target group, children are comparable to women and people of color, to Jews and gays; but their group contains all the other target groups: young women and girls, children of color, Jewish children, gay children and the children of gays. Children have in common that they are all born dependent and relatively helpless. After birth they experience a period of developmental immaturity, to which different cultures assign different physical or biological and mental descriptions and phases, and to which different cultures give different endpoints (often puberty, when the children become sexually mature or capable of producing their own offspring).

But beyond these shared features, the biological group

comprising children is also subject to social, cultural, and political construction, evaluation, and distortion—the same kind of conceptualizing that Prejudice Studies identifies as central to the creation of every other target group. On a continuum, children are valued and loved at one extreme or they are not valued and not loved at the other. They are wanted or not wanted, adored or rejected, protected and provisioned or forced to fend for themselves. They are treated violently or wrapped in cotton wool. They are provided with the finest education available or allowed, even encouraged to become truants. Overall the continuum runs from love and nurturing all the way to negligence, hostility, and what has become classified as child abuse and neglect. Prejudice overtly rationalizes or justifies the behaviors at the negative end of the continuum, but it can subtly suffuse the positive behaviors as well, revealing their ambivalence or making them ambivalent.

The prevailing images or stereotypes of children that individual adults and societies use to rationalize their feelings toward them are, taken together, their childism. Consider the following sentiments, which are probably uttered every day without thought in the United States: "Kids are just wild unless you keep them in line, and that includes hitting them"; "If you don't smack them, they don't get tamed"; and the time-honored "Spare the rod and spoil the child." These viewpoints are childist: they construct children as wild animals that should be physically controlled—they must be broken or they will not be obedient, useful possessions. The parent who hits a child in order to protect it from danger—to teach the child not to run into the road, for example, is doing something very different from the one who disciplines the child in order to break him or her; this discipline is rather a violent contest of wills, resembling the discipline that used to be thought necessary for animal trainers or cowboys but is now recognized as brutality.

That prejudices operate by making a distinction between features a group actually shares and those that are attributed to it is by now common wisdom, and that understanding has made its way into contemporary dictionary definitions of the various prejudices, which are distillates of common wisdom. But dictionary definitions also reveal an area that has not been properly explored in Prejudice Studies—the various motivations of victimizers. Prejudice Studies has tended to treat all prejudiced people as having similar motivations, which are simply focused on different targets. This bias has made it difficult to look beneath the surface of a prejudice, the cliché level, into its motivational depths, where the negative and distorting evaluations originating in fantasies of target groups are rooted.

To come up with a working definition of childism that can point the way to an understanding of the origin and ongoing motivations of the prejudice, we need to look at how typical current definitions of prejudice avoid the territory of motivation in the same way that the field of Prejudice Studies generally does. Dictionary definitions routinely identify a target group and then gesture toward the grounds on which the target group has been *prejudged* (*prejudice* comes from the Latin *praejudicium,* "prejudgment"). But as the definitions approach the grounds of the prejudice, they often become circular, closing the door to deeper thinking with a cliché. For example, the *Oxford English Dictionary* (*OED*) defines *sexism* as "prejudice or discrimination, esp. against women, on the grounds of sex." There is a wall of incomprehension and resistance in that "on the grounds of sex." And it is just the wall that people hit when they try to analyze their own prejudices, which they cannot see because they are looking at their prejudices through the lens of their prejudices. Prejudices are inherently self-justifying.

We can push against the wall by agreeing that, yes, a prejudice is a classification dividing people into groups and stereotyping them "on the grounds of" some feature—but that "on the grounds of" must be explored. It is the road leading to the classifier's habits of thinking, speaking, and behaving that favor some people (and the traits and activities attributed to them) and condemn others. In the *OED*'s definition "on the grounds of sex" is really just a way of saying "on the grounds of their being women/men." But if the definition read "on the grounds of *beliefs about the sexual differences and inequalities of people,* esp. females," it would point readers in the direction of considering what purposes the prejudice sexism might serve.

Dictionary definitions of prejudices become circular when they build the prejudice they are defining into the definition. Nonetheless, by identifying the target group, they do at least identify the question: What is it that is being targeted about this group? What does the *sex* in "on the grounds of *sex*" refer to? And they do suggest that a prejudice is a belief, not a scientific or objective classification of a group, although prejudices can be presented as if they were science. Prejudices are not motivated by the desire that spurs genuine scientists: a desire to be as open-minded and inclusive as possible. Scientists seek theories that will explain the interrelatedness of all the elements that make up the universe— the whole cosmic ecology, as it were. (*Ecology* once referred to the study or science [*-logia*] of all living beings in their home or habitat [*oikos*], but it now refers also to the interrelatedness itself, the web of things and beings that create and live in the same habitat. The definition itself has opened out.)

By contrast, the narrow-minded purpose of a prejudice is to defend the prejudiced person (or group) by dividing, separating out, disconnecting, or privileging one part of the interrelated whole: one class of beings, one individual, one group. In the group sphere, it separates "we" from "them." Prejudice defends "we" against a "them" that has been marked off as separate, other, not of the same family or ecosystem. Consider a cliché which is often used to explain sexism but which is itself an example of sexism: "Men are from Mars, women are from Venus." Men and women are not of the same family; "where they are coming from" is different, and difference is destiny. This is like the older cliché "anatomy is destiny"—men and women have different futures based on their anatomical differences.

Prejudging subverts the frame of mind—the commitment to openness—in which scientific judging takes place, in which knowledge is a process, constantly subject to revision in the light of new knowledge. The development of knowledge is the basis of scientific judgment. When that development is disrupted by prejudices, the result is corrupt classifications, which fall short of the holistic, impartial developmental ideal. That ideal is hard enough to approach under the best circumstances because all searches are influenced by the subjectivity, partiality, and limitation of viewpoint and view of the searcher. But scientific minds are parts striving to investigate the whole of which they are parts. A mind, as Friedrich Nietzsche once observed when considering the place of science among the ancient Greeks, is "a microcosm swelling up to the macrocosm."

Absence of defensiveness, too, is a scientific ideal that is never fully attainable. Prejudice corrupts understanding through a combination of partiality and defensiveness by setting up a hierarchy or a hierarchical binary "on the grounds of X." A prejudgment that one class of beings is privileged over another extends to the idea that the class is superior, and fit to rule or dominate over another (or even dominate over the whole ecology). The hierarchy asserted in childism is obvious: adults should rule over children; adults' needs should be privileged over children's needs. But "on the grounds of what" is not as obvious.

The European scientific tradition began with the works of Aristotle, and we can put the "on grounds of what" question to him. In the *Nicomachean Ethics,* where he described the nurturing love and education (*kai trophes kai paideias*) a parent owes a child, Aristotle set out to define, as inclusively as possible, what *all* human beings have in common. Humans share a common desire to live together in a city-state (a *polis*), he noted, and to be happy (in a state of *eudaemonia,* "inner harmony"), while practicing virtue. Acknowledging that there are different human character types, each with a different guiding notion of how happiness is to be pursued and attained, Aristotle nonetheless kept in view as he classified the character types the unifying notion that all humans seek happiness and harmony, within themselves and in their relations with others.

A claim might have followed from this framework that all human beings are born *equally* desiring happiness in their relations with others—the philosophical assumption that began to appear consistently in post–World War II studies of children by child developmentalists and clinicians. But no such claim was made by Aristotle, whose excellent definition of the natural relation of children and parents is actually set in a childist frame. Aristotle first privileged one of his three character types, the contemplative man, over the other two (moralists and materialistic hedonists/proprietors), and then privileged one class of human beings, free male citizens of the polis, over everyone else, including all women and children. Contemplative men were, asserted Aristotle, the most evolved in the spheres of character and political action.

So the classification, it turns out, was not universal: it did not include *all* men or women or children as those who were born seeking happiness. Slaves fell outside of the classification altogether, on the grounds that they were not free men or citizens. Stateless slaves were property. And women also fell outside of the classification on the grounds that they were inferior humans—colder, weaker, fitted primarily for bearing children, and lacking the reason possessed by citizens that could be exercised when they were acting within city-states. Women have virtues, said Aristotle, but not the higher, male virtues. Although he could eloquently describe a child's need for cherishing and education and a parent's natural responsibility to give that nurturing, children as such—and this is to the point of how to define *childism*—were omitted from Aristotle's characterology. This is because he thought of children politically as belonging to their male parent, just as slaves belonged to their masters, and he thought of them developmentally as similar to childbearing women, that is, without the reason needed to guide their search for happiness. Boys might become rational at age seven or so; girls never would.

Aristotle's assumptions about children—that they are possessions and lack reasoning ability—are childist. Nonetheless, they fit well with the common assumptions of the Greeks, and they were easily built into the European tradition after Aristotle, where they continued to intertwine with sexism and justifications of slavery (which eventually became racist). The idea that children are by nature meant to be owned by their male parent and that they lack reason has justified treating them like slaves and like immature, unformed persons without the active qualities, the developmental thrust, the proto-reasoning and choosing, and the individuality that contemporary developmentalists now recognize in them. These are the same qualities that the framers of the U.N. Convention on the Rights of the Child saw in children when they included participation rights in accord with their evolving abilities as one of the 3 Ps.

The need that limits Aristotle's worldview is a desire for control and domination. Children are born wild and undomesticated and must be controlled, and women, as unreasoning beings, are not able to do this controlling. Women have wombs where children gestate, and they keep the households in which children continue to grow, but in those households men should be in charge of the male children's domestication, just as male citizens will later be in charge of their education. Not surprisingly, Aristotle also subscribed to a biological theory common among the Greeks that the conception of a child occurs when a male implants in a female's womb a seed, a *sperma,* that grows there for nine months. No ovum from the female is involved; she simply houses the tiny seed-being while it grows. A woman is like the soil in which an acorn grows to be an oak sapling.

The Greek theory of conception as a male act was eventually abandoned in the Western world. But the desire informing theories that deny the female contribution to reproduction, which is a desire to see men as responsible for reproduction, as well as for the cultivation or domestication of *their* seed, remains current in some quarters. It is still key to the prejudice sexism, as it is still involved in childism; and it also helps keep sexism and childism intertwined.

The desire behind the childist and sexist Greek theory of conception is not ancient history. The theory it underpins has been superseded, but the wish has not been abandoned.

You can see that desire at work now, for example, in the arguments of anti-abortionists, who claim that child ownership begins at the moment a sperm fertilizes an egg and there is "life" (a vague, polemical word in this context). Anti-abortionists insist, further, that decisions about the fertilized egg be made not by the women who gestate the child and give birth to it but by those who control the definition of *life*. In America today, a woman who judges that she physically cannot, or lacks the resources or feelings to, nurture a child she is carrying will find herself accused of being a child abuser. On roadsides all over the country and outside every abortion clinic, billboards and placards condemn "unborn child abuse."

When anti-abortionists make their highly charged accusation that abortion is unborn child abuse, they are constructing themselves as the child-savers, and a mother who chooses not to carry a child to term as the child abuser or murderer, party to a physician-assisted infanticide. They seek to legislate who controls reproduction, who owns the unborn child, who defines *life,* and who defines *abuse.* They present the anti-abortion position as the only one that puts the welfare of the child first, that makes the best interests of the (unborn) child primary. But this assumes that "the best interests of the child" encompass nothing more than life—regardless of what sort of life it will be, or with whom, or how its life is viewed by the mother, without whom the unborn child cannot gestate. A conflict is set up between the anti-abortionists' ownership claim to the unborn child and the claim that they try to impose on the mother: to be or not to be a child murderer.

I am not talking here about the ethics of abortion, only about how prejudice has dictated the public terms into which the abortion debate has become confined, so that the ethical issues are obscured in a power struggle. From this angle, what the abortion debate shows is what happens when two parties or two institutions both claim ownership of the child and the right to impose their idea of "the best interests of the child." It becomes nearly impossible to talk about the best interests of the child outside of the conflicting ownership claims. The idea that has disappeared from view in the current abortion debate is that there would be little need for abortions—which neither anti-abortionists nor pro-choice advocates wish to see become more common—in a society in which sex education and safe contraception were freely available, enabling both women and men to refrain from conceiving children they do not want and cannot provide for—children whose irreducible needs they cannot meet. Similarly, in a society not racked by claims and counter-claims regarding who controls reproduction, mature, careful (including medically careful) decisions could be made by the mother about the welfare of her child not because she owns the child but because the child cannot live or thrive without her and her body. In a freethinking society, this mother would not be judged by sexist standards and the child would not be subjugated by a childist ideology that insists "we [including non-kin adults] control reproduction," "we own the child."

These reflections on Aristotle's classification or pre-judgment habits and his views of women as not-parents and children as lacking reason, which still reverberate, can send us back to the dictionary method of identifying a target group. The *Oxford English Dictionary*'s definition of sexism as "prejudice or discrimination, esp. against women, on the grounds of sex" does point readers to the victim group, women, but not specifically to a belief or to the question of what it is about *sex* that supplies the ground for the prejudice. For many readers, the vague phrase "on the grounds of sex" will evoke the visible anatomical differences that more or less mark women off from men in appearance and biological function. But anatomical differences do not explain the desire to control reproduction and its product, children, which becomes manifest if you look into the sexist theories themselves, ancient and modern. Nor does "on the grounds of sex" leave a path open for exploring the fear or envy of females, and specifically of female sexual activity and reproductive capacity, that sexist theories and beliefs might reflect. How does a sexist come to behave defensively toward women, to say, in effect, "You are a female, therefore you must . . . " and to believe that he is owed obedience: "You must stay away from public spaces (remain 'in a separate sphere' of the household or private realm, where you can be controlled)"; "You must do this (laboring or reproductive) task and not others"; "You must play that sexual role, live under these conditions, assume that identity"—even "die that death."

Just as many people think that sexism is about observable anatomical differences and biological functions rather than about justifying the assertion of control—physically, legislatively, medically, or in some other way—over women's sexuality and reproductive activity, many believe that racism targets certain groups on the grounds of external appearances: skin color, shape of face, shape and color of eyes, body type, and so forth. Appearances certainly mattered to the eighteenth-century European ethnographers who divided the world's peoples into three "biologically separate" families or races: Caucasian, Negroid, and Mongoloid. But their classification, which had no more scientific validity than did the fifth-century B.C.E. Greek theory of reproduction, was not ultimately about appearances. They were concerned to identify who counted as family and who ruled within a family. Racism, according to the *OED*, is "a *belief* [italics added] in the superiority of a particular race," and "antagonism toward other races on the grounds of this belief." The definition rightly stresses that racism is a belief system. But it incorrectly accepts the eighteenth-century ethnographers' assumption that the human species is divided into biologically separate races or families. To avoid building racist theory into its definition of *racism*, the dictionary should have defined the term as "a belief that there are biologically separate races and that a particular race is superior to the others."

Racism focuses on the idea that disparate peoples did not descend from a common human ancestor family. Racists usually forbid intermarriage between the biologically different families (calling this miscegenation), and they deny theories like Darwin's that emphasize the common descent of humans. Psychologically, racism is a belief system that allows people of an allegedly "superior" family to fantasize about sex with people safely deemed not-family, not "blood relatives," not incestuous objects. Racists can act on these fantasies as long as they do not *marry* the inferiors or acknowledge the children born of these unions because to do so would break down the not-family, incest-avoiding fantasy as surely as if they had married a monkey. (In the most extreme version of Christian creationism, the white "race" was created when God made Adam from the dust of the earth and then Eve from Adam's rib. Humans did not evolve from earlier life forms; the first humans weren't even the result of sexual intercourse. Some extreme creationists believe that the white "race" should dominate the others on the grounds of its priority. People who contend that this creationist variant should be taught to schoolchildren are racist and sexist and childist all at once.)

Sexism and racism often intertwine. But sexism directed at women of a racially marked out-group (which might be called sexist racism) is more about dictating roles to those "others" and keeping "other" women in their nonfamily places (as mistresses or prostitutes, for example) than is sexism directed at women who are racially the same and may be wives—that is, in the family. Sexism directed toward in-family women is a clear example, a fundamental example, of a form of prejudice that denies the identity of a victim considered one of us.

A sexist, that is, treats in-family women narcissistically, as extensions of the sexist's self, identified in whatever way he needs them to be. As psychoanalysts have pointed out, even while a male sexist consciously accentuates female anatomical or mental differences, he unconsciously needs the women with whom he has sexual relations to be like him, narcissistically mirroring, perhaps phallic, but most crucially sharing the condition (that he will not acknowledge in himself) of being not reproductive in her own right. If she were acknowledged as a reproducer, it would mean that she could have children with any man she had sex with. But her children must be *his*. So the mother must be trained or coerced into submission and into the conviction that she is all about him. And this form of prejudice is something many children experience: they discover that to their parents they are all about their parents. Even though the children are in the family, they are granted no identity of their own: they are considered their father's possessions. (Or their mother's, if she is claiming for herself the prerogatives conventionally claimed by men or by the paterfamilias. Generally, female sexism operates on a different model from the male model described here.)

Few modern Prejudice Studies works on sexism have made it clear that sexism crucially involves beliefs not about sex (a vague noun that can refer to acts, primary or secondary sexual characteristics, chromosomes, and others) but about control over reproduction, and this confusion explains why the dictionary definition is so circular. By contrast, most studies of racists and racist theories have made it clear that racism is a belief system focused on how races deemed inferior have different origins and a different developmental course. The allegedly inferior races have supposedly remained *primitively* "other" in comparison to the superior and civilized. The *childlike* inferior people are held to be naturally fitted for intellectual and sexual subordination and slavery, and this belief reflects the fear that they are sexually animalistic: powerful, wild, and prolific. Racists do focus on the victim's appearance: "You are of that inferior race, looking like that, therefore you must . . ." But the commands racists issue actually reference their deeper beliefs: "Maybe you are human, but you are not of the same family of humans as I am; you are childlike, not adult as I am." So "stay away from our living spaces but in quarters close by so that you can be enslaved to do this task (and not others) for us; play that sexual role in which your power can be harnessed and appropriated; live in these conditions; assume that identity; die that death." The racist is a role dictator, writing a script.

The *OED* defines anti-Semitism—to take a third example—simply as "a prejudice against Jews." The dictionary drafters did not even try (one has to sympathize with them) to summarize the belief system or the grounds for this obsessively convoluted prejudice, involving so much fantasy construction of the target group's characteristics. Perhaps no dictionary could gesture in a phrase at the whole strange history of how the Jews came to be classified in the nineteenth century as "the Semites." The Semites were once a common-ancestor group that included Arabs and other peoples who spoke the languages (the Semitic languages) common to a dozen sibling groups around the Mediterranean. The dictionary simply builds into the definition the result of a long history of constructing one of these groups as "the Jews."

Going circularly, the definition does nothing to signal to a reader that there is a belief system consisting of the fantasized functions and purposes "the Jews" serve for those who are prejudiced against them. Some contemporary studies of the prejudice have struggled to reveal that "the Jews" serve as a target group that can be accused of accumulating resources and money at the expense of other groups, practicing usury, becoming wealthier than others, or eating away secretly at the bowels of a society into which they have been fantasized as boring their way like germs, pollutants, parasites, blood-suckers, vermin, spies, thieves, secret agents (and, more recently, terrorists). "They" are the murderously bad— dirty, diseased, and wily—inside "us."

Anti-Semitism is a prejudice against Jews on the grounds of a belief that they are infiltrating "us" (as an "international Jewish conspiracy," for example). By secrecy, cunning, and the use of devious, calculating, money-oriented intellect, hypocrisy, and disguise, Jewish interlopers have penetrated the institutions of Gentiles and are changing the legal authority (with their agenda of world domination). One of the most obvious features of the commands that modern anti-Semites have issued to "the Jews" is that they must be rounded up (ghettoized) and separated off entirely, for if they were to live near the anti-Semites (as the victims of racism and sexism live near their oppressors) they would drain away the anti-Semites' strength, resources, and legal authority. Jews may have to be *eliminated*; there may have to be a "final solution."

Behind every modern conspiracy theory is a prejudice that takes this basic eliminationist form. One target group after another can be assigned the fantasy role of "the Jews."

Japanese-born American citizens were so characterized during World War II, and therefore they were ghettoized, interned; later, Japanese business interests were so viewed in the 1980s when they bought up American businesses and real estate, and therefore protectionist legislation was developed to contain them. The Jews, too, like every other group, can have their fantasies about being infiltrated. This is, of course, particularly true now that they have a homeland of their own, with borders that can be penetrated by tunnels, rockets, and bombers. They have a society that can be infiltrated by the secret agents of the Arabs, the Palestinians, or the Muslims. "The terrorists" are now everybody's infiltrating Jews.

In 1980s America, a variant of this obsessional, anti-infiltrationist, eliminationist prejudice began to be directed at teenagers. Youths were described as domestic terrorists who carried guns to school, conducted drive-by shootings on a daily basis, dealt drugs, joined terrorist organizations, and generally ran amok. But only among the few adults who speak of "ephebophobia" (fear of youth) does this prejudice even have a name, although one scholar studying today's youth has accurately called them the Scapegoat Generation. The ghetto into which most children said to be thieves or terrorists are being put is the juvenile detention center or prison. In particular, as noted earlier, America is now ghettoizing its young male population, many of them African American, sequestering them in prisons for life. Inside families, children face ghettoization if they are construed as undermining the family, eating up its resources; or they may be rejected by one parent for being the favorite—the chosen one—of the other.

In the three examples given above, a definition can be constructed that identifies the target group and suggests that a prejudice is a belief system, not a knowledge system, about the group. To go where dictionaries are not designed to go—

to explore the grounds of the prejudice—we must look into the details of the belief systems, listening clinically as if to the elements of a dream, or a nightmare. Each system involves images or stereotypes of the targeted groups that, while they usually reference immediately identifiable group-distinguishing appearances, attach more deeply to activities and functions attributed to the group by way of fantasies.

As I have implied, there seem to be three elementary forms of fantasy that feed prejudices, and each is reflected in one of the three prejudice forms of which sexism, racism, and anti-Semitism are representative. In brief, there are fantasies about being able to self-reproduce and to own the self-reproduced offspring, fantasies about being able to have slaves—usually sex slaves—who are not incest objects, and fantasies about being able to eliminate something felt to be invidiously or secretly depleting one from within.

Each of these three prejudice forms is "on the grounds of" beliefs that articulate such fantasies and can lead to commands and actions that fulfill the fantasies by erasing another's identity, by exploiting or manipulating another (particularly sexually), or by physically removing another. Some prejudices consist almost exclusively of one form of fantasy and its corresponding beliefs and actions; others contain elements of all three, such as a prejudice like homophobia. Actions against homosexuals forbid reproduction in homosexual unions, caricature their sexuality while at the same time seeking to exploit it or participate in it, and try to eliminate homosexuals and their invidious secret "agenda" by ghettoizing them or attacking them, even murdering them. I shall argue that childism, too, can involve all three forms of fantasy, belief, and action.

I began my discussion of Prejudice Studies by presenting childism as a prejudice that rationalizes or justifies acts that harm children or fail to meet their basic needs. But at the more fundamental motivational or fantasy level, childism can be defined as a belief system that constructs its target group, "the child," as an immature being produced and owned by adults who use it to serve their own needs and fantasies. It is a belief system that reverses the biological and psychological order of nature, in which adults are responsible for meeting the irreducible needs of children (until the adults grow old and, naturally, reciprocally need support from children). Adults have needs of various kinds—and fantasies about those needs—that childist adults imagine children *could* and, further, *should* serve. The belief that children as children could serve adult needs is a denial that children develop; the belief that children should serve adult needs is a denial of children's developmental needs and rights.

In differing degrees throughout history, children have been fantasized and set in belief systems that require them to serve the needs and fantasies served by allegedly inferior women, allegedly inferior "races," or alleged infiltrator groups. In childism, as in homophobia, all the psychological mechanisms that have been discovered to operate in prejudices on the sexism, racism, and anti-Semitism models can operate. There is an observable, investigable range of attitudes of the anti-Semitic form indicating that "children (and this child) are bad or burdensome, taking our resources, depleting us or corrupting us, and they should be pushed away, placed out, or even eliminated (by quick or slow infanticide)." There is a range of attitudes of the racist form that could be summarized as "children (and this child) are dangerously, wildly sexual and should be repressed or given a pseudo-adult role, used, enslaved, prostituted, trafficked, turned into pornography." A third range of attitudes is of the sexist form and particularly salient in our current society in relation to older children or youths: "children (and this child) are threatening and disobedient and should be controlled, indoctrinated into a cause or a religion, forced to assume an identity, kept from overthrowing or supplanting adults, kept from asserting their rights over or against their parents' rights."

Each of these three forms has variants that apply to newborns and infants, to young children, and to youths or adolescents (who are easier to construct as rebellious or parricidal than young children are). Each form of childism also has a shadow or cover-up set of images, too: images of angelically innocent "good" children and youths; ideally socialized and sexually purified servant children and youths; and children and youths obediently honoring their fathers and their mothers without a trace of protest. (Aristotle's childism was a relatively mild version of this last, controlling sort, designed to make of male children well trained and good citizens; but he did not go so far as to demand unconditional honoring of parents. Parents—fathers—were expected to be responsible for the child's nurture and education. There was reciprocity between the male generations.)

Drawing on a comparative study of prejudice forms, then, childism can be defined thus: a prejudice against children on the ground of a belief that they are property and can (or even should) be controlled, enslaved, or removed to serve adult needs.

In the modern field of Prejudice Studies, a broad consensus has developed among researchers that prejudiced people's negative images or stereotypes are projections outward of hated or feared traits, aspects, functions, or fantasies of the prejudiced person's own psyche or history. Once the target group has been projectively constructed, the projector experiences the projections as traits belonging to the targets and coming *from* the target group, which is blamed for them.

Among modern social scientists, this projection theory was first advanced by Freud in his study of paranoia; it was then developed by Freudians and given the name projective identification. But the understanding is ancient and can be found, for example, in texts by the same Greek philosophers who were so sexist and childist in their understanding of human reproduction. As students of human thought processes, and as creators of descriptive psychology, the Greeks understood projection quite impartially. They knew that people project their hated and feared traits downward toward inferior people whom they have constructed as such in order to oppress them. The philosophers even understood as critical theologians that people project their positive traits upward, creating not just heroes but also powerful deities. The tragedian Euripides, writing in the fifth century B.C.E., was especially gifted—and shocking—as a debunker of deities. But a century earlier than Euripides' play *The Bacchae*, the philosopher Xenophanes had noted in measured tones: "The Ethiopians say their gods are short-nosed and black, the Thracians that theirs have light blue eyes and red hair," and that other groups assign their own characteristics to their own gods. The Greek writers of comedies constantly mocked religious—or pseudo-religious—projective behavior. Menander, for example, pointed out that impious people are so self-absorbed that they create gods that reflect their own characters and thus worship themselves. The Greeks were aware that powerful deities, like the people who created them, would be imagined as protecting or favoring some people and not others—that is, that the deities would be prejudiced in favor of a "chosen people" and against that chosen people's enemies. This insight disappeared during the ascendancy of the Abrahamic monotheistic religions, and returned again only during the Renaissance, when the humanists recuperated Greek and

Roman thought. People who worship a single god find it difficult to imagine that their one god will not favor one people—themselves. A Hindu like Gandhi, reared in a polytheistic tradition, did not share this frame of mind—he considered it intrinsically violent and antithetical to a nonviolent way of life.

The modern projection-theory consensus in Prejudice Studies includes the idea that a target group in whom downwardly projected negative traits have been stored must be controlled or assigned a role or even eliminated in order to keep the projections away, to make the target group permanently "other" and less threatening. Again, this is ancient wisdom that modern scientists have rediscovered. It was clearly recognized in many ancient traditions that making a sacrifice functioned to extirpate an unwanted or guilt-inducing past experience or trauma. The sacrifice was a *pharmikon* (to use the Greek term from which we get the word *pharmacy*). The pharmikon was a therapeutic object that, when it was removed, took with it something bad or unhealthy. Children or animals could be used to represent symbolically the unhealthy or sinful past that should not be allowed to carry into the future. So Oedipus was sacrificed twice: first when he was exposed as a baby to protect his father, Laius, and then, after his guilt was discovered, to protect Athens. The goat, a common choice of sacrificial animal among the ancients, supplied modern languages with words meaning "sin goat" or scapegoat: *Suedenbock* in German; *capro espiatorio*, "expiatory goat," in Italian. Children are often scapegoats.

To this old idea that people use a pharmikon or scapegoat to get rid of their bad parts or their bad past, psychoanalytic theorists have added the idea that target groups can operate as phobic objects. In this situation people with phobias project unwanted aspects of themselves onto some object or place and then come to fear the object or place that "contains" those rejected aspects: a snake or a spider, a bogeyman or a witch, a bridge, a plane going up or an elevator going down, an expanse or a narrow defile, rats, vermin, germs. Or frightening children: powerful, rebellious gremlins, goblins, or little devils, insinuating dwarves, or wild putti shooting arrows of disruptive eroticism. Adults fear these objects, but they are also compelled by them or obsessed by them.

Prejudiced people cannot say to a therapist, as phobic people can, "Help me! I know that this fear I have is crazy, but I am in the grip of something I do not understand." The prejudiced person feels justified in his or her prejudices; they raise no questions. "There are too many children in the world; they will eat us out of house and home," thinks a greedy person who hates that greediness but also wishes that his or her children would feed him or her, treat him or her as a child ought to be treated. We do not hate or fear ourselves if we can with justification hate or fear in others what is hateful or fearful about ourselves.

Psychoanalytic theorists have also pointed out that prejudiced people can resemble perverse people or be themselves perverse but be unable to realize their condition or ask for help. People who are perverse relate to others by focusing their desire compulsively on some part or aspect of another, to the exclusion of everything else or to the exclusion of the whole person. They then experience the fantasies projected onto these parts or aspects of another as coming back like a boomerang. The returning projection is taken in (introjected) so that the desire can be satisfied. There is no real, whole other person involved in this loop of projection and introjection. A fetish, for example, is an object associated with a part of a person—usually a sexual part—to which the perverse person gives compulsive attention, needing to take it in, wear it, sequester it in a pocket or a pouch or special box, or (nowadays) hide it in a computer file. A voyeur, for another example, becomes fixated on what can be seen of another person from a distance, from a position of concealment. Any other way of being with people—talking to them, touching them—terrifies voyeurs, who need to remain isolated, touching only themselves, wrapped up in their (usually) sexual fantasies. People of target groups can supply or be these fetishistic objects or these voyeuristic objects. Children can become such objects. They become fetishes especially for pedophiles, who desire children sexually, but they can serve the purpose for anyone who desires someone who is less than adult or not completely adult physically or emotionally.

People project onto children different aspects of themselves that they cannot tolerate or need to get rid of, and these aspects can be classified generally as burdensomeness or badness, wildness, or rebelliousness. Each of these is an aspect of immaturity, of what is not yet, of future development. So it is, basically, their own immaturity and not-yet condition that adults project onto children, whom they then hate and fear for their immaturity and for what they might become when they mature. Children are "childish," which is a negative adjective marking something an adult should not be. Being a grown-up is imagined as separating from what is childish by denigrating it and calling it shameful. Because in their fantasies childist adults really want to remain children and to be taken care of, they perform this denigration of childishness with guilty vehemence: "When I was a child, I spake as a child, I understood as a child, I thought as a child," Paul of Tarsus told the Corinthians (1 Cor. 13:11), self-righteously invoking his own uplifting conversion to Christianity. "When I became a man, I put away childish things." The essence of Christian childism is this rejection of children as sinfully childish. Adoration of a sinless, holy child, Jesus, who is superior to all adults and who will rule over all children ("Suffer the little children to come unto me") is a rejection of disrespectful children. Jesus was never a human child, never fallible or imperfect like all other human children, who, in some later Christian theological treatises, were presented as originally sinful—that is, born sinful. To my knowledge, the idea that children are born sinful is uniquely Christian. They are "bad seeds," who must be commanded (as the Israelites were) to "honor thy father and thy mother," for they will not do this naturally if they are well cared for, as Aristotle assumed they would.

But it is a crucial part of childism's distinctiveness as a prejudice that children are in reality, not just in guilty adult projections, developmentally immature; they have not yet become their future selves. At birth they are helpless and dependent on the care and assistance of adults. They need that adult care for a longer period of time than any other mammal. Being the least guided of all the animals by "animal instincts," they are the most dependent on imitating adults and being educated by adults and apprenticed to adults. Adult projections of child immaturity in the form of images of their burdensomeness or badness, their wildness, their rebelliousness are always mingled to some degree with interpretations of children's *actual* immaturity. But some interpretations of child immaturity support childism more than others.

Some people will look at newborns, for example, and see in them a complete lack of abilities or capacities, or only potential abilities, a "blooming, buzzing confusion," in William James's phrase. This insistence that a child is an empty vessel or chaos in a vessel at birth does not arise in cultures in which people looked on newborns and saw a reincarnation of an ancestor, a transmigrated "old soul" with an extensive prehistory of living in ancestral bodies or "astral bodies." Similarly, a newborn would not look like an empty vessel or a chaos to a modern scientist who believed in innate linguistic capacities or innate universal grammar or the innate thrust toward development assumed by most contemporary child development researchers. Contrasting interpretations of the child have always clashed and competed in the Western tradition. Socrates found out by questioning him that the uneducated child Meno had an intuitive knowledge of Pythagorean mathematics. By telling this story in the dialogue *Meno*, Plato created an ideal of education as a drawing out (*ex ducare*) of a child's inborn capacities and ideas. But this was precisely the ideal that he then rejected in his *Republic*, where children are empty vessels to be filled up by adults. Thus did the father of Western philosophy leave a legacy for childists and a legacy for critics of childism alike. (Aristotle assimilated to both modes, imagining male children as evolutionarily destined to exercise their reason, but not until after age seven, and apt to fail if they were disobedient. Female children were perceived as empty.)

Even if they do not have the word *childism* with which to criticize images of children as empty or chaotic, contemporary developmentalists who study children have recognized the prejudice and countered it by showing ways children have been underestimated and their contributions to human life underappreciated. They reject the notion that a child is a blank tablet, a person who can become bad, wild, or rebellious unless properly written on or subjected to some "higher" adult purpose. Edith Cobb, for example, inspired by Johan Huizinga's classic study *Homo Ludens* (1950; translated into English 1955), argued in *The Ecology of Imagination in Childhood* (1977) that in children's play we can observe the quintessence of human spontaneity and capacity for renewal of the world and creation of civilization. To make her case, Cobb drew on research into the complexity of a baby's capacities at birth and during the first year of life, when the brain develops more, and more quickly, than at any other period. In the field of psychoanalysis, the English pediatrician-analyst D. W. Winnicott was the most clinically experienced explorer of children's inborn capacities for play and creativity. Contemporary developmental neuroscience has itself developed to the point where Alison Gropnik's 2009 book summarizing its findings was titled *The Philosophical Baby*. (And a philosophical baby is one who could, of course, teach a philosopher prejudiced against babies a thing or two—like a modern Meno.)

The distinctiveness of childism as a prejudice in which immaturity is projected onto a group that actually *is* relatively immature has made all study of what constitutes human maturity very complex, and it is difficult to conduct such study without prejudice. We hardly know how to describe *adult* maturity scientifically, although there are libraries of efforts to formulate standards of ethical maturity. But a scientific description of maturity is, I believe, crucial to being able to understand how adult immaturity underlies childism itself and all the kinds of acts and policies that manifest childism. We can begin an inquiry about this topic (for which children's own statements will be important) by observing that children themselves project.

By finding others naughty or dangerous, children themselves can get rid of either what they find naughty or dangerous in themselves or what adults have told them is naughty or dangerous about them. The others onto whom children project *become* their badness or their anger, their shame, or their humiliation at being called bad or at having bad thoughts. Often, children use the nearest "inferior" people to hand—like their younger siblings—as objects of fear and hatred, as rivals. (Not all "sibling rivalry" is direct rivalry for the parents; some is among children over who is going to be the "bad" one and fall out of favor or not get any favoritism from the parents or other adults.)

The projections people make as children provide a foundation for projections they make later as adults—including childist projections. Adults who are prejudiced against children are carrying a layered history of prejudice experience, which will usually include experiences of disappointment in their own parents, who were immature in ways that could be read, understood, and sometimes assimilated to. Children can internalize the childism around them as women internalize sexism or people of color internalize racism. Jews are said (prejudicially) to have a special gift for being "self-hating Jews." Homosexuals are said to be especially good at being homophobic. Later, I shall provide clinical evidence of the ways children who have internalized childism become divided beings, carrying inside themselves an oppressor adult and an oppressed child. Their ability to mature is deeply compromised as they build up what Winnicott called a "false self" out of their conscious and unconscious reactions to their being targeted.

The remarkably comprehensive *The Child: An Encyclopedic Companion* (2009) has an entry on prejudice that discusses how *children* become prejudiced, but nothing in this article suggests that children are *targets* of prejudice. One of the key mechanisms involved in children's becoming prejudiced has thus been omitted. The insight, with us since the Greek tragedians, that people do unto their children a version of what they feel has been done unto them is very frightening. (Oedipus, exposed on the mountain by his father, Laius, later unknowingly kills Laius.) That children can grow up to do unto others (or sometimes unto themselves) what they have experienced makes the future frightening. So it is not surprising that every known literate culture has some version of the Golden Rule that warns people "Do not do unto others what you would not have done unto yourself." It is a formula for preventing childism from being acted upon.

I have noted that adults and children both project. But they do not do so randomly. Their projections reflect their individual experiences (both in their own psyches and in the world) and their individual make-ups, which psycho-analysts, working in the Greek tradition that stems from Plato and Aristotle, call their *characters*. Our characters are the sum of our inherited or inborn characteristics interwoven with the psychic habits we develop from childhood on into adulthood. Our habits include habits of working over in ourselves traumas we have undergone, habits of assimilating to what we have been taught, and habits of projecting. Our characters encompass both our biological nature (sometimes called temperament) and our "second nature," acquired in and from our familial, social, and political culture.

In the field of Prejudice Studies, the projection theory is accepted by most researchers; however, the idea that character forms or shapes projections is not part of the consensus. When Gordon Allport of Harvard University summarized the projection consensus in his classic *The Nature of Prejudice* (1954), he asserted that all the prejudices are alike—all are a form of racism or "ethnocentrism," a majority in-group hating a minority out-group—while making no distinctions among projections or projection formations. He identified anti-Semitism as a type of racism; sexism was ignored alto-gether, perhaps because women are not a minority group. The idea that character shapes projections and thus prejudices comes from psychoanalysis, where the differences among people along characterological lines are as significant as they were for Plato and Aristotle and all the heirs of their study of human nature.

Like his Greco-Roman predecessors, Freud—the Aristotle of modern psychology—assumed that on the one hand, every human makes a unique developmental journey to maturity, while on the other, there are typical paths to that journey, typical interweavings of what psychoanalysts call "developmental lines." Character types are the configurations or clusters of traits resulting from a *unique* maturational journey with *typical* features.

As I noted before, Aristotle recognized three basic character types among men: those who pursue happiness through the enjoyment of physical-sensual pleasure and the acquisition of material goods (the hedonists and the proprietors); those who find happiness in exercising their ethical reasoning (the moralists); and those for whom thinking is happiness (the contemplatives). Although Aristotle privileged the contemplatives, he acknowledged that men of each type can be happy as long as they do not pursue their goals to excess—as long, that is, as they are virtuous. "Moderation in all things" was Aristotle's advice for avoiding what in contemporary psychiatric language would be known as a character disorder. It's fine to be a moralist, but tyrannical to be a moralist who tries to control all who disagree with you.

To Freud, who made basically the same classifications, the three characters were called hysterical, obsessional, and narcissistic. It is unfortunate that Freud gave these character types such pathologizing names, because, like Aristotle, he assumed that people of each type could be happy and healthy as long as they were not immoderate in their desires or extreme in their inner conflicts. Freud and his early followers found that the types themselves were quite useful for recognizing common orientations toward the world and the actions that follow from such orientations. And they used the types to guide their therapeutic work, their efforts to prevent damaging actions flowing from and channeling into character distortions.

A person's character develops as he or she successfully contains conflicts and developmental difficulties and challenging interactions with the world, achieving a degree of eudaemonia, or inner order and peace. But Freud thought that each character type was susceptible to the neurosis from which it derived its name—hysteria, obsessional neurosis, or narcissistic neurosis. People can become extreme and distorted or disordered as they struggle to contain their neurotic conflicts or their developmental difficulties or their interactions with the world. Their containment efforts can also break down, and they can regress into a neurotic state; their character formations can be overtaken by open, acted-out neurotic conflicts that they cannot contain, or traumas can weaken them.

To put this another way: a neurosis could be described as a breakdown or a running off the road (to a greater or lesser degree) during a characterological journey toward maturity. Characteristic distortions result, and I would add that characteristic prejudices result, as a person struggles to regain harmony. A prejudice is a neurosis or developmental problem played out projectively in the world, among people. (A psychotic goes so far in the direction of projective functioning that he or she cannot relate to people, losing contact with reality, fragmenting inwardly, and attributing various unreal characteristics to others, to the point of paranoia.) One of the key ways people have of keeping themselves on an even keel is projecting their conflicts onto others; they throw their baggage overboard in a storm. The result is a prejudice rather than a neurosis.

In simple terms, what Freud was observing and describing in those of hysterical character was the containment of a neurotic split or dissociation into conflicting "selves"—a good, chaste self and a bad, lascivious self, a real self and an impostor self, a conventional self and a renegade. When the containment is not successful, a hysteric can be an upstanding citizen who is also compelled to be an outlaw or to make scenes, acting out the bad self by creating a turmoil, a drama. Hypocrisy becomes a way of life for such a person because it allows him or her to repress, or disavow, or dissociate from the activities of the bad "other" half, projecting them either outward or onto themselves. The "classic" hysterics described by Freud, most of them female, projected their uncontainable wildness onto their own bodies and produced bodily symptoms (known as conversion symptoms) like eating disorders, paralysis, fatigue, swooning, sexual dysfunction. But other hysterics project onto the bodies of others—in extreme cases, making others ill, beating them, or focusing various kinds of violence upon their genitals, from castration to rape. Much less extreme hysterics arrange people in scenes and dramas, dictating roles to them but not necessarily abusing them physically or sexually. These "drama queens" (to use a pop word) are "histrionic" (to use the word employed in contemporary psychiatric diagnostic manuals).

Hysterical characters commonly grow up in milieus where the family life is double- or two-tiered. In what sociologists call a Creole family, typical of the middle-class Viennese of Freud's time, a network of domestic servants is woven into the primary family—there are two mothers, two fathers, two sibling groups—and the hysterical character can assign one "self" to each family. The lower and darker self of a dominant family person goes to the low (in class terms) or dark (in race terms) people, for purposes that Aristotle called hedonism and acquisition—acquiring sensual pleasure or material goods or both. Competitiveness is the name of the game. The lighter and higher self idealizes the light and high people. Incestuous desires and rivalries over sex or goods can be acted out with a parent or sibling who is not the biological parent or sibling (and the same thing can happen in contemporary merged families that combine two households). So the prejudices of such characters are endlessly sexualized, as is typical in racism. The hysterical character's victims are imagined as archaic, primitive "natives" of grotesque sexual appetite and inferior intellectual abilities. Children can easily be manipulated in such families to play all kinds of roles, including sexual roles, in this drama.

The Freudian obsessional character is the Aristotelian moralist—that is, he or she is marked most saliently by rule-boundedness and love of order. The obsessional is a conformist, constantly splitting emotions off from intellectual operations, and thus presenting a kind of cold rationality or hyperrationality. This type flourishes in families and institutions that promote order for order's sake, "Prussian" values, sexual suppression, monetary discipline, envy, and affectless intellectualism. Among the family types that sociologists identify, those in which sexuality and the acquisition of money are evaluated most negatively and moralistically are the ones that most commonly contain obsessionals. Christian European families, for example, were traditionally more anti-sex and anti-money (especially anti-usury) than Islamic West Asian and North African or South Asian Hindu or Confucian East Asian families. The process by which the acquisition of money became acceptable among many families who share this Christian European background—from robber baron

capitalism to Christian fundamentalist entrepreneurship—
has involved strenuous projection of money-greed onto others, which is to say, strenuous prejudice on the anti-Semitism
model. Children in such families are often seen as greedy,
spoiled, demanding, undermining; they need to be strictly
monitored and punished.

Among cultural commentators and analysts, obsessionals and obsessional families have been described more
clearly than the other two character types and social-familial
types because their behaviors are more stereotypical, and
markedly full of suspicion. In *The Paranoid Style in American
Politics,* the critic Richard Hofstadter saw this type dominat-
ing public life in the anti-Communist 1950s, while the sociologist William Whyte in *The Organization Man* saw it domi-
nating the 1950s corporate world. This was Richard Nixon's
milieu. After the upheaval of the 1960s youth rebellion, the
paranoid-obsessional style was ascendant again in the Reagan
era, when a new kind of McCarthyism flourished, in which
new left youth were being branded as Communist agents of
the Evil Empire. But the 1980s were also (as I shall show with
clinical material in Chapter 6) a time of ascending narcissistic assertion of control of children's identities and insistence
on the delinquency of the younger political generation.

A person who is characterologically narcissistic can
be either grandiosely inflated or grandiosely deflated; either
"the best" physically or mentally or the best at being bitterly
wounded. Male narcissists are identifiable by their grandiosely complex phallocentrism: they worship their own phalluses, which they often think of as magically reproductive.
Sometimes they attribute phalluses to women whom they do
not want to imagine as reproductive. They lack empathy or
the ability to see things from another's perspective, and they
radiate the expectation that they be privileged, lucky, indulged,

or taken care of when they are hurt—often by children. Their sense of self or self-esteem requires them to dominate or erase another's self—often the self of a child over whom they claim ownership and complete authority.

All types of family systems that are patriarchal—and almost all are—foster male narcissism, but in different ways. The traditional Confucian family system, common in China, Japan, Korea, and Vietnam at different historical periods, for example, emphasizes filial piety. The father-son relationship is central, and the sons—particularly the oldest or an only son—are privileged, often adored by the parents. The son resides in the paternal home after marriage, and so is never separated from his mother but has power over her as well as over his wife. The son is expected to become the center of the family universe, but the price for this power is that he has to do exactly as his father, the current center, says. So his individual identity can be effectively erased if his father needs it to be for his own narcissism. Many pre-industrial European and Russian aristocratic families were "Confucian," as one can see in Turgenev's *Fathers and Sons* or in Freud's case studies of the Rat Man and the Wolf Man.

In the Freudian theory, people's characters do not *cause* their prejudices. Rather, their projections of shame and of guilty self-hatred or their distorted, fantasy-driven desires cause the prejudices. Each individual's prejudice is thus distinctive, discoverable only through a focused study of his or her fantasies and projections. But because people's characters determine how their projections form into prejudices, there are common features to the prejudices of the hysterical, the obsessional, and the narcissistic characters. Further, their characters determine how people use preexisting, culturally available prejudicial stereotypes with which to reinforce and justify their own fantasies. That is, individuals fantasize and project out of their unique internal lives, but they also find in their family cupboards, societal bazaars, media outlets, and cultural storehouses collections of ready-made stereotypes or images within which they can package their individual projections. And they add with their projections to the collective store. Sometimes they find or help create full-blown ideologies, which are like systematized prejudices.

Character is a synthetic concept: it situates individuals, with their unique intrapsychic lives and stories, within groups: first a family group, then a social or political group, and on to larger clusters of groups. As I have tried to indicate in sketching the three character types, there are families and societies where hysterical, obsessional, or narcissistic people predominate or control the main social, economic, and political institutions, organizing and operating the institutions according to their characterological needs and prejudices. So there are, then, societies organized around hysterical dramas, scenes full of conflict, and moral panics or mass hysterias; societies organized around obsessional rituals, control mechanisms, and paranoid ideas; and societies organized around grandiosity, identity-assertion propaganda, and efforts to dictate the future. Sometimes societal character is lasting, staying relatively constant over generations, but sometimes— particularly under contemporary conditions in which the media have such influence—societal characters shift and change in less than a generation. Characterologically homogenous groups come quickly into being and fade just as quickly. What is known as a "generation gap" is a time of rapid social character shift, often spurred by a group revolt of the young against the prevailing characterological constraints of their elders.

Both individuals and groups will need their prejudices more in various kinds of aggravating conditions, particularly conditions that make them fear that their familiar order is being threatened and that they are either going to lose something they value or not get something that they deeply wish for. Then prejudices become crucial as mechanisms for defending the status quo, recovering lost security and prerogatives, or demanding attention. On a continuum from mild to severe, the commands given to "inferiors" on the basis of the prejudices become more strenuous and more violent, more abusive. The technique of projection may also become more complex: some kind of "badness" may be projected onto others, for example, by means of an elaborately announced expectation that they will be "good" followed by disappointment when they are not and obsessional policies aimed at removing them: "Such-and-such a group was meant to be our ally, but they all proved to be dangerous to us and they should be separated from us and purged." People prejudiced against children in the identity-erasing narcissistic way will often say something like "Children are supposed to continue our glory into the future, but they are ungrateful and rebellious, so they must be punished," or "Kids today are so much less good than we were as kids." "Our society is the most child-centered in the history of the world, so I cannot understand why anyone would keep harping on our child poverty rate." Hysterical childists say things like "We brought the children up to be natural and free, and instead they are all drug addicts."

Like any prejudice, prejudice against children conveys disrespect and hatred as it takes its characteristic forms; but childism, like the other prejudices, may be suffused as well with envy. Most anti-Semites envy what they see as the financial power of their victims, racists their victims' alleged sexual or physical prowess, and sexists their victims' reproductive capacity. Envy of the young for their youthfulness and energy cuts across all forms of prejudice. But prejudices can also convey patronization, a particular kind of disrespect that says the victims need help or rescue; the prejudiced person needs to tell them how to do things they would otherwise be unable to do. The Christian theologians who patronizingly thought up the place called Limbo where unbaptized children go after death felt that this was a kinder and gentler place for those children than the flames of Hell that awaited unbaptized adults. Currently, Americans who claim that America is the country that gives most protection to abused children find it hard to think about the needs and rights of all children, the 3 Ps of Provision, Protection, and Participation outlined in the Convention of the Rights of the Child. They construe abuse of children as an exception to the norm, rather than as an extreme at the negative end of the continuum of the ways to nourish and educate children.

The natural dependency of children has been one of the key reasons for the prejudice against them not being recognized as such or its being so easily rationalized. Adults who argue that children do not and should not have rights, for example, base their arguments on children's natural dependency, making assertions about their lack of agency or capacity for choice, expression of interest, or reason. But such arguments are prejudicial against children's *development:* by declaring that children do not have these capacities, the arguments are really contributing to the difficulties children have in developing the capacities. The arguments are like a standardized test that children have to fail. Even the mild progressive philosopher John Locke, one of the first to make the radical proposal that children should not be thought of as the property of their parents (because, he added, they belong to God), justified corporal punishment because children have no reason; they are blank slates. Their capacity for sensation is the only available channel to get the message of discipline through to them. The effect of this view is to thwart the very development that is anticipated. Hitting a child does not get a message of discipline through to the child; the blow lays down a pain pathway neurologically and provokes the child to feel, "You do not love me," and very often, "I am not lovable."

Patronization is also typical of what might be called adult childism, the variant of childism that casts adults as children. Generally, every time a group within a society wants to control, role-cast and script, or eliminate another, the victims are first charged with being childish, immature, limited, or not capable of being like the victimizer group. When childism intensifies, adult groups are also going to be more intensely charged with being childish. Often the targeted adult groups will also be charged with childishly indulging children or advocating for children or encouraging children to be bad or wild or rebellious. Progressives who have worked for children's rights have time and again been thwarted by opponents who call them immoral, naive, or opposed to family values. Child advocates are set aside through charges that they are subverting parents' rights.

In summary, the definition of childism that I have been developing draws on what Prejudice Studies teaches us about the basic mechanism—projection—that operates in all forms of prejudice. But it goes farther by suggesting that the forms of childism are basically three, shaped by three character formations. The character formations, in turn, are promoted by familial, societal, and cultural character formations. Any analysis of childism needs to take these layered definitional elements of the prejudice into account: individuals' fantasy projections, individuals' characters, and corresponding social character formations.

To understand when and how a prejudice operates, these definitional elements also have to be placed in a historical and political analysis focused on trends and conflicts in relations between those who claim ownership of children—chiefly families and states. Trying to prevent or ameliorate a prejudice depends on understanding how it can change and be changed *in historical context,* and specifically in the context of ownership conflicts in which children exist like the third part of an Oedipal triangle: father, mother, children.

In this chapter I made a preliminary theoretical map of existing approaches to the question "Why do parents sometimes turn against their children?" Now I will use that map to introduce you to a mistreated child who learned in psychoanalysis to articulate her understanding of the motivations of the adults who mistreated her. I have chosen Anna because she experienced all three of the forms of childism that I have discussed, and experienced them brutally, at the extreme negative end of the child-treatment continuum, where the effects of the forms of childism are very clear, like physical and psychic brands. Anna has given me permission to tell her story, believing that my case study of her is part of her own quest for what she calls "the whole story" and part of her own mission of writing educationally about child abuse and neglect. We have protected her confidentiality, using a fictitious name and disguising various details about her family and her involvement in legal proceedings.

Anna grew up in the 1970s, as did a group of her peers whom I shall present in Chapter 6. They share a historical context: their parents reached adulthood in a decade of political and cultural experimentation (the 1960s) and then brought them up in a decade when the experiment had begun to fail (the 1970s and 1980s). This is when the field of Child

Abuse and Neglect (CAN) emerged to address that failure but also as a symptom of it. A long imperialist war in Vietnam had ended in 1975 with a humiliating defeat; conservative forces had begun to work for a restoration of the "family values" of the 1950s era that the parent generation had been rebelling against. Programs supporting child development were being rolled back, leading to the development of the field of Child Advocacy in protest.

During the years she was in psychoanalysis with me, the decade after September 11, 2001, Anna began to think that she would like to write a play about her experience and create a troupe to perform it. But before she could do that, she, like the other young people we shall meet later, had to piece together a narrative of her experiences in the context of her family, in the context of her society, and in the context of something more, a vaguer something for which neither she nor I had a name when we began: childism.

CHAPTER TWO

Three Forms of Childism
Anna's Story

IN 2001, A BEAUTIFUL YOUNG WOMAN IN HER LATE TWEN-
ties, sexy in her tight blouse and long, flowing skirt, came into
my consulting room, looked around as though she were in a
museum, and asked me where she should sit. I gestured toward the chair opposite mine. She sat there but fixed her gaze
on my couch. "This is where your patients lie?"

"If they want to," I answered her.

"I have no idea whether I want to," she said pensively.

Anna took a deep breath and looked right at me,
steadily, composed. "That is my problem. I want to be able to
desire. But I can't. I can't let myself." Speaking in clear, rich,
thoughtful prose, she told me that she had first gone into
therapy when she was fourteen and had stayed for several
years. The therapist had been helpful and kind but ultimately
"too cognitive," and Anna had not recovered her ability to desire during the sessions. "I still could not feel my feelings." Anna
stared at me in a way that I felt as vaguely seductive.

"I guess I had better tell you what happened. Why I
needed help then, and why I need help again now. I think it
is psychoanalysis that I need because it has to go way back to

when I was a little girl, when everything went wrong, and I became a very capable child but all confused."

"Do. Do tell me what happened," I said.

"My mother was not even twenty when I was born. My father was older, married. He was having a fling with her. She was a crazy, wild girl, prostituting herself. But they decided to get married, and he left his wife and kids. Ridiculous, I mean really ridiculous. Juvenile. The marriage lasted about six months, and then they parted. I stayed with my mother, but most of that time—until I was two, almost three—we were with my grandparents, her parents, who tried hard to be good parents to me, I think."

As Anna continued with her story it became clear that her infancy had receded behind a major drama, so startling and frightening that it had created a stark Before and After in her mind. Before, in the good time of her infancy, she was primarily in her mother's care, with the grandparents as auxiliary parents. But After, in the beginning of the bad years, she was with her father, and her mother was gone. Lost.

On a lovely summer day when she was two and a half, she was sitting at a little table in the backyard of her mother's unkempt, ramshackle house making imaginary tea with her plastic tea set. Her mother was inside the house with a new boyfriend. A wild dog wandered through the yard, parting the thick, uncut grass, prowling past the trash and broken lawn furniture. He came up to the table and stared at her. "As I remember it, I wanted to serve him tea, and that's what I was doing when he leapt and caught my head in his big jowls."

With great intensity, Anna watched me wince. Then, calmly, she got up from her chair and came toward me to show me the scars she has on her temples—pale puncture marks, tooth marks, on both sides. Then she returned to her chair and to her story. She was offering me proof—the evidence of her body—that what she was telling me had really happened. That she was truthful.

"I screamed, and my mother's boyfriend came running out and pulled the dog off of me, pried his jaws open, and released my head. I was all bloody. They picked me up, and we went in his car to the hospital, where I got a lot of stitches." She paused. "I don't remember being scared; I remember it was like a game that I was playing with the dog, and then suddenly he attacked me."

I made a mental note to myself: as she remembers this incident, she was happy, having fun, and then she was brutalized—and she has no memory of the feelings she had during the brutalization. This pattern was precisely repeated in the next incident in her narrative.

"My father held my mother responsible for my being alone and unsupervised in the backyard, so he went to court and got custody of me. The judge said my mother was neglectful. So my father took me to live with a woman he had married, in a house they shared with all her grown children. Once he told me that he had married her just to have a mother for me—but who knows whether that's true. Sometimes my father's children from his first marriage were there, too. A lot of children, all much older than me—I was really the only child in that house. But those kids were really damaged people. Not one of them could really grow up properly. I can see that now. That house was complete, total chaos. They did all kinds of drugs; some were dealers; they drank; they had no rules; they were violent; the boys sexually abused the girls; they were all messed up—all of them. Later I used to say to myself that I was sent to hell."

She took another deep breath and looked warily at me. I know that look. I have seen it many times on the faces of people who were abused as children. It is a cluster of questions: Do you believe me? Are you going to be able to hear what comes next? Are you strong, or are you crazy yourself? Are you judgmental and easily repulsed? Or are you kind and forgiving? Do you settle for sympathizing? Will you find me shameful and repellent?

She hesitated but did not look away. So I invited her to test her little bit of trust in me: "What happened to you in hell?"

"The oldest of my stepbrothers—he was twenty-one—didn't go to school or work like the rest of the kids did. So he was my babysitter all day until my father and stepmother got home. I was three. He sat around all day reading porno magazines. And one day I was looking at the magazines. I can remember what they were like because I looked at them with him a lot after that, too. They were very exciting, and I got all flirty and excited and danced around singing, 'I love you, I love you.' Imitating the girls in the magazines, you know, being sexy. And he raped me. For the first time."

I was stunned, and Anna registered that reaction, gazing at me intently. In her story she had been having fun, playing out her fantasies, and suddenly she was brutalized. She did not draw a connection between the dog story and the story of her stepbrother's wild-dog behavior, but the pattern of her emotions did, and she had set me up to hear the connection. "As far as I can remember, there was no treatment, no going to the E.R. I was in pain, but nothing happened. No help. Later I got treated for various problems, infections, tears in my vagina. The one time I remember my father doing anything was when I was seven or eight and a doctor gave him some cream that he was supposed to put in my vagina, to help the healing." She looked at me again, checking my reaction, then she commented, "So my father got to molest me."

"Why was it your father who put the cream in you?" I asked her, feeling enraged.

Calmly she informed me, "Because my father is in their field, in medicine. He does meds." With intense sarcasm, she added, "He is a healer."

I—a healer—got the message. Her father could not be credited with ignorance; he was a medical man himself. But she obviously did not want to tell me anything more about him. "I could not get out of my father's custody until I was almost fourteen," Anna went on. "And it was a horror the whole time. That stepbrother continued to rape or harass me whenever he wanted—almost every day—until I was about eight. Then it was now and again. He did it in my father's bed for some perverse reasons of his own. And the others abused me in other ways. I was like a slave who did all the housework. Or some kind of toy. I can't even remember a lot of what the boys and their pot-head, crack-head friends did. My stepmother had no interest in controlling any of them; she spent most of her time in bed, depressed, issuing orders. In fact, I think she got off on it in some sick way when they tormented me. My name in that house was 'Ugly.' The whole time I was there, I dressed like a boy, a scruffy boy, and I have believed it all my life, that I am ugly." Her face collapsed as though she were going to sob, but she didn't; she pulled herself up short and went on, stoically, her emotions hidden.

"I went to live with my mother a couple of years after my stepmother died. Before that, there was a year of transition living with a woman my father took up with, later married, who was pretty good to me, at least not abusive. My mother had married that boyfriend who saved me from the dog, and he was feckless but at least not abusive. It was pretty safe there. He had kind of calmed my mother down, and she had two children with him. After a while, she divorced him. I turned into a second mother for those kids, doing all kinds of housework like I had back at my father's. I did really well in school, even though I worked so much at home and also at jobs, for money."

Later I came to recognize this phrase "at least not abusive" as being the most she hoped for from people. But even while she was telling me that she did, finally, get away from her abusers, her expression said that she still expected abuse. I felt sure that she expected me to disapprove of her, but I also wondered what else she expected me—the healer—to do or say to hurt her.

"I did a time in high school of drinking too much and doing pot and having sex with boys I didn't really like, but basically I was steady, and the therapy helped me a lot. So after I left there to go to college, I took a big step. I took my stepbrother to court, and I got him put away. He did six years in prison. I did that because he had married and he had a little baby girl. I was convinced that when she got to be three he was going to rape her. I absolutely could not stand that idea. And the mother of that girl was a child herself; she never would have been able to protect her daughter."

Anna paused again and once more stared hard at me. "You have to understand that the trial was very, very important for me. It empowered me. And I got my therapist and my father and his wife—he had married the woman I lived with for a year—and my lawyer to help me. But the trial also created a problem for me. Because we had to assemble evidence to prove a case, and that meant we had to tell a very specific story about rape, leaving out lots that happened, lots of abuse from other people, lots of memories. And now that specific story, which was quite true—and documented with all kinds of medical records and pediatrician's reports saying 'suspected sexual abuse' and everything—that rape story is standing in the way of the whole story. It has blocked me from getting at the whole story. I have come to you because I think that I need the whole story in order to get well. But I cannot find it by myself."

She rested for a minute. "No, it's even worse than that. I cannot, anymore, really trust my memory. I worry that I make things up. My lawyer said that what had happened to me was 'too horrible to be true,' so we had to tell only the true—the provable—part. He kept warning me, 'Enough is enough.' I think he did not believe me except about the rape. It made me feel like I am a liar, or a hysteric, or just some drama queen who has to always be telling everybody the story of her abuse. I disgust myself. And I assume I will disgust you. I disgust everybody, eventually, even though at first I charm and seduce everybody, even very bad people. I am like my mother in this."

Glancing at the clock and realizing the session was coming to an end, Anna went into a torrent of self-denigration. "My story has a mythic quality to it. The dog story has a mythic quality to it. Little Red Riding Hood and the Big Bad Wolf. Even though it is *true*. And when I tell it, it's like I tell it for myself—there are no listeners, really, or they are all alike; I make them into no one in particular. I'm terribly narcissistic. And sometimes when I am telling it, I feel myself turn into a person I call 'Tiny,' a little girl, that little girl who was abused. I was with my new boyfriend at a Chinese restaurant the other night, telling him the story of my abuse, how everything had gone wrong, and suddenly I felt that the chopsticks in my hand were too big, that my hand was a little girl's hand."

I asked myself, of course, whether I was hearing the name of an alter—one of the "selves" in what used to be called Multiple Personality Disorder. So I asked Anna if Tiny was with us while she was talking, and she said no. I said, "Well, if she shows up again, maybe after this session, tell her she's welcome here."

In this one session Anna told me a great deal: I got an unusually full, richly articulated child-abuse story—one that the adult Anna indicated had been prepared in advance. But along with the prepackaged story was a signal that Tiny, the abused child, had not yet—had never—told her story. Her voice would, of course, be less intellectual, less crafted, more emotional, rawer, closer to the unconscious. Closer to the bone. There was going to be much more, and I was being told not to behave like the earlier, "too cognitive" therapist or like the lawyer, not to focus too narrowly on the rape or doubt that she had been in multi-abuse hell because her story was "too horrible to be true." She had been testing me to make sure that I was not afraid to discover—or, like her, afraid to feel—the whole story.

That first session also presented me with the complete cast of characters. The crazy, wild young mother, the rapist stepbrother, the controlling father who abused rather than protected her, the two stepmothers, the groups of stepsiblings, boys and girls. The scene was set: a 1970s merged household, chaotic, without boundaries, generally abusive and negligent, offering no safety of any sort. I had also been alerted to the two times when the outside world, in the form of the courts, had stepped in and shaped the story. A judge had found her mother "neglectful" and delivered Anna over to her father's ownership, a terrible decision that could in no wise be considered "in the best interests of the child." A second judge had sent the rapist to prison, making Anna feel empowered but also confused, unsure of *her* truth, which her lawyer had insisted she not tell as it was not about "sexual abuse." While I wrote up the session—creating in my process notes as much of a verbatim transcript as my memory could provide—I kept wondering about Tiny. And I warned myself not to prejudge this story or use any of the negative projections that Anna, as Ugly, had taken in from others, who had their own purposes—not to use any of the classifications that had cut off her need to understand. These warnings to myself were, I later came to understand, the dim outline of a theory concerning the source of her abuse: childism.

The second time Anna came to see me, she lay down on my couch, although she did not say that she had made a decision to do so; she did not mention the matter at all. I waited to talk about this decision until later, wanting her to know that she could act on her desires without a reaction from me, even if she had expected one. I did not want to intrude on her. We talked for most of the session about her mother.

After she was placed with her father and stepmother by the court, Anna was allowed to visit her mother at her grandmother's place several times a year, and she remembers waiting for these times as for another life—or a life at all—and crying bitterly when she had to return to her father's house. Her father chose to interpret her tears as evidence that she had been mistreated by her mother during the visits, and he returned to court to press for a reduction of her mother's visitation rights. He projected his own abusiveness onto the mother. "He just wanted the world to be the way he saw it," Anna said, but she was afraid to tell him how much she wanted to be with her mother for fear of losing his "love," such as it was. Similarly, she was later afraid to tell anyone about the stepbrother's abuse because he (as is typical of abusers) threatened to punish her if she did. She was also afraid that she would lose her father's love if she accused the stepbrother; and this meant, I thought, that at some level she knew that the father did not want the rape to stop, that he was colluding in an open secret.

In her trap, in her enforced silence, Anna made her mother into a deeply idealized figure (and as such her main figure for identification, as is apparent in the fact that Anna tried to look like her mother, tried not to be "Ugly"). "She was so beautiful! When she came for me, she wore elegant dresses, soft, sexy, I was almost afraid to touch them. Chiffon. I wanted her to hold me on her breasts. I clung to her like a little monkey. And when they took me back it was like I was being ripped away. I screamed and she wept for me."

I learned later that Anna began in this time to develop a whole language to communicate what she could not say otherwise for lack of words and because of her fear. She would scream, and later she would keep the scream inside herself, where it came out in her dreams. ("I have a dream life like Munch's painting *The Scream*.") She started to invent creatures and spirits in her fantasy who visited her, saved her, talked to her, loved her, as well as creatures who harmed her—terrifying insects and animals, abusive evil spirits. This was her private salvation and damnation language—Tiny's language, I supposed—in which she both helped and abused herself. When she was about four years old, she invented two imaginary friends, a boy and a girl, with interchangeable names. When she talked aloud to them, she was ridiculed and mocked in her household, so she kept them to herself and spoke to them in a private language. As a latency child of about ten years old, she was also visited by her "ancestors," wise older people such as her grandmother and grandfather who, although they had suffered and bore scars, were kind to her.

One of the most important roles I came to play for

Anna was that of lexicographer. I was like an anthropologist gathering up the interior language and all the dialects she had developed for her different interior characters. In her dreams, this language was, pictorially and verbally, spoken in another country, an underworld, a dissociated world: Tiny's world. I found that the pain in that language and in Tiny's world were bearable only because in their wild, desperate creativity I imagined that I could *hear* Anna's resilience, her strength, her future life. She was, as she told me many times, "a feral child," and my task was to bring that child into my world without hurting her, caging her, interfering with her strength, and to teach Anna—literally—her native tongue.

When Anna left her father's house at age thirteen, she lost her fluency in these dialects; they could not help her outside of that hell. She longed for her mother even more strongly. But when Anna was able to rejoin her mother a year later, she was shocked. "It was like she was a wreck, all worn out and old and tired. And still so unhappy and sexually frustrated. She drank too much. She worked frantically to be a mother to my sister and brother. I felt like I should try to help her be a mother and save her." Anna's most elemental feelings were about her mother, and even before we had done much analytic work she could state them simply. Later analytic work allowed her to see her mother more complexly, and to understand how much mothering her mother needed, but her core feeling never wavered: "I see now that my mother was always a very chaotic, confused person, sometimes hurtful to me, but I never doubted, ever, ever, that she loved me, and I depended on her love no matter where she was or how angry I was that she wasn't with me. Otherwise I would be dead."

I asked Anna during the second session whether she had told her mother at any point before the trial about the stepbrother who raped her and the ways in which she was being emotionally abused and neglected in her father's house. She replied that the whole time she was living in her father's house she had been afraid and ashamed, assuming that she must deserve the abuse everyone heaped on her, and she had not wanted her mother to know what an ugly, bad girl she was. She was afraid that her mother would think she was so bad that she would not be allowed to visit with her, or perhaps some day to stay with her. But when she went to live with her mother at age fourteen, she did tell her a circumscribed version of what had happened (as at her trial, this was not "the whole story"). It was that version that prompted her mother to get her a therapist. "It also made my mother afraid for me, afraid *of* me, like I was a wild animal, so she tried to monitor me a lot and warn me about the dangers of men, about sex. She had a lot of fear and hatred of men. I tried to be as good as I could be, and I kept my adolescent experimenting out of her sight." When her mother married the father of Anna's stepsiblings, a middle-aged guest at the wedding danced with her and then took her outside and tried in a drunken haze to rape her. Anna was now strong enough to fight him off, but she never told her mother. "I was really terrified at how much I wanted to kill that bastard."

I learned some days later that she also performed "the good girl" role for her father. To make herself into the kind of girl her father wanted her to be, she had done what she was told in her father's home. She had also thrown herself into the lessons and school activities her father sponsored. As a straight-A student in school, she pleased him because he admired academic success. When she was about six she joined a young people's dance and theater company, where she found a good substitute mother in the director. This remarkable woman nurtured her, mentored her, and provided her with a home away from hell throughout her elementary school years. There she was not Ugly, and the world of the company was the complete antithesis of that of her stepmother: everyone was disciplined, hard-working, dedicated. "My salvation was performance. Everyone there thought I was wonderful. Occasionally, I believed them." Her father allowed her the experience of performance and the love of the good mother, and he paid for the classes, but he made it clear that dance and theater were not serious, not academic, not part of his vision for her, which was that she become a doctor, like him, and like his own tyrannical father, a surgeon.

When she fled to her mother after her stepmother's death and the mother arranged for her to see a female psychotherapist, Anna experienced another type of good mothering. The therapy focused on the childhood rape experience and on the stepmother, who in Anna's mind at that time was the one most responsible for not protecting her. (Later in our work the full scope of the father's lack of protection could come to the surface.) In the categories used in the field of Child Abuse and Neglect (CAN), which the therapist adopted, the stepmother's main maltreatment of Anna was neglect, which is known to be highly correlated with depression (especially in women, who make up the majority of in-house neglecters). In our therapy, too, we acknowledged that the stepmother was a depressed woman (as well as weakened during her later years by an illness). Although she spent much of her life at home in bed, growing fat and ordering her children around, Anna knew from her stepsiblings that her stepmother had once been an accomplished, attractive, college graduate with a profession in the medical field. But in her first marriage the stepmother had lived in a commune with her children's father. "Free love" was the style, drugs flowed, and the whole family became sexually chaotic, without boundaries, and abusive, as they continued to be later in hell. The daycare in the commune had been completely un-structured, and as the children grew they and their mother became more and more addicted, agitated and depressed, angry. They developed the kind of psychic economy that re-searchers know to be typical of a neglectful family: there was never enough love provided, and everyone believed that love was a zero-sum game; if one person received anything the others were jealous, feeling that they had been deprived, and they competed for everything. In a perverse, neglectful fam-ily, everyone tries to throw someone else out—or even throw everyone else out. "Survival of the sickest," Anna once com-mented sarcastically about this elimination mode of childism.

As Anna and I talked, we learned that the stepmoth-er's neglect followed a common pattern: she singled out her rival, the hated stepdaughter Anna, whom she viewed as the sun around which her husband orbited, the one who stole his attention. Her own children all shared her envious and rival-rous feelings about Anna to some degree. "They all thought my father cared more about me than he cared about any of them, that he spoiled me with all the dance lessons, the schooling, and they hated me for that. They all wanted me dead." The stepmother did not neglect her through what child-abuse researchers call "passive acts of omission"; rather, in the most active, direct, often sadistic fashion, the stepmother neglected Anna by not feeding her. If she found that Anna had taken anything from the refrigerator or bought candy on the sly, she punished her. "I have never been able to feed myself properly; I starve myself and then, when I am fam-ished, I cannot find anything that I want to eat. But I love food! I love to be served food in restaurants like a princess."

The stepmother's neglect was also built into her role as a colluder (along with the father) in her son's sexual abusiveness. She practiced what is called "medical neglect" in a particularly sexualized sadistic fashion, not by refusing Anna medical treatment but by controlling the medical treatment she received. Anna told me—hesitantly, not sure that she could (like a courtroom lawyer) "make the case"—that she thinks her stepmother formed an alliance with the family pediatrician, who was in her child's eyes "some kind of pervert" who leered at her and mocked her in his office with remarks like "Aren't you a sexy little number!" He made no attempt to report her case to the authorities, as he was legally required to do. "I didn't want that pediatrician to touch me, he was, like, a very weird guy, very sicko." He took pictures of her genitals, and she later wondered whether this was for child pornography. In the meantime the stepmother "was messing with my mind, making me feel like I was only on this earth to be abused by men. When she did ever buy me clothes, they were either little baby doll things, Kewpie doll things, or they were boy's clothes—and the others mocked me for being Ugly in those boy's clothes. That family operated like a cult. I think the pediatrician was in that cult."

From this remark, we got our first clue, confirmed after a lot of work, that the way in which the stepmother expressed her desire to eliminate her little rival was strangely gendered: she narcissistically created a prettified little girl for public display and then erased her by insisting that Anna dress as a boy at home. She then erased the little boy-girl by mocking her for being ugly and unfeminine. Anna could not win; she was effectively degendered. As soon as her stepmother died, the eleven-year-old Anna made her father give her money for clothes, which she chose for herself, so that she could have a self, gendered as she desired it to be. But she was not always sure which gender to choose, and she wondered whether she was bisexual. Like many female adult survivors of child sexual abuse by men, Anna found it easier to think about being with women sexually, but she was not really sexually attracted to women and often found herself, after an initial surge of love for a woman, afraid that the woman would neglect her and start behaving in a crazy fashion. She liked to hang out with her women friends in a small group—that seemed safer to her.

At home, Anna experienced herself as being cut into pieces, and this feeling became attached to the way she split her own body into the lower part, which was abused and which she wanted to get rid of, and the upper part, which she thought of as better, less dirty and polluted, where her breasts, of which she approved, grew relatively unmolested, clearly feminine. Her father liked to touch her breasts when she was pubescent, but she was able to scream at him in protest over this, which she called "his fetishizing." She was, that is, better and more actively able to protect herself in the area of her body where she felt clearly gendered and less hurt, more "normal."

Her experience of herself as cut into pieces became a fixed image in her mind one day when her stepmother was driving her (dressed in her little femme clothes) someplace in a car. Anna leaned her head out the window to enjoy the breeze and the stepmother used the automatic window control on the driver's side to raise the window: "She almost choked me to death; I felt like she wanted to cut my head off." The stepmother was neglectful some of the time from a depressed, lethargic, apathetic position, but some of the time she was neglectful in an active, sadistic way, focused on eliminating Anna's gender and her mind, cutting off any pleasure she felt.

Immediately after the stepmother's death, Anna spent the transitional year (age twelve to thirteen) in the home of the woman who became her father's next wife under that woman's non-abusive care. Early on in the analysis, Anna told me, "She fed me properly. For the first time in my life, I ate regularly, and I transformed really fast from a skinny, skinny kid, a boy-kid, into someone with a woman's body." She went on, "My puberty was a drama. It is strange that I experienced a kind of collapse *that* year, when it was safer . . . It's like they broke me in my father's house, but I didn't fall apart until I left. I think I was psychotic that year. I had nightmares every night that I can remember so vividly. Sometimes I still have them, the same ones. I just had to go to my mother's, and finally my father did let me go. I think he was too afraid of what was happening to me, how crazy I was, how deviant from his idea of the perfect girl." She learned the terrible lesson that a psychotic episode could repel people and frighten them into giving her what she wanted—her mother, mothering. "Is it any wonder I am a hysteric?" she asked me; and she always berated herself for being manipulative and abusing people to get them to do for her what she assumed they would never do without being frightened.

Anna always believed that when she was "psychotic" with me that she was manipulating me. I didn't agree. I assumed that at such times Tiny was speaking in the only language she had. And I assumed that it was in this period of Anna's puberty "psychosis" that she had come to rely on "hysterical meltdowns." It felt to me as though the meltdowns meant that her hysterical dissociative defenses were not working. She was desperate. A child who does not run away from home may instead retreat into a dissociative state, and when this does not work, she becomes desperate.

It has often been observed by psychoanalysts that children who have been abused in various ways relive (and sometimes re-create) their childhood abuse at puberty, as they become more adultly sexual. But what Anna relived were not the various actions of the abuse; she repeated the basic pattern of her response to the abuse. Even when she found relative safety and began, as she put it, to have desires again, she would anticipate attack, anticipate a lack of protection, and would kill off her own desires before they could bring her into danger or lead to disappointment. In her worst moments, she wanted to kill herself: she imagined herself retreating from all human contact, pushing away anyone who tried to love her ("to save them from my toxicity") and "shriveling into nothing." She contemplated suicide by disappearance or deflation, but also by falling in front of a train, "like Icarus," who had tried to fly too high. In the first sessions we had after the World Trade Center was destroyed, she talked about the people falling and jumping from the towers and the horrifying white dust cloud floating over to Brooklyn. All that she had been able to feel that day, with deathly calm, was "Well, of course, it's the Apocalypse. I have been waiting for it."

In these deathly states, which came on especially strongly whenever anything good or pleasurable happened to her, she was unable to eat and often became physically ill (but never self-mutilating); her nightmares recurred and she felt "hallucinogenic." Fantasy images (fashioned on a core of memories) flooded her: herself covered with horrible insects or being enslaved. In one recurrent nightmare she was being held at a farm where women were cultivated to have orgasms with the masters. There was no escape.

In the course of our work, it became clear that Anna had always hoped that her father would become like her idealized mother and give her the once expected, always longed-for *mothering*—that he would help her, rather than being a devious master. He had, in fact, been the parent who provided the material support that allowed her to get an education and a graduate degree, and on my recommendation he paid for her psychoanalysis. ("Reparations," I called these payments.) But she felt—rightly—that he used his money to buy her loyalty and her obedience. Her understanding of him (which took her a long time to articulate) was that he attached himself to young women whom he allowed to sexually manipulate, dominate, and control him while he played both the victim and the rescuer: he tried to rescue and redeem *them,* thus inflating himself into a great healer (and, in the process, illegally dispensing prescription drugs). It was after Anna had articulated to herself his behavior pattern that she realized how he had "perversely" tried to make her into such a woman, too, particularly as she reached puberty. He later formed an alliance with her college boyfriend, who was also a "rescuer" (and who had been sexually abused by his father). For the five years she was with this boyfriend, her father was able to use him to become her vicarious boyfriend and to continue to rescue her in that sexualized role. Only when she came to this insight could Anna begin to understand why her father had not stopped her stepbrother's abuse of her.

But I pointed out to her—helping her find words for something she was already aware of—that her father attached himself to two kinds of women: the young, chaotic ones like her mother and the older, maternal ones like her first stepmother. His psychic maneuver was the one long ago identified by Freud as the most common among men: he split his love object into a whore and a chaste maternal figure. Her father tried to keep his younger women in a state of perpetual youth, and he neglected the older ones, sexually as well as otherwise, until they declined into a depression, eventually becoming lethargic on tranquilizers that he supplied. (He helped turn the older ones into his own cold, neglectful mother.) When he rescued Anna with support for her education, for example, his unconscious design was for her not to grow up; she would have to remain under his direction. (We had to be careful to preserve our work from any interference from him because he was paying for the therapy.)

Rescue, in Anna's book, is very different from protection: rescue is masculine and involves control and manipulation, while protection is loving, maternal, and ideally means "Grow freely! Have desires!" A second long-term boyfriend was able at the beginning of their relationship to be fairly consistently maternally protective, and, as a survivor of adolescent sexual abuse by his cold, oblivious mother's best female friend, he had his own experience to provide a basis for understanding Anna's. Anna and this second long-term boyfriend could mother each other in a kind of mirroring or twinning transference. But they also had a very charged, experimental sex life in which she was—intermittently—excited and pleasure-seeking, though never without pain, anxiety, and self-denigration.

Over the course of about five years (the same length of time she stayed with her college boyfriend), this relationship deteriorated. The boyfriend, who had come into her life about six months before she first came to see me, began to expect her to take care of him, and she did so, even acting as the financial provider, indulging his wounded narcissism. She thus became, again, a slave, unable to leave him because he was the only source of love, as her father had been for the five years (age three to eight) of her childhood rape experience.

In the analytic transference, I was called upon to be the good, non-neglectful mother, and Anna tried to accept my assurance that we would make our way through and out the other side of what she called "that inner jungle, where

I am a feral child." She was usually loving toward me, but when she did reject me, she did it in her characteristic way: she assumed that I would hurt her too much, that I would not be able to help her, and that I would become critical and disgusted, tired of having "all [her] woe-is-me histrionics dumped in [my] lap." She assumed that I would leave, become unavailable, as her mother had become unavailable when her father took her to the hell of his house. She would have liked to cling to me like a little monkey, but that was, Tiny knew, dangerous.

Anna eventually brought the whole complex cast of hurtful characters and forms of abuse in her life and in her body and mind directly to me, and I learned a great deal from this "dumping," as she called it. When I was "too silent" as I sat "listening and then just going about the rest of [my] day" after her session, I seemed to her to be like her father in his "incredible passivity," in which "he did nothing to protect me and just busied himself with being a healer and telling me what to do in every detail": "He never protected my body, but he orders me exactly how to get my goddamn car repaired!" (Several years into our work, she realized why her father micromanaged her car repairs: her stepbrother had trained as an auto mechanic, and her father had become accustomed to using him as an agent for controlling her.)

As an adolescent at her mother's home she had formed the unconscious conviction that there was a "Force of Perfect Love" in the cosmos, a ground of hope that meant that "there is ultimately some point to my life, some purpose, that will make all this pain worth it." (This was Anna's version of a common abuse survivor's salvation fantasy that a perfect childhood is going to be bestowed upon him or her to make up for the horrible one.) When she experienced me as ruining this conviction she was deeply hurt. Her mystical conviction had the power to protect and inspire her only when it was largely unconscious, so when I—and her psychoanalysis—revealed it, she felt the therapy as "lethal." Without my protection, and still unable to protect herself, she backed off, isolated herself, closed down—although she never stopped coming for her sessions. Her first real turn away from this instance of her basic pleasure-inevitably-brings-pain pattern came when, in one of her suicidal self-castigating states, she was driving her boyfriend away, and she telephoned me to ask for help outside of our regular sessions. Adopting the humorous childlike tone she used whenever she was in great pain, she ended that conversation with: "I promise, cross my heart, not to abuse him or neglect him. Or myself. Or even you."

When Anna had, finally, after much vacillation and anguish, detached herself from the once-mothering, once-protective boyfriend, who had come to seem more and more like her narcissistically injured and abusive father, she soon found—or was found by—a third boyfriend. This one was not a rescuer, unable to tolerate her unless she needed rescue and allowed herself to be overpowered by the rescue. And he was not a twin: he did not come from a world of abuse. He was a nurturer, a man who, literally, liked to cook for her. They promoted each other's work, and he asked for no financial support from her; on the contrary, he was generous and kind, the son of a Mediterranean mother who considered stocking the refrigerator the ultimate act of love.

It fascinated me—and filled me with joy—that she had had a prophetic dream about just such a man more than a year before she met him: the dream presented what I call her relationship ideal, a nonperverse relationship, which grew out of her sense of her infant love for her mother. When she had that dream, it also gave her the beginnings of a positive image of herself in the future: she was going to be a woman of accomplishment and mothering nurturance, and she was going to be a person with what she called "power images" of herself as a male dancer, "at home with the phallus, not a frightened little boy-child, a dirty masturbator." (Both her feminine and masculine dimensions had to be able to grow up, to become powerful.) I could see, as she could, where we were going, despite the fact that her past, repeating itself, fell like a shadow over her positive visions every time she allowed herself to have them or took any pleasure in them.

Along with the prophetic dream of the nurturing man came a series of dreams in which she gave birth to a baby. In my experience, there comes a point in every analysis when a series of dreams tells the dreamer's developmental story and looks to the future. Anna was beginning to imagine herself as a mother, but the babies she produced were all versions of herself as a baby: pictures of Tiny and Tiny's abuse experiences. In the first dream, she gave birth with difficulty to a boy. She was lying in a dirty bathtub in the chaotic household of her childhood hell. There were medical people around who watched her give this baby CPR because something was the matter with him. As she did so, a brownish-black ooze came out of his mouth, and in this ooze there was a tick, as big as his mouth and with a face on its back, like an Egyptian scarab. She and the baby had a conversation, and she was amazed that he could talk. "Of course I can!" he told her proudly. As the dream went on, the tick reproduced, and she felt powerless against the many little ticks and their "ancient magic." Toward the end of the dream, as some people— perhaps the medical people—were setting up a triage station to deal with the danger of the insects, she became confused; she could not remember any more of the dream: "I don't remember what happened, but I want to say that the baby became a toddler and something happened . . ."

Soon after this dream, which stopped short either before her own toddler rape experience or at the experience itself, she had a dream in which she gave birth to a "tiny, tiny little" girl who was "temporary," a kind of trial baby. There was some test that this baby was going to have to undergo. In one scene of the dream, the baby sat on the lap of Anna's father in the car, still as a Buddha, but Anna felt relief because she knew that her father did not do really bad things to little girls, only to young women. The baby spoke, trying to explain why she was only a test baby and could not stay around; she had been sent from another world to teach Anna something. "Maybe that I really can love a child, that I have plenty of love for a baby? And then I felt so sad that she would go away and a real one would come later."

Because she felt protected by me at this point in our work, and anticipated protection in the future relationship she was able to imagine, Anna had let Tiny appear in her dreams, which were, hesitantly, reparative. Tiny was a "wise baby" of the kind described by Freud's colleague Sándor Ferenczi: a baby who has been abused but can, notwithstanding (or even because of) the horrible experiences, gain wisdom and speak like an adult, talk to the analyst. A third dream came. "The baby in this dream was larger, and a boy, sitting on a counter with his upper body straight and his lower body stretched out in front of him so it was also kind of a tray on which there was a yellowish liquid with some kind of fibers in it. It wasn't urine, it didn't stink like that. The baby was sort of a clown." Lots of things happened in this carnivalesque dream, not many of which she could remember, but she did retain a vivid image of the clown-baby singing a rap song. The long, cynical, comical poem came out of her own mouth simultaneously, although she felt that she could never have composed it. It was the boy's brilliant creation. She was a ventriloquist while he was "like Allen Ginsberg doing 'Howl.'" Perhaps she should record the rap song, preserve it, it was so great. "This poem coming through me like a streak of light made me feel powerful, and there wasn't any question that I was capable of being his mother. He was totally unafraid of offending those he criticized in that poem."

During the period when the new, more deeply protective relationship with the third boyfriend began and was developing, Anna did not need my mothering so much, and she converted me more and more into a good-teacher figure—a successor, I think, to the theater director who was the good mother during that crucial five-year period of her elementary school life. For the first five years of the analysis, I received in the transference the whole complex of her feelings about abusers and types of abuse; then, as she had worked through so much of that experience and become a more integrated person, much less fearful of criticism and of abuse, she needed me more for her work of synthesis and consolidation. We had had our five-year inside-the-abuse relationship, and then we began to do what she had never done: we began to outgrow the abuse experience as student and good teacher.

In my new role, I was given the news that the cosmic vision she had earlier told me had been destroyed by psychoanalysis was coming back to life in her. She began to have the "good" dreams that she had had recurrently in her childhood and adolescence. Many of these dreams featured ancestors, especially from her mother's side of the family. She viewed the maternal family as alcoholic, hurt, and damaged, but not cold and perverse like her father's family, which was dominated in her imagination by her father's hypercritical and physically abusive father, who had had a surgical, cutting style of dealing with everything in his life. Her mother's family was full of "psychics," and very influenced by her Native

American great-grandmother's intense psychical power. To help me appreciate the maternal psychic legacy, Anna gave me several books on Native American rituals and dreams. But she nonetheless feared that I would find her interest in shamanism "flakey," that I would dismiss her as "histrionic," a "wannabe Indian."

The ancestors who appeared in Anna's dreams were people who needed help to come to life: they lived in a border world, half death, half life, and they needed to be released into life. They needed rituals and ceremonies to help them overcome their pain and suffering and be restored. In her waking life, Anna viewed carnivals and shamanistic ceremonies as abuse-overcoming communal rituals, and she created versions of them in her dreams, something she had done since her childhood. When Hurricane Katrina ripped through New Orleans, Anna was terrified that without their carnival the people of New Orleans—especially the "Black Indians"—would not be able to keep themselves and their ancestors in life. To her, the United States government's failure to protect the people of New Orleans from the vulnerability of their levees (their bodily entrances and exits, their passages) and the harm that befell them in the hurricane was racism, but also adult childism, treating them like exploitable or dispensable children. "We live in such a cruel country. Our leaders are cruel."

While Anna was using me as a teacher rather than a protector, reflecting on social policy and people's attitudes toward groups, I began to reflect on my own earlier career as a teacher and a writer—particularly as the author of *The Anatomy of Prejudices*—in my countertransference. Her evolving understanding of her abusers' motivations stimulated me to more theoretical, more reflective, associations. I was listening to her but also learning from her, and bringing what I was learning into the field of the concept I called childism. I realized, too, that this conceptualizing was how I had contained my initial rage over Anna's abuse at the hands of her stepbrother, her father, and her stepmother. I was asking myself why parents or family members turned against their children and how they justified their actions with beliefs, with prejudice against the child and against children.

Anna is an artist and an intellectual, and intensely, proudly verbal. Tiny's "psychic" understanding of the world and the people around her (of their unconscious minds, their unconscious motivations, even more than of their conscious minds), on the other hand, was acquired and expressed bodily. She experienced people in her body, and she experienced their bodies. One of the most important insights that she, and then the adult Anna, had, which later helped Anna a great deal as she slowly learned to enjoy adult sex, was that her stepbrother the rapist and her father the pervert were different kinds of men or men-in-bodies. These were the two kinds of men the adult Anna had to be most careful to recognize and protect herself from.

Tiny was speaking when Anna said that her stepbrother was a beast (like the dog who attacked her); he was a "scary gorilla"; he "followed his penis around brainlessly." In her young adult academic rendition of this feeling, Anna said he was "The Phallus." Tiny had remembered that in the fixed ritual of his abuse of her, everything served his penis. He always abused her in the afternoon. During the first years that Anna came to see me, as that afternoon time approached she would feel "something" in her go to sleep—this was Tiny entering into a preparatory state of dreariness and apathy, sinking self-protectively into a dissociated state to avoid that penis. All her life, Anna told me, she had became "unfathomably tired" at this time in the afternoon. When she wanted to avoid a sexual encounter, she became lethargic, immobile.

Tiny would hear her stepbrother in the kitchen getting ready: he would put cooking oil into a small plastic bag, which he would carry with him as he marched her to the parental bedroom. The oil was to lubricate her little vagina and his big penis, "for his sake, not mine." It took Anna several years to tell me that her stepbrother raped her anally as well as vaginally; this was more shameful to her, although she once said that she wasn't sure whether, as a small child, she had much sense of her different sexual parts. "It was like all one place, my ass, my bad ass." That was Tiny's experience, and in Anna's dreams there were often circles and round spaces with blurred sections in them that represented all holes as one.

When the raping was over, Tiny would need to go to the bathroom and the stepbrother would follow. "It hurt me so much to pee; and I always felt like I needed to shit, but couldn't. He said: 'That's just my cock in there, you don't need to shit.' He teased me about it." The Phallus hurt Anna deep inside herself, and the body memories of this hurt were located very specifically in her cervix and her rectum. The Phallus was the forever occupying army which commanded those places, those underworlds.

As a young adult, Anna often went to gynecologists to reassure herself—that she was not permanently damaged, that she would be able to have children, that she was not diseased (because she had had to endure treatment as a child for Chlamydia, genital warts, and urinary and bladder infections, as well as for vaginal and rectal tears). She struggled with constipation, even though she had trouble eating, and she went to internists and "gastro men" for help. Often she felt a kind of pounding in her cervix: "It's him, still hammering on me." The many kinds of body workers that Anna visited (without telling them her abuse story) tried to relieve her of her tension, her pain, the knots deep inside her. She saw massage therapists, chiropractors, reflexologists. But during the years that I worked with her, the only one of these auxiliaries to our therapy who really helped her was a Chinese acupuncturist who practiced near my office in the East Village. He spoke very little English and had nothing to do with her father's kind of medicine. When she complained to him of her abdominal pain, he placed his needles on her body and recommended a combination of herbs, but he never touched her directly. He contemplated her problem in his mind (as I did), mentalizing. When she was leaving, however, he spoke to her in what I call body-psychic language, while pointing to her abdomen: "Bad man come here, very bad sex man." When Anna told me about this good doctor—she came straight from his office to mine—Tiny exploded in a catharsis of tears.

Even as a three-year-old, Anna knew that her father was a different kind of man from her stepbrother the Phallus. An Oral Man, as she put it in her academic classificatory manner (which she and I shared more and more as the therapy progressed, like allied psychoanalytic explorers speaking in code). He talked a great deal ("he can't keep his mouth shut"), and she experienced his talk as deviousness and often lies—certainly as denial. He has never been able to listen to her speak about her experience or admit his own role in it, much less express sorrow or guilt about it. He rationalizes, making things seem other than they were, making the world what he wants it to be. "He is not about the phallus, he does not dominate that way, he is about oral sex, sweet talk, oily charm. Vampire Man. He always twists things so that he is the victim and women are supposed to take care of him." As though she were a psychoanalyst herself, Anna explained Oral Man as someone who had been deprived by his cold, unfeeling mother and physically abused by his harsh, critical father. As Tiny summed him up, capturing his projection of oral aggressivity: "He stuffed pills down my throat."

After Anna had described to me one day how her father manicured his hands and kept them soft with creams, I pointed out that he, like her brother with his bag of cooking oil, was "an oil man," but he lubricated his hands and used oily words. "Yes. Disgusting words, sleazy words—he is always making embarrassing crude sexual jokes, crude oil." This prompted her to tell me about something that Tiny used to do as a child that she had never been able to understand: she would draw on her own little hand, with crayons or markers, a circle divided into three equal parts, one third colored green, one red, and one blue. She would redraw the circle whenever it was washed off. I asked Anna for her associations to this symbol. At first she could not get back to Tiny's world. It was, she said, like a brightly colored baseball, and she had loved to play catch as a kid. It was a pinwheel, such fun at the country fair. Maybe it was a mandala, such as Jung studied. A sacred mandala, like the Tibetans have—she had seen them at Asia House. She went off on an erudite riff about these symbols but then stopped herself. "It is *my* hand that is power and does not invade anybody. It does not need any words, it signs. It is a hole with different parts in it protected by me."

Tiny had made signs from a very early age. Her mother told Anna that when she was two—*before* the first rape—she had used her crayons to cover as much of a wall as she could reach from her crib in round shapes, circles, with six legs, three on each side, like spider's legs. Her mother had been astonished but had no idea what these dozens of insectlike creatures meant. "Do you know?" I asked her. "Does Tiny know?" "No, I have no idea. Those were the good days—I didn't need signs of power like the mandala." When this wall drawing came up, we had to let it go, a mysterious rune out of Tiny's world. But nearly three years later, we got an important clue to its meaning.

Anna had spent a few days with her mother's other daughter, who was ten years younger than she. Her stepsister told her some things that their mother had confided concerning the first two years of Anna's life, while Anna and her mother were living with the maternal grandparents. That was the period that Anna had always thought of as the good days, Paradise, before the Fall. But "apparently, my mother was into drugs then, and left me a lot in my grandmother's care. She went out, she went back to prostitution—what she had been doing when she met my father." Anna was disillusioned, but she understood that her mother's unavailability had made her want her all the more, that she had wanted to cling to her all the more. Then she suddenly understood Tiny's stratagem: "I guess I needed to have sixty times six little legs, and sixty webs, to capture her. Lots of hands to hold tight onto her." The baby is a clinging insect. So we also knew, then, why good insects appear in her dreams as well as bad ones that suck like vampires. I reminded her that she had always said that she clung to her mother "like a little monkey—that's four arms to put around her." Anna responded, "Sometimes when I am sewing a dress I imagine I'll put it on her—all around her—and she'll be all mine." (As every attentive parent and grandparent knows, the age of two is the era of "Mine! All mine!" in a child's life; parents and possessions alike are ferociously loved, and all rivals are despised.)

Because Anna recognized so clearly and viscerally that she needed love, she had a clear sense of the forms of damage done to her by her stepbrother, her stepmother, and her father. She was able to explain to me how the forms related after she had liberated herself somewhat in our work from her father and felt herself to be "in free fall" without his familiar abuse: "I've been thinking he is the main perpetrator . . . but that's because I loved him, and identified with him, and wanted most from him in that house. He became the gatekeeper of the horrors. He permitted the rapes, he permitted [the first stepmother] to dress me up and say inappropriate things like 'if you are going to masturbate, wash your hands.' They all talked about him when they abused me. 'You're a Daddy's girl'; 'He spoils you.'" She knew that the Phallus was not the figurehead, he was the machine. A wild beast. "His rage and his own abuse history and his drugs all funneled through me to attack my father and his mother. That was powerful, but the bigger relationship—the Godhead—who hurt me the most and could have helped me the most, that was my father. In my relationships now, he is there. But also not there— because this therapy is about us breaking up, divorcing . . ." Tiny expressed this complex understanding very simply several days later: "I got cut up inside and he put salt on it so I could not heal." (That is, Tiny experienced the salve her father put on her vagina as painful, sadistically meant to keep her in pain, to keep her being abused.)

Toward her perverse obsessional stepmother ("wash your hands before you masturbate," she ordered), the one who wanted her eliminated, Anna used Tiny's body language and imagery, which were all about emotional control. Her stepmother was Control Central, both pulling things into her and pushing them away. Her presence was a swamp: Tiny could have fallen into her and drowned, or her fumes could have driven Tiny away, made her vomit. When her stepmother took her shopping to buy the "girly" clothes, Anna wanted desperately to feel this as love and caring, but she could not. In her adult, academic language, Anna explained: "My stepmother was a shopaholic, who used my father's credit card and just drove him into the ground with her purchases. He made lots of money, and she spent it all. A Big Bad American Dream."

Our picture of her hell became richer over the years of our work, but there was a period in Anna's life that remained full of blanks, and I came to feel that this period, from ages seven or eight to twelve or thirteen, had something in common with Tiny's pre-rape period, age two to three. Both periods were profoundly disorganized. Tiny was baffled and lost throughout the first of them, and the preadolescent Anna was baffled and lost throughout the second.

During the five years of her early adolescence, Anna experienced a new kind of abuse in which her stepbrother, her stepmother, and her father did not play the role of key perpetrator. This abuse escalated after her stepbrother stopped raping her consistently (at age eight) because he had become afraid of being caught. He had been reprimanded once, lightly, by Anna's father, who had discovered her diary and become afraid that she would publicly expose the open family secret, at school, perhaps, or at the theater company. During this period, the rest of the family increased their verbal abuse and enslavement of her, of Ugly. She had clear images from age eight to eleven of her stepmother controlling what she wore, refusing to feed her, and ordering her around, but she could not remember many specific details of what was done to her by the other stepsiblings at that time or after the stepmother died when she was eleven. She had vague images of herself going to bed in a sleeping bag in order to keep the boys from being able to touch her while she was asleep. A vague memory of one of her stepbrother's friends getting her high on pot and groping her. Vague images of being bullied and ordered about: she had to meet with the boys' drug dealer, for example, so that they would not be caught purchasing pot or cocaine. Another memory came forward strongly one night when the third boyfriend held her close in bed and "kissed her head all over." "I was repelled, and I think it goes back to when one of my stepbrother's friends wrapped me in a blanket and kissed my head, mocking me, teasing me—it was pseudo-affection. I can't remember what it was all about. Maybe some kind of perverse game." The strongest image from this period was of being made to get on her knees and clean up the dog's shit from the always filthy floor. When Anna described this memory she told me, too, that as a little girl she had eaten dirt in her grandmother's yard, and perhaps also at her father's. Pika (the medical term for compulsive dirt eating) runs in her family, she said; her mother, too, ate dirt.

In my estimation, this early-adolescent period was vague and full of blanks because so many forms of abuse were mingled up in it: so many people, so many motivations. It could not be navigated with the clear map that young Tiny had made of her bodyworld and the motivational world of her abusers. Tiny knew what her stepmother wanted: to eliminate her. She knew what her stepbrother wanted: to make her play a sexual role for him. Later, Anna could add that he banged on her—in her—like a hammer in order to keep her sexuality down and make sure that she did not become her father's darling and get all the goods. To make sure that her sexuality, her femaleness, did not win her any favors, the stepbrother commanded it brutally; he made her Ugly. Tiny knew what her father wanted: to jerk her around like a puppet, to use her as his in-house trophy girl, the incarnation and representation of her mother, not for sex per se, but as a sexualized creature and a self-flatteringly redeemed young goddess. She served his narcissism.

But as an early adolescent, out in the general chaos of "emotional abuse," with so many abusers around, Tiny became disoriented, unable to use her psychic powers, jammed. While her stepmother was alive she had controlled this world and its goods—particularly its food—and her father had let it happen by being absent and being the man whose money everyone wanted. But basically it was anarchic, a mapless jungle. Anna was experiencing something that came to be known in the 1980s child-abuse literature as MV/MO (multiple victim/multiple offender), similar to what can happen in a cult or a sex ring. I would not be surprised to learn that the boys who abused her were aware of the contemporaneous satanic ritual abuse panic that was all over the American news media, with its bizarre imagery.

Later, when Anna was trying to live in the world as an adult—to work in various kinds of workplaces, perform in theater troupes, and make her way in New York City—she encountered variations on this baffling multi-abuse jungle over and over, although she also met her three abuser archetypes. We found that we could consider her experiences as they came, in the present, without having to reference them to that unclear period. But we received a powerful lesson in why multi-abuse, multi-abuser scenes are so terrifying—they can defeat the need for understanding and truth. We also had to recognize that a good enough psychoanalysis, like a good enough parent, can be—as she always said—"empowering."

After eight years of work (at varying frequencies, from four times a week to once a week, depending on Anna's work and travel schedule), we decided that Anna was doing well enough for us to end our sessions. But I told her that I would like to work for a few months more at greater frequency (using the analytic couch) because I felt that we needed to revisit the story—"the whole story"—that we had put together and lived through. While she was on a vacation with the third boyfriend, I read back through my notes on her, which included an extensive collection of her dreams. (I had the uncanny experience, which I have had with other analytic patients as well, of realizing on reading my record of the first session that it was a miniature version of "the whole story," although neither she nor I could have known that at the time.)

"We had a wonderful trip," she said as she came into my office and went over to the couch, where she curled up on her side, so she could look at me. "My sinuses were so clear in the dry air! I could breathe! The mountains were so beautiful! I was so beautiful! My body was strong, hiking was easy, and I just strode along, not at all like a driven, crazy New Yorker. As much like a Native American as I could be, at home in the wilderness." She went on happily, but then grew sad. "Since we got back, I have been completely depressed. It started a little on the trip. In the afternoons. Last night, we went to the theater and saw a fabulous *Macbeth*—all in Polish! On the wharves in Brooklyn! I was so excited. But then by the end of the evening, in bed, I was completely unavailable. I don't know what is the matter. It's not my hysteria, it's depression. No drama. I am of course just going about my days, getting stuff done, taking on the new job. There's going to be a big challenge there, because they have hired a pervert, a sleazy pervert, about thirty years old, and they don't know it, or won't know it. Really, people are so thick when it comes to perversion, they absolutely do not see the obvious. I'll have to handle it, protect the young people. But inside I feel dead."

We understood pretty quickly that having a wonderful, relaxed time on vacation with her boyfriend had made

Anna apprehensive, and that she was also apprehensive about ending the therapy. She was asking herself when the pleasure was going to be followed by pain. When was the boyfriend going to reveal himself to be in reality a pervert, an abuser of some sort? When was she going to lose her figure because she was working too hard and had no time to go to the gym, "so I'll be just another fat ass and he won't love me anymore, he'll go off with another woman, an undamaged one"? Anna could correct herself, could reassure herself, but she could not get out of her state of anxiety.

Soon afterward she experienced a new abuse, which allowed us, once more, to listen to her pain—but this time through our hard-won perspective. She visited her mother and the mother's current boyfriend, and during the visit the man logged onto Anna's computer and accessed her e-mail and files. He read through her correspondence with her second boyfriend, some of which was highly erotic, and explored her current business and personal correspondence. Several days later, when she told me about this violation—"this huge, huge boundary violation"—Anna had already made up her mind what she was going to do about it and had acted. She had confronted the man, told him that she had been able to track in detail the tour he had taken of her computer, and informed him that she would never again come to his house or let him in hers. He had responded by saying that she was making "a big deal out of nothing": she was being "oversensitive," and her reaction would cost her her relationship with her mother, who would never stand for this kind of "verbally abusive attack" on him.

Anna held her ground, trusting that she was not at fault or being hypersensitive, and trusting also in her mother's capacity to judge the situation correctly and not let herself be bullied, which turned out to be the case. And that experience, in turn, allowed Anna to recognize two things: something she had been unwilling to admit about her third boyfriend and something she had been unwilling to admit about how she behaved with me. "I have been trying to impress you, to be a really good girl for you, so you would love me forever, even after we stop. Too much performance! So I didn't want to tell you that I am not really so happy with my boyfriend—I am, but I'm not. He is a good man, who can be a nurturer. But he is using me. I'm his obsession. He is controlling, and very jealous of any man who looks at me, and even of my work whenever it involves people looking at me. It's not perverse like my father, but he does want me to be the woman he wants, and that includes sexually—he wants to set the terms. I always feel crowded out, or smothered." She allowed herself to tell me in detail what felt wrong without assuming that she herself was making things feel wrong or refusing to accept happiness. We could talk about whether, in her fear of not living up to my hopes for her, she had been experiencing me as demanding that she play the role of the good patient, the good psychoanalytic explorer, hiking boldly into the wilderness.

Anna broke up with the third boyfriend and then had a period of more than six months in which she was not sexually active—for the first time since she was three. We did not stop working but instead reduced the frequency of our meetings. During this period, she corresponded with a man she had met on a business trip and had found interesting. They began to talk in the evenings via the Internet. "All he can see of me is my face on Skype. Not my body. This is not about sex. He wants to know me. He enjoys my mind. We meet in love for the theater, but it is way more than that." Their relationship grew, and she told me about it each time we met, now once every two weeks.

She visited her friend's family home at Christmastime and met his parents, his siblings, and a troop of little nieces and nephews, all in a simple, warm, orderly house that stirred memories of her childhood performance school and its remarkable director. The family loved her and were physically affectionate with her, even the mother, who, Anna said with great knowingness, "needs to be perfect and is tempted to kiss in order to win admiration." But then she laughed: "There are way worse reasons to kiss!"

"This really was the right way for me to learn to love— to start with a long time of caring and affection and shared interests and 'getting to know you' and meeting the family, and then to have sex. So the sex is not about power, not about being used or abused. It's about celebrating the love once you are sure of it. I'm not saying it has to be that way for everybody, but it needed to be that way for me because I should never have sex with somebody *hoping* there will be no perversities and that any problems can be handled. It shouldn't be for me that I *hope* love will find a way, or love will conquer all, and all that romantic stuff. I need to be safe! Safety first! And then we can go sailing freely and maybe not sink." Anna stared at me for a while, told me a bit more about why she trusted this man who had patiently, understanding his own needs as well as hers, engaged her in a six-month conversation before he touched her. Then she laughed: "Well, I suppose that is what I learned here—talk, talk, talk honestly for as long as you need to. Then you can leave and go on and look for the right person, for real, you know, in reality, really in life. Real person to real person, no performance. Or leave performance for the theater. But it will be for real there, too!"

CHAPTER THREE

Child Abuse and Neglect
A Study in Confusion

IN ANNA'S HOME—IN ANNA'S HELL—THE ADULTS WHO abused her shared a childist belief that she, the one young child in the household, was theirs to do with as they pleased. They felt no responsibility to cherish and educate her, or to put her needs first. As a child, she was at their service to satisfy their needs and desires. But they had individual needs and desires, and Anna had to work hard to figure out what those needs were. And as she carefully studied her abusers she internalized both their shared prejudice that children are servants of adults and their individual projections onto her. She repressed her own desires and needs and became the child Tiny and then the adolescent Ugly, feeling that the abuse she endured was shameful, and that she was bad, toxic. Later, during her teenage therapy and in psychoanalysis with me, she continued to try to understand her abusers, but now she sought to uncover the motivations of her abusers' actions as a way of escaping her victimization. But Tiny and Ugly were paralyzed and self-castigating, trapped by the beliefs with which the adults justified their actions and their motivations— their childism. "I became a competent child, *but all confused*," she had told me the first day she came to my office. Until the end of our work, she struggled not to perform for the adults, and not to perform for me either.

It was during the last phase of my work with Anna that I began saying to myself that the therapy would eventually have to encompass the whole of her understanding of the motivations and prejudices of the adults who had harmed her, for those motivations and prejudices were inside her— she had turned them against herself. Therapists speak of "abreacting" a trauma, allowing it to be expressed in the therapy and with the therapist so that it can be confronted and worked through. This is shared clinical wisdom, like the wisdom of tragedians that they must engage their audiences in a catharsis of fear and pity. But I was also telling myself that the trauma was not just "what Anna suffered in hell" but the beliefs—the childism—with which the adults legitimated what they inflicted on her. Without this abreacting step, she would continue to inflict suffering on herself and would never be able to protect herself.

Anna's experience, and the experiences of other patients I was treating at the same time (some of which will be discussed below), prompted me to think about how we deal with child abuse in the United States. Was childism something like internalized racism or sexism? There is an entire field of studies known as Child Abuse and Neglect, but I began to wonder whether the founders of the field had made a distinction between acts committed against children—as a group and individually—and beliefs justifying those acts and their motivations, as was the case in the field of Prejudice Studies. Even in Prejudice Studies the acts/justification distinction became important only when those who experienced racism or sexism insisted on it. Was it part of either field in 1978, when the three-year-old Anna was first raped, and when the mandatory reporting of "child abuse and neglect" by childcare professionals was also three years old? I knew that reporting had been a major requirement of the federal Child Abuse Prevention and Treatment Act, which went into effect in 1974, with variations across the fifty states. But *what,* exactly, were reporters—including myself as a professional therapist—mandated to report? Only knowledge of or suspicions about specific acts? Or did the obligation include suspicions that a child had been a victim of something like what later came to be called "a hate crime," an act directed by a prejudice like racism or sexism or homophobia?

To answer these questions, I began to read in the vast CAN literature, which by 2001, when Anna came into treatment with me, had grown to hundreds of books and journals, including the flagship international journal from the 1970s, *Child Abuse and Neglect.* Every book or article I took up began with a description of the field's foundational moment, which those in CAN designate "The Discovery of Child Abuse" or, more accurately, "The Scientific Discovery of Child Abuse" (as child abuse was, of course, known in all societies for which there are records).

What everyone was describing was an article published in the *Journal of the American Medical Association* in 1962. The lead author, Dr. C. Henry Kempe, a psychoanalytically trained pediatric psychiatrist at the General Hospital in Denver, suspecting that about 10 percent of the infants and toddlers admitted to his pediatric emergency room had been physically abused, had begun an intensive investigation. Working with his colleagues and his wife, Ruth, a child psychiatrist, he had reported his findings to his peers at their national meeting in 1961, and then in this article, titled "The Battered Child Syndrome." The article was later reprinted in a 1968 book, *The Battered Child,* which is still—in its fifth edition—basic reading in the field it helped found. The book is like the Constitution of CAN.

"The discovery of child abuse" was not a clinical discovery in which health care professionals listened to abused children (or to adults who had been abused as children, or to abusing adults). It was a research discovery made for a very specific purpose with a very specific population, infants and toddlers brought to an E.R. The children seen by the Kempe group presented not with their stories—most of them were preverbal—but with bruises and broken bones. The parents who brought them to the E.R. explained that they had fallen or been accidentally dropped or injured by a careless babysitter. But the emergency room staff suspected that the babies had been beaten and battered intentionally. The purpose of their investigation was to find a way to prove that the children had been physically abused. Proof would support legal action against the abusing parent(s).

The proof was also very specific: X-rays taken of the children's skulls and long bones that could reveal a pattern, like an archaeological site; multiple fractures of different vintages on one arm, now broken again; a break that could only have come from a violent twist; a swelling under the cranium (subdural hematoma) indicating that the cranium had been hit, even if it showed no fractures. When a child had been battered frequently—and it often turned out that the child had been treated at different hospitals —X-rays could reveal the palimpsest of skeletal damage or scar tissue. A metabolic bone disease resulting in broken bones would never reveal such a pattern. And such a pattern could not be the result of an accident or a single instance of careless handling or the onetime work of a stranger or a bully. The X-rays photographed a crime scene, and the pediatricians learned to investigate it.

What the Kempe group had done by interpreting their X-rays in this way revolutionized not only pediatric radiology but pediatrics generally. It opened doctors' eyes to what they had been unwilling to see. The effect is clear in a memoir by a pediatrician named Abraham Bergmann:

> Etched in my memory is an x-ray conference during my internship at Boston's Children's Hospital in 1959, before the "discovery" of child abuse. A film was displayed of an infant with multiple fractures of varying ages. The debate among the eminent clinicians present was not about whether the diagnosis was a metabolic bone disease, but which one. The sole dissenter was the radiologist Martin Wittenborg, who said simply "This is trauma." He was ignored. The classic paper by two distinguished pediatric neurosurgeons on subdural hematoma in infancy came from the same institution. Ninety-eight cases between 1937 and 1943 were described. With our present [post-1962] state of knowledge, most of these infants would have been considered to be abused, yet that possibility is never mentioned in the paper.

The discovery of child abuse, then, was also the discovery of blindness to child abuse. Looking at what they thought were symptoms of bone disease, pediatricians had asked "which bone disease?" as the key to finding the specific cause, eliminating it, and thus eliminating the disease. Rickets had been dealt with this way early in the twentieth century: once its cause—nutrition deficiency, insufficient vitamin D—was addressed, rickets disappeared. When pediatricians became able to read an X-ray and say, "This is trauma," they could look for the cause of the trauma—identify the perpetrator—and then put the perpetrator in prison or remove the traumatized child, using separation or foster care in the same way they used quarantine to isolate people with contagious diseases.

The Kempe group's medical or public health model founded the field of Child Abuse and Neglect as a kind of public health field, with epidemiological researchers who located outbreaks of child abuse and neglect, explored their causes, and worked to eliminate those causes. Their outbreak information came from emergency rooms, and later from mandated reporters, and later still from a vast corps of Child Protective Services (CPS) investigative personnel following up mandated reports. But the problems and limitations of this approach inevitably came to the fore.

The cause of an abused or neglected child's "disease" is (usually) a parent or family member or someone close to the family. Is the solution to remove all abusing or neglecting parents from their homes and their parenting roles, or to remove the children from their parents (say, into foster homes)? Or are some abusing or neglectful parents less than criminal and correctable—imperfect but not deeply or recurrently traumatizing to their children? Where should a line between poor parenting and intentional abuse be drawn? Is there a gray area? Would a change in the conditions in which children and their parents lived—for example, poverty conditions or chronic stress conditions or marital abuse conditions— eliminate the cause, the way changing the hygiene systems of human habitats can, to a great extent, eliminate the microbial causes of infectious diseases?

Reading the CAN literature some forty years after the field was launched in the 1960s, I could easily see that the medical or public health model the Kempe group subscribed to and then helped establish and institutionalize throughout the United States was flawed. People are not germs. A blow that breaks a child's bone is not a bacillus. Identifying a parent as a perpetrator is a frightening and complicated matter for all concerned, not least the child. People who cause a child harm have causes *in themselves,* not just from their habitats, for their actions, although their living conditions may be miserable and frustrating and conducive to violence. People have motivations, and they have beliefs that justify their motivations and their actions. Those parental motivations and prejudices lodge in their children along with the physical blows and attacks or the verbal blows and emotional attacks. In Prejudice Studies, researchers would say that children "catch" projections that parents have used to rid themselves of their own inner pain and conflict, and children suffer within the systems of discrimination that adults create to keep their projections lodged within their victims, out of sight, out of mind.

As I read further in the CAN literature, I could see that it had never intersected with Prejudice Studies; it had remained a public health field, and a very narrowly set up one, unable to deal with the complexities of human motivation and discrimination. CAN researchers looked for a single cause that operated like a germ; when they could not find it in one place, they looked in another. But the field shared this reductionist tendency with an aspect of Prejudice Studies that was—and still is—reductive. As I noted in Chapter 1, until the victims of prejudices like racism, sexism, and homophobia began to insist on making their own stories central to the field, a too-simple model had prevailed: that model identified all prejudice as "us vs. them on the grounds of x." All prejudice was seen as ethnocentrism in which one group (one *ethnos*) projected needs and desires and conflicts onto another (or even all others).

This grand edifice of theorizing had been toppled when women insisted that what they experienced was specific to them and that it needed its own name, "sexism." African Americans insisted that the racism they experienced was not the same as anti-Semitism. What had been learned about anti-Semitism should not be transferred into the study of racism, determining its questions and answers. Nor should "racism" be appropriated and used for understanding anti-Semitism. Definitions of prejudice began slowly to reflect this shift in thinking in the early 1960s, just when the Kempe group began its own research. So when CAN was founded, it was not common knowledge that the victims of an attack must be consulted in order to analyze that experience, or that researchers needed to look beneath acts to the complex, multiple motivations and beliefs guiding those acts.

The field of CAN did not, at its inception, have in it the voices of abused and neglected children. The battered children the Kempe group studied and treated were too young to tell their stories verbally, and, besides, what the Kempe group wanted first and foremost was the evidence of their bruises and broken bones as X-rays could present them. With the best of protective intentions, the pediatricians wanted to make a case against the physical abusers. I kept thinking of Anna's description of her lawyer helping her in the mid-1990s to prepare a case against her stepbrother. The lawyer wanted to present evidence of a specific act, rape. He assembled her early medical records from the 1970s with their descriptions of her injuries and infections and with "suspected sexual abuse" duly noted (although no reports had ever been filed). Proof would get the perpetrator sent to prison. When she wanted to tell the lawyer the whole story as she then knew it, he stopped her. "Enough is enough." "It is too horrible to be true." The trial, she had told me, had empowered her. But she was also left confused and unsure of her own ability to speak the truth, to tell the whole story. The lawyer thinks I am a bad girl and a liar, Ugly thought; it really *is* all my fault, Tiny felt.

As I reflected on "the battered child syndrome," it seemed to me that the Kempe group and the doctors who learned from the group had been initially tremendously empowered by their discovery, their ability to assist prosecutions and, later, to assist legislators in formulating mandatory reporting laws and eventually shaping the Child Abuse Prevention and Treatment Act. But the situation had become confused because the doctors did not—perhaps could not, given their mission—look for the whole story. Perhaps it was "too horrible to be true."

The history of the discovery of child abuse and of how that discovery was built into legislation to combat child abuse and neglect, and from there into social policy to protect children from abuse, is crucial, I think, to addressing the disastrous consequences all these well-meaning efforts have had— and continue to have—for children. Because CAN did not understand adult motivation and childism, childism was built into the whole field and its legal and policy advocacy. It is time to tell the story about "the discovery of child abuse" from the point of view of those who experience childism.

In a decision that had far-reaching ramifications, Dr. Kempe had offered a name for the abuses he investigated: "the battered child syndrome." Relying on his medical and public health model, he construed the children's injuries (emphasizing battering rather than any other type of physical injury) as a disease *of the child*. Not a disease *of the abuser* that is manifested on the child, though he had originally considered "parental abuse" as the general name for what he was exploring. The battered child has a *syndrome*, which implies medically that there is a *single* cause, a *typical* course, and (potentially) a *single* cure (like a vaccine) or treatment modality that will eventually lead to a prevention program that can eliminate the cause and with it the problem. The name thus from the start took attention away from abusers and their motivations; and it implied that children could be helped without their abusers being helped. The abusers were, on the contrary, to be *identified*—they, too, must have identifying features typical of their class of "abusers." So the idea grew up that all abusers must be similar, just as the idea had grown up in Prejudice Studies that all prejudiced people must be similar and similarly prejudiced. At the least, it was hoped that people who were "high risk" for abusing could be identified after a description of "the abuser" was generated. As far as "the abuser" was concerned, CAN began to operate like a police department building up a profile.

Kempe's group started gathering data on the parents they met in their E.R. and came up with a preliminary report that offered a two-part working classification based on the *Diagnostic and Statistical Manual* of the American Psychiatric Association, which had been in use throughout the 1950s. Some 10 percent of abusers are psychotic or psychopathic, the report suggested, and abusing is a symptom of their pathology or psychopathy. They are schizophrenics whose children have become part of their delusional system, or they are psychopaths who direct their criminal intent toward children (though no reason was given for this preference). In the early 1960s, and even today, psychopaths (sometimes called sociopaths) were considered untreatable. So the conclusion followed that no child should ever be left in a psychopath's care, and for their crimes against children psychopaths should be put in a prison or a psychiatric facility. (No conclusion about schizophrenics was drawn in this report.)

The other 90 percent of abusers, the report indicated, did not meet DSM criteria for any particular clinical diagnosis. They were "normal." However, they were said to have in common a "defect in character structure which allows aggressive impulses to be expressed too freely." The character structure that was said to be defective was typical of a person who was "immature, impulsive, self-centered, hypersensitive, and quick to react with poorly controlled aggression." No other character types appeared in the Kempe team's preliminary analysis. Further, there was no indication of why this type, which resembled the extreme or distorted psychoanalytic "hysterical character," would target a child. People with poorly controlled aggression are aggressive, the report said, offering the kind of circular definition that has plagued Prejudice Studies, too. But this circular definition did not explain *child* abuse.

The preliminary report had nothing specific to say about what might be causing an abusive person to abuse, and to abuse a child rather than another adult—that is, there was no sense that children are a target group. But Kempe did realize that his report was only preliminary and needed follow-up. So he asked his psychiatrist colleague Brandt F. Steele, who was joined by Carl B. Pollack, to talk to the parents of a battered baby in the pediatric ward to see whether they could discover more about "the why and wherefore of this distressing type of behavior." Steele and Pollack later wrote: "This first patient, an effusive, *hysterical* [italics added] woman with a vivid, dramatic history and way of life, turned out to be a challenging 'gold mine' of psychopathology." (Her "psychopathology" was not specified: was she psychopathic or just an extremely neurotic hysteric?) Over five and a half years, the team studied sixty families, some referred from the pediatric ward or the psychiatric clinic, some from social work agencies. One couple "was first seen in jail after we read newspaper reports of their arrest for child beating." But the researchers kept to their original goal: isolate the single physically abusive type that we can identify by his or her character defect and aggressivity; if we can identify this type in advance of any battering, perhaps we can prevent the battering.

Steele and Pollack acknowledged candidly that the population they studied was not in any way representative, and that they had used no non-abusing, good enough parents as controls for their research. They began with subjects who had physically abused their children quite severely, and thus the children qualified without question for the diagnosis "battered child syndrome." But then, realizing that "we were dealing with only the extreme of a much more widespread phenomenon," they turned to subjects whose abuse was closer to "the gray area between 'real abuse' and the 'accidental' signs of appropriate, albeit severe, disciplinary punishment." Along the way to this gray area, they ruled out of consideration child murder by psychotics, which they felt was quite different from "the battered child syndrome" because murder involves a single violent episode rather than a behavior pattern. They did not discuss whether an episode and a pattern could be similarly motivated, nor whether a "normal" person, a neurotic, a psychotic, and a psychopath could share similar motivations and beliefs.

This narrowing of focus was crucial: just when they had identified battering as a specific act and noted that they needed to investigate "a much more widespread phenomenon," they began limiting their study. They did not say: We should be talking about all the kinds of traumatization of children, by all the varieties of means or acts, including the ones for which we cannot offer the definitive evidence of X-rays. If we looked at this as a disease among adults called "traumatizing children," rather than as a syndrome among babies, we could seek out motivations or causes of every sort of traumatizing behavior. Instead, they turned away from the bigger picture that had started to emerge and began narrowing their focus once more, first by ruling out murder. It was as though they had said, There will be no Medeas in our study; in our theater, there is no infanticide. "Enough is enough." "Too horrible to be true."

Further, by considering murder as "an episode" rather than an aspect of the disease, the researchers ignored murder by other means than battering, such as murder by neglect (for example, by slow starvation), which is a chronic occurrence and sometimes takes years to reach its finale. (Later researchers would report that the majority of maltreated children are neglected and, further, that the majority of children who die of maltreatment die of homicide by neglect.) Then, in yet another narrowing down, Steele and Pollack decided to focus only on babies and toddlers, which meant ruling out any longitudinal study of effects of abuse over time or of differences between the experiences of younger and older abused children. In a corollary move, they decided not to consider physical abusers of children ages four, five, and older because they considered abuse of older children as possibly being "much more involved with matters of sexuality than is attack on small children." They did not explore the idea that physical abuse and sexual abuse might (and often do) go together. To simplify their study, they also decided not to interview adults who were both physical and sexual abusers, thus ruling out any inquiry into how physical abuse and sexual abuse might serve the same purpose and have the same motivation for an adult.

By the time Steele and Pollack had finished ruling out areas of study, they had also effectively ruled out the possibility that they would discover anything they did not already think they knew—and they had closed off important fields for Child Abuse and Neglect Studies. The distinction between younger abused children and youths, for example, which is important in all types of abuse acts, was not followed up in later literature on physical abuse. Remarkably (indeed, tragically), the ages of physically abused children are almost never reported, unlike reporting of sexual abuse, which usually distinguishes among infants and toddlers, prepubescent elementary school children, and pubescent adolescents. The "battered child syndrome" always referred to very young children only; there is no corresponding "battered adolescent syndrome" in the literature. The research bias against attending to age, of course, also precluded exploring what abuse (other than sexual abuse) means for children at different developmental stages, what children of different developmental stages mean to their abusers, and what different age groups are capable of understanding about their abusers and could describe to researchers. Developmental child study was not originally a part of CAN at all.

With regard to the study of abusers, the Steele and Pollack research, with all that it had ruled out, was so narrow in focus that it admitted no questions about the plurality of character types that might be involved in abuse, about the social or cultural attitudes that might impinge on it, or about any other motivational contexts. The pioneering scientific discoverers of "child abuse and neglect" ended up making impossible their original vision of approaching "child abuse and neglect" as a public health issue, in which causes could be identified and cures found that would diminish the problem over time and eventually lead to prevention. Their narrow notion of "cause"—modeled on the idea of the germ—was self-defeating from the start.

And the researchers' ruling-out method also led them to rule out research that did not conform to their own methodology. In the 1950s—before the "discovery of child abuse"—

child abuse had already been studied scientifically by social workers, but at that time social work methods were not considered truly scientific, and they were not organized on the medical model. On the shelves of the New York University library where all the CAN books are kept I found a dusty volume, not checked out for decades and long out of print, that is to my mind far superior to any published in the years when CAN was launched as a field. Based on a decade of previous work, *Wednesday's Children* (1964) was by an Ohio social worker named Leontine Young. Real children and real adults appear in this book, and clinically trained social workers—obviously psychoanalytically trained—listen to them as they describe their experiences.

An extensive case study opens *Wednesday's Children*. We meet the Nolans, a college-educated couple living without financial worries in a comfortable house, generously supplying their four children's every material and educational need. Like a character out of Betty Friedan's pioneering study of sexism, *The Feminine Mystique* (1963), Mrs. Nolan is subservient to her husband, the family provider, adoring him and according him complete control in the household, although she finds his violence confusing and distressing. He beats the children, particularly her favorite, Donald, who is nine. Donald is the "scapegoat," routinely terrorized and beaten until he collapses. Because a neighbor has reported Mr. Nolan for brutalizing his children, he has found himself in front of a social agency caseworker talking about Donald's younger brother:

> He is explaining that he loves his children. His wife indulges them too much, but that is really the only problem. Of course, the children have to obey his commands, and when they don't he punishes them. One evening recently

he told his four year old son to go into the basement and stay there. The little boy went down the stairs and ran quickly back. It was very dark and he was frightened. "I spanked him and told him to go back," explains the smiling father. "He went down the stairs again and ran back to the light, frightened, so I spanked him again and sent him back. He returned four times and each time I spanked him harder. The last time he stayed down."

When asked what the little boy has done to deserve such severe corporal punishment, Mr. Nolan is taken aback. He cannot remember what the child did, and he clearly does not think that spanking him is a severe punishment. When she is interviewed, Mrs. Nolan, although she clings desperately to the abuser—as is typical of women in this kind of marriage—does acknowledge his tyrannical tactics and even recognizes that a family triangle is involved (a rivalrous Oedipal triangle, the Freudian social work clinician noted). Mr. Nolan wants to "break the children," especially Donald, a child who keeps his emotional distance. "Donald is like me," Mrs. Nolan notes. "He doesn't need outside recognition. He gets his security from inside himself. He only needs to know I care about him." She is worried, though, because Donald is still wetting his bed at night; sometimes he wakes up screaming; he is tense, and if someone comes upon him unexpectedly, he will cry out and then fall into a stony silence.

A few months after Donald ended up in the hospital with a broken leg that his father said had been caused by falling down the stairs, Mrs. Nolan tried to kill herself. She was depressed, Mr. Nolan explained. As he was pledging to the social workers that he would take over more of the childcare in order to relieve his wife of the strain of looking after four children, particularly Donald, he let drop in an unguarded moment that he hated Donald "because he is like his mother."

In their triangle, his wife and son were allied and identified, and his authority was being undermined. So he reasserted that authority brutally.

"This is the outline of abuse," Young commented, and she went on to offer a general characterization of the physically abusing parent in which the key psychodynamic or motivational word was *perverse* (and the unspoken one was *sadism*). Physical abuse

> is not the impetuous blow of the harassed parent or even the transient brutality of an indifferent parent expressing with violence the immediate frustration of his life. It is not the too severe discipline nor the physical roughness of ignorance. It is the perverse fascination with punishment as an entity in itself, divorced from discipline or even the fury of revenge. It is the cold calculation of destruction which in itself requires neither provocation nor rationale. . . . The one invariable trademark of the abusing parent regardless of economic or social status is this immersion in the action of punishing without regard for its cause or its purpose. . . . The violence created terror and panic for the child, but it did not teach him any rational means of avoiding that violence. Like an earthquake, it struck without warning, and this was part of its terror.

As was typical, I found, of all the clinically astute researchers of this period, Young focused on physical abuse—just one area of the vast field of child maltreatment. (In terms of social context, I think she was responding to the upsurge of male physical abuse of women and children—soon to be called "domestic violence"—that came with the return of traumatized soldiers from World War II and the Korean War, and with the incipient feminist revolt against the middle-class family structure, which Betty Friedan was then describing in *The Feminine Mystique*.) Young also singled out only one feature that was commonly observed in male physical abusers: perverse fascination with punishment itself, used to make sure that no one gained power inside the household or refused to recognize patriarchal authority. But she did not see this perverse fascination as a trait typical of *obsessionally* organized sadists and torturers, domestic storm troopers set on eliminating their victims with "the cold calculation of destruction." She could see clearly a character structure shaping Mr. Nolan's obsessional desire for dictatorship in his household, but she did not emphasize it or name it.

I found only one isolated effort among clinical social workers at the time to create a broader characterological picture of physical abusers, and it came from a group in the Massachusetts branch of the Society for the Prevention of Cruelty to Children, who reported their work through a brief American Humane Society pamphlet published in 1962. Drawing on a clinical interview study of 115 families with children who were referred to his agency in 1960, the reporter, Edgar Merrill, suggested that there were basically three clusters of personality characteristics—that is, three character types— to be found among both men and women who physically abuse children, and one subgroup cluster specific to men. Although his subjects were physical abusers, Merrill said little about the specific types of acts they engaged in; his goal was to show multiple features in the abusers and distinguish them— in effect, creating a characterology. But he made it clear that the three character types he described also channeled quite individual, intrapsychic hatred and self-hatred and made quite specific defensive projections.

The first group of abusers described by Merrill were angry and hostile toward both specific targets in their environments and the world in general. They were constantly simmering with anger, which could be heated up or triggered by specific daily troubles and difficulties. Their anger could be traced to their childhoods and conflicts they had had with their own parents. "Take for example the mother who came from a home where emotional rejection and deprivation were severe, where hostility and attack were the acceptable forms of behavior." Merrill noted that "fathers are more apt to express their hostility by acts outside the home as well," and also that "some of their abuse had more serious consequences." Merrill did not use the psychoanalytic phrase "narcissistically wounded," but the angry, accusatory people in this group seemed to be, each in his or her own individual way, suffering from fluctuating self-esteem and frustrated ambition; they were all using their children to right the specific wrongs they perceived themselves to have suffered. One mother, for example, had four children but beat only one, her son. With therapeutic help, she was able to see that she identified this boy with her brother, who had been favored and indulged while she was neglected. She imagined that her son was going to marginalize her as the brother had, so she erased his sense of himself with blows. Each of the parents in this group had individual agendas of success or failure for his or her children to fulfill, and all felt righteously entitled to exact the fulfillment. That is, they justified their behavior by their narcissistic childism, their belief that their children existed to serve their needs.

A particular group of men in Merrill's sample seems to be a subgroup of this first angry, wounded type. "These fathers were fully or partially unable to support their families due to a physical disability of some degree," and most of them were at home with their children in the traditional mothering role. "The atmosphere of the home was seen as angry, rigid, and controlled. Strict discipline and control were exerted, and punishment was swift and severe." The fathers in this group were "often intelligent, young men with acquired skills" and social status who had been accustomed to performing well and providing capably for their families before their disability deprived them of the status of family provider. The loss of status was their narcissistic wound, which reopened a specific earlier wound from childhood. (I wondered how many of this group were disabled veterans with undiagnosed post-traumatic stress disorder—a diagnostic category that only came into existence in 1980 after the Vietnam War.)

The second group that Merrill identified were cold, rigid men and women of marked compulsiveness or obsessionality who were unable to feel love or protectiveness for their children. They lacked any "reasonableness and pliability in their thinking and their beliefs." Tending to blame their children for whatever troubles they experienced, they viewed them as interfering with their own aims and pleasures, as undermining them. "These parents were extremely compulsive in their behavior, that is, there seems to be almost an 'I can't stop what I am doing' quality to them." This was shown in their compulsive housecleaning, the demands made on their children for excessive cleanliness, and their negative attitude toward sex, dirt, and bodily processes generally, which they tended to characterize as dangerously bad, to be feared and avoided. "Many of these parents had great difficulty in relaxing, in expressing themselves verbally, and in exhibiting warmth and friendliness." In these households, the motto seemed to be Total Control. All unwanted, bad feelings were projected onto a child or the children, who were pushed away and punished for their "badness." (These were parents with "the cold calculation of destruction" that Young had observed in Mr. Nolan, and that I observed in Anna's stepmother.)

Finally, a third group of men and women "showed strong feelings of passivity and dependence." These parents were unaggressive or intermittently aggressive, reticent about showing their emotions or desires but characterized by a general depressiveness; they "seemed continually sad, moody, unresponsive and unhappy." Immaturity and lack of a clear identity were typical: "They questioned whether they wanted to be married, have children, or even have a place of their own. Some of them were still dominated by their families, a fact they did not always resent and frequently were openly seeking." In keeping with their "I won't [can't] grow up" tendency to seek parenting for themselves—to seek people on whom they could depend and who would tell them what to do—these parents competed with their own children for love and attention, creating rivalries with their spouses. They would episodically snap out of their usual passivity, becoming explosively angry when they were not getting enough attention, and taking revenge by acting impulsively or throwing a tantrum. They kept households where an economy scarce in emotional goods prevailed and histrionically making scenes to grab attention was the norm. Physical abuse was not perversely enjoyed or felt to be satisfying as a means of erasing a child's threatening identity; it was part of a script for getting attention in which children were to play assigned servant roles. (The hysterical abuser who was a "'gold mine' of psychopathology" for Steele and Pollack was apparently of this type, impulsive and explosively aggressive, like Mrs. Nolan and Anna's stepbrother.)

In the characterology proposed by Freud and developed over the course of psychoanalytic history, people of these three types—the angry, wounded, frustrated type; the cold, rigid, repressed type; and the dependent, love-starved, depressed type—became known as narcissistic, obsessional, and hysterical characters. Although he was clearly psychoanalytically trained, like the majority of social workers in the early 1960s, Merrill did not refer explicitly to the Freudian character types, but he does seem to have been aware of the Freudian tradition of studying character types and linking them to social issues. This tradition had flourished after World War II and continued through the 1960s in American universities. In the series called Studies in Prejudice, the model study, *The Authoritarian Personality* (1951), produced by a team of psychoanalysts and empirical researchers, presented a character who was prejudiced against all groups not his own and saw conspiracies everywhere; this was an obsessional character type (mixed with many narcissistic features), and it thus resembled Merrill's second example, the cold, obsessive type. But Merrill did not link his abusing character types to types of prejudiced people.

In the rich social work research tradition that Leontine Young and Edgar Merrill worked in and developed, where the people being studied were seen in their homes, not in emergency rooms, there was no assumption of a *single* character type or generic abuser. Physical abuse, although it was the focus, was not the only kind of abuse observed. Donald Nolan was obviously emotionally tormented, not just battered or thrown around; his little brother was also terrorized. When they began their research, Steele and Pollack and the pediatrician researchers who followed them basically ignored the social work approach. But when they later widened their research a bit and talked one to one with older, verbal children who had been physically abused, they came into agreement with a key social work insight.

By listening to children, the psychiatrists determined that all the abusing parents had in common an "underlying attitude of demand and criticism" in relation to their children. Considering the parental "attitude" (which I would call a prejudgment or prejudice), the researchers were able to identify "role reversal." The children had been called upon to give the parents the love and attention that the parents had not gotten from their own parents. Writing about the physically abused older children in *The Battered Child,* Steele and Pollack noted about role reversal that

> all [the abusers] had experienced . . . a sense of intense, continuous, pervasive demand from their parents. This demand was in the form of expectations of good, submissive behavior, prompt obedience, never making mistakes, sympathetic comforting of parental distress, and showing approval and help for parental actions. . . . Performance was expected before the child was able to comprehend fully what was expected or how to accomplish it. Accompanying the parental demand was a sense of constant parental criticism. Performance was pictured as erroneous, inadequate, inept, and ineffectual. No matter what the patient as a child tried to do, it was not enough, it was not right, it was at the wrong time, it bothered the parents, it would disgrace the parents in the eyes of the world, or it failed to enhance the parent's image in the eyes of society. Inevitably, the growing child felt, with much reason, that he was unloved, that his own needs, desires and capabilities were disregarded, unheard, unfulfilled, and even wrong. . . . Everything was oriented toward the parent, the child was less important.

When they had pursued this role reversal, Steele and Pollack came into psychological territory that their single character/single defect causal claim had been unable to navigate. The idea of role reversal brought them to the crucial observation that abusers, expecting their children to parent them, insisted that they must own or have complete authority over the children who were to do this parenting for them. Put another way, the parents insisted that the children serve their

needs, without regard for the children's own needs or development. They had made their child into a servant. Role reversal and the way it operates in the intergenerational transmission of traumatizing demand and criticism brought Steele
and Pollack up against the concept of childism.

Expecting service from one's child is the essence not
of abuse per se but of the childism that justifies abuse: "I
have a right to the child's service," thinks the parent in an
obsessional, a hysterical, or a narcissistic way. But though
they did not make this distinction between abusing and justifying, the Kempe researchers began to see motivations they
had been unable to uncover using their old methodology.
They noted "obsessive-compulsive personality traits into which
parental criticism had been channeled at an early age." They
could see that some abusing parents had been narcissistically injured in childhood rivalries with siblings whom the
abusers felt had received more parental love; and they could
describe rivalries in the present with a spouse or with the
child designated for abuse. But while their view widened beyond hysteria to obsessionality and narcissistic injury, bringing them close to Merrill's characterology, they still insisted
that there was a single abusive type—the impulsive, aggressive hysterical type. The confusion this caused can be seen
in the passage following, where they describe how the basic
childist expectation can take both passive-hysterical and
active-obsessional forms: "We occasionally see a child who is
both abused and neglected. Yet there is a striking difference
in these two forms of caretaker-infant interaction. The neglecting parent responds to distressing disappointment [of
expectations directed at the child] by giving up and abandon-
ing efforts to even mechanically care for the child. The
[physically] abusing parent seems to have more investment
in the active life of the child and moves in to punish it for its

failure and to make it 'shape up' and perform better." There is a clue here to what comparative work with different forms of caretaker-infant interactions and relationships might have yielded, but Steele and Pollack chose to consider only parents deemed hysterical and only acts of physical abuse. They forced their "active" and "passive" parents into that single box, ignoring the nonhysterical character types and also ignoring neglect or any combination of physical abuse and neglect— even though they had before them children who had suffered many kinds of abuse and were able to describe them.

Battering done in Denver, Colorado, circa 1960 could be imagined as a spot on a map of a huge territory that could be called "all the ways people of diverse character types have found to turn against and traumatize their own or others' children and to use childism to justify themselves in doing so." Or "all the ways that people have ever found to interfere with children's normal growth and developmental needs and rights without understanding what they are doing or receiving any social or cultural support to help them question their actions and motivations." But neither Kempe nor later CAN researchers has ever tried to draw that map and to classify the forms of maltreatment after determining which distinctions or classifications would most effectively reveal the origins of or the purposes served by the myriad forms of harms and interferences. There was never an overview, a broad map, and never a critical look into how to go about making a classification of abuse *relationships*. So the CAN research could not result in a multi-causal analysis that might have produced a useful public health approach, or in the prevention work that useful public health approaches can lead to.

Nonetheless, there was a great deal of legal work. After the original paper on battered child syndrome was published in the 1962 *Journal of the American Medical Associa-*

tion, Kempe went to Washington, D.C., where he met with officials at the federal Children's Bureau, then part of the Department of Labor, the source of most existing legislation supportive of children, starting with anti–child labor legislation. His "battered child syndrome" designation was taken up—and his expertise drawn upon—while the Children's Bureau officials drafted a law requiring all professionals dealing with children to report suspected abuse. The law, which they offered to state legislatures in 1963, covered battered child syndrome only, ignoring other kinds of abuse.

Meanwhile, Kempe's article was summarized and popularized in major magazines such as *Time, Good Housekeeping,* and the *Saturday Evening Post.* Soon the idealized television doctors James Kildare and Ben Casey were treating physically abused children in their hospital emergency rooms before the appalled eyes of millions of American viewers (myself as a teenager included). Because both legislators and the general public had been so effectively sensitized to the "battered child syndrome," it took less than five years after the Children's Bureau reporting law was drafted for a version of that law to be on the books in each of the fifty states. All professionals dealing with children were mandated to report suspected physical abuse (neglect was not added until later, and sexual abuse later still). Priests and religious teachers were exempted from the reporting requirement—and this meant that children were completely without protection in churches, and particularly in the Catholic Church, where priests are celibate men who lack hands-on experience or training in child development. Assuming that religious professionals could not be child abusers, and that their institutions did not have to be included in the reporting requirement, of course, had horrifying consequences.

Kempe had launched one of the swiftest transitions

from identification of a social problem to legislation in America's history. His advocacy work is also amazing testimony to the power of giving a name—even if a misleading one—to a problem no one had wanted to acknowledge existed in any stratum of society. The states all increased their vigilance by establishing or strengthening Child Protective Services (CPS) departments. But since CPS was created as a rescue service—a child-saving service—not a *family* service supporting child development generally and helping parents, greater efficiency in prosecuting parents was achieved but not greater understanding of them, educating of them, or working with them therapeutically to prevent child abuse.

Further, the reporting legislation exacerbated the problems created by the syndrome's name and the abuse's conceptualization. Fifty different reporting systems, incorporating fifty somewhat different definitions of physical abuse (and, at first, no mention of neglect) based on different types of acts were created in 1968. The reporting quickly produced startling statistics on the incidence of physical abuse across the country. (The same phenomenon occurred in the other Anglophone countries that adopted American reporting techniques, even when they refused, as Great Britain did, to make reporting mandatory.) But no system of services was created to treat the children, to treat the parents, or to work for prevention. There was no provision for expanded services for children within their families, and no consideration of what new services might be needed either for at risk children or for children following an intervention. Child Protective Services was set up as an *investigative* service, which could override family privacy and family authority. Few of the families reported by CPS felt that the government was trying to help them; they felt that the government was trying to ruin them. This fact became one of the seeds of the "family values" argument that arose in the 1970s in favor of limited govern-ment "interference."

Along with staff in the Children's Bureau, in 1968 some progressive congressional representatives recognized the prob-lem in implementing the legislation and began to work to-ward a more thorough and constructive approach, which could be linked to President Lyndon Johnson's War on Poverty and Great Society initiatives like Head Start. The child advocates who had gathered at the 1970 White House Conference on Children and drew up the Comprehensive Child Develop-ment Act believed that child protection needed to be set in the context of concern for child development. Child abuse and neglect needed to be conceptualized as disruption of child development; maltreatment needed to be seen as the negative end of a continuum of childrearing, and the positive end needed to be supported by family services, including welfare, to place or keep children on healthy developmental tracks.

But the progressives trying to fold the child-abuse re-porting legislation into the Comprehensive Child Develop-ment Act hit a formidable obstacle: Richard Nixon's veto and the emergence and consolidation of the form of child-ism it represented. We need to look at this story, which is—ironically—about the triumph of "family values," because it is key to understanding why the ideal of comprehensive de-velopmental support disappeared from public awareness and why, during the 1970s, protection from abuse and neglect be-came the only public focus on children's developmental needs outside of schools.

Although there had been a number of development-oriented comprehensive programs for children in the western European and British Commonwealth social democracies after World War II, the Comprehensive Child Development

Act was the pioneering effort in America. What made it unique were its emphasis on prevention and, especially, its focus on all aspects of child development. Previous U.S. policies concerning children that took a prevention approach had specifically targeted physical diseases, and they had been the purview of the public health services. Diseases from smallpox to polio had been contained, and many had been eliminated, with the support of the majority of American citizens. The prevention approach had included vaccines, but more broadly it had focused on "primary prevention": cleaning up physical environments that fostered pathogens and keeping facilities—schools, hospitals, camps, playgrounds—hygienic. Children took a class called Health in school that included nutrition counseling and the emphasis on physical fitness that President John F. Kennedy had supported so effectively in his brief tenure. Parents were educated in how to protect their children from physical diseases. Few citizens complained that the public health programs interfered with their "family values" or religious convictions. Or that they overstepped the bounds of "limited government."

In medicine, prevention was an established concept—even if not then and certainly not now the guiding concept, except in the realm of contagious physical diseases (though not yet, importantly, HIV/AIDS, which passes from adults to children). But *development* was not a household word in America in the 1960s. Work that drew upon the psychoanalytically inspired effort to describe children's irreducible developmental needs was just becoming well known among child psychotherapists and advocates, but not yet among citizens or legislators. The influence of the development-oriented pediatrician Dr. Benjamin Spock, who first published his parenting manual in 1946, was growing, but not without controversy. Child study work had been more advanced in Europe, particularly in England, because necessity had been the mother of its invention: modern developmental child study had grown out of state-sponsored wartime programs for dealing with children who needed residential care or evacuation during the Blitz, such as the Hampstead Nursery run by Anna Freud or the treatment schemes for evacuated children run by D. W. Winnicott in Oxfordshire. "Attachment theory," which focused on children's needs for secure attachments, had grown out of the psychoanalyst John Bowlby's reports for the British public health services on the condition and needs of postwar mothers and children. In 1945, the British established the National Health Service.

The Comprehensive Child Development Act addressed preventable failures of universal, "normal" child development, but few citizens knew what that phrase meant, and quite a number of professionals worried that it was too prescriptive. Further, in Section 522 (b)(5) the act looked forward to services that would support the development of *all* children, not just those from impoverished or at risk households or those already singled out as abused or in need of protection. It looked forward to "universally available child development services." But if *development* was a word in need of explanation, *universal* was a well-established Cold War trigger. In America, it meant socialism and disrespect for, or even the abolition of, families.

Recognizing that the act would raise questions about the relation between responsibilities required of local and national governments and those of families, the act's drafters carefully charted a path toward family-*strengthening* by calling for parental involvement in all the services they wanted established. That involvement was to take two forms. First, parents were to be included in the services: parenting education, in-home visitations to help parents with their children and with their own development, were part of the program for child services. Second, parents were encouraged to become involved in the administration of the services through local councils made up of parents and a jobs program for parents whose children were in the preschool programs. In sum: "direct parent participation in the conduct, overall direction and evaluation of the programs," as the bill phrased it. The idea was to bring families, as families, into child development daycare and education services that the government would fund. The act would have been a positive step in the direction of protecting children from abuse and neglect, and protecting parents from becoming abusers and neglecters. If Anna had been a daycare or Head Start child, she might never have been raped by her stepbrother, for she would not have been at home all day.

After the act was approved by narrow margins in the House of Representatives and the Senate, President Nixon vetoed it, faulting it on three points: "fiscal irresponsibility, administrative unworkability, and family-weakening implications." The act had stressed decentralization or local control over services as the most workable approach and the most fiscally responsible because it would be able to harness the many pounds of savings that an ounce of prevention can bring into education and health systems, as the contagious physical disease prevention programs had made very obvious. But Nixon was not terribly concerned with the first two elements in his veto argument; his focus—like that of his allies in the congressional debate—was on the "family-weakening implications."

Like his Republican allies, Nixon argued that it would be a serious error to commit "the vast moral authority of national government to the side of *communal* [italics added] approaches to child rearing over and against the family-centered approach." *Communal*, like *universal*, was a code word for *socialist*, as everyone knew. But Nixon did not stop with innuendo. He countered with a proposal of his own, which he described as family-centered: this was a program of federal subsidies for daycare that would be offered only to two married parents who were both working while rearing a family. His program, which in effect defined "a family" as two parents (no single mothers need apply) and their children, required both parents to work and thus not to go on welfare, in this way reducing the federal welfare budget. But the proposed program also meant that these working parents would not be available either for stay-at-home daytime parenting or for participation in the kind of services the act had called for, which were designed to keep parents and children together (as much as possible) and "in close proximity during the day." Nor did the subsidized daycare Nixon proposed have a developmental dimension—it was babysitting, and the people offering the care were to be paid a babysitting wage and would not be trained. Daycare was not imagined as a professional service for child development. There was no suggestion that employers might sponsor professional daycare in workplaces to keep parents and children in close proximity during the day. Nixon was articulating the standard American conservative line that the state owes children minimal protection against abuse, but neither provision for their developmental needs nor participation (through their parents as their representatives) in decisions that directly affected their well-being. Of the 3 Ps in the U.N. Convention on the Rights of the Child, only protection was even being considered.

Nixon, the proponent of "family values," thus promoted an anti-family, anti-child measure that privileged working over parenting and privileged limited government over child support. His approach was said to be good for the bottom line of businesses that employed parents (they did not have to create workplace daycare programs or grant childcare leaves), and it was said to be good for keeping governments out of the welfare business. But it was not good for children, and it was not good for parents who wanted more time with their children, either immediately after the birth or during the preschool years. Nixon obscured the distinction between programs that help families provide for their developing children and programs that help parents give their primary allegiance to their jobs. It was at this moment that the American discussion of what counts as "anti-family" began to get very confused, and the interests of children, parents, and the state were made to seem irreconcilable.

But I would argue that Nixon's veto met with little protest from voters not just because they were confused about its implications but because the veto channeled a widely shared prejudice against children. That prejudice had been revealed clearly in the arguments made by Nixon's allies in Congress, who had charged the authors of the Comprehensive Child Development Act with being infiltrators and secret agents out to corrupt *corruptible* children—a standard obsessional accusation. Representative John Rarick of Louisiana made a speech that is still, in 2011, so valuable to the conservative Family Rights Association that it is prominently featured on the association's current Web site: The developmentalists who framed the act, he charged, "provide for programs to keep the child away from the parents. . . . This power grab over our youth is reminiscent of the Nazi youth movement; in fact, it goes far beyond Hitler's wildest dreams or the most outlandish of the Communist plans. . . . The law is clear that where it is impracticable to replace the parent with the State, then the bureaucracy would train those functioning in the capacity of parent as a paid agent of the State." The act would produce "federalized children," he had warned. Representative Tom Pelly of Washington added, ominously, that the child developmentalists who drew up the act would have "a giant laboratory to tinker with children's minds." The act was "a massive governmental invasion of this last stronghold of the home" (that is, the years before children must submit to "compulsory schooling"), said Representative John Schmitz of California. Proof of these assertions was that the Harvard pediatrician Dr. Urie Bonfenbrenner, one of the developmentalists who testified in hearings on the act, had spoken about the virtues of communal childrearing and economic collectives. A Jewish socialist! A kibbutznik!

What the conservatives were drawing upon and feeding was the standard Cold War free enterprise versus socialism debate, in which socialists are perceived as creeping into the stronghold of the family and capturing the children for the state. "The intention is clearly to put government in place of the parent—the ultimate threat to the family," as Schmitz said. To this kind of childism, in which trying to ensure that parents were responsive to their children's developmental needs was seen as anti-family, the framers and supporters of the act could not reply, "This is childism." They lacked the concept of childism to address the root of the controversy and so remained on the defensive, trying to win a "disinformation" propaganda war. A futile project.

After the 1971 veto, the Comprehensive Child Development Act's main Senate sponsor, Walter Mondale (D., Minn.), decided to push the problem of child abuse forward on its own. "Not even Richard Nixon is in favor of child abuse," he quipped. After hearings and much deliberation, Senator Mondale's proposal eventually emerged in 1974 as the Child Abuse Prevention and Treatment Act. But because it was crafted to avoid another Nixon veto, the act cautiously skirted around anything that might be seen as a threat to "the family-centered approach" or so-called parental rights. Even the act's title was a decoy: it seemed to mean that "Treatment" would be offered to abused children (and even Richard Nixon could not object to that); but the problem the bill was really wrestling with was whether and how to investigate and treat *parents* who are reported for or charged with abuse. The bill counted on sympathy for battered children, but it did not address their batterers, much less the social and motivational contexts in which batterers (or any other type of abuser) operate.

It was unfortunate enough that passage of the 1974 act ensured that legislation to address child abuse and neglect would develop outside the context of a more comprehensive approach to children's needs and children's rights. But the way the 1974 act was crafted had the further consequence of aggravating the confused state of the emergent field of Child Abuse and Neglect. Because developmental services, family-support programs, and welfare were off the table, the legislators concentrated on *therapeutic* help for parental abusers—and for this they needed to find out what CAN experts knew about abusers and their treatability. Mondale sent a delegation to Denver to consult with Dr. Kempe, who repeated the kinds of confusions about abusers that were built into his original battered child syndrome article and into Steele and Pollack's research. And these confusions, which were eventually enshrined in the 1974 act, have remained with us to this day.

Recall that Kempe's original 1962 article had claimed that only 10 percent of the abuser population was psychotic or psychopathic and thus (allegedly) untreatable. But later in his article, Kempe had made a vague statement that gave the impression that *all* abusers are untreatable, not just psychotics and psychopaths. While admitting that not much was known about "the character structure of abusing parents," he said:

> We know of no reports of successful psychotherapy in such cases. In general, psychiatrists feel that treatment of the so-called psychopath or sociopath is rarely successful. Further psychological investigation of the character structure of attacking parents is sorely needed. Hopefully, better understanding of the mechanisms involved in the control and release of aggressive impulses will aid in the early diagnosis, prevention of attack, and treatment of parents, as well as give us better ability to predict the likelihood of further attack in the future. At present, *there is no safe remedy in the situation except the separation of battered children from their insufficiently protective parents* [italics added].

The obvious implication for policy in this paragraph was that *all* physically abusing parents are impulsive, hysterical, aggressive, *and untreatable,* so that removing children from their homes into foster homes is necessary. In effect, it looked like an argument for increasing reliance on foster care, not for establishing treatment programs for children or parents.

This interpretation of Kempe's work came under immediate criticism from other CAN researchers, and some of those critics appeared at Mondale's congressional hearings to argue, on the basis of their research, that only about 10 percent of abusers were untreatable psychotics and psychopaths (exactly the figure that Kempe himself cited in his paper). No CAN expert questioned the judgment that psychotics and psychopaths are untreatable; but also none questioned the assertion that there is only one character structure (with a defect) lying behind child abuse. The experts, sidestepping the question of treatability, left the senators to debate the Child Abuse Prevention and Treatment Act without addressing the most important issue. It was as though they were discussing environmental protection without bringing in the idea that people produce environmental damage and thus have to be educated and legislatively encouraged not to do so.

More illuminating and persuasive was the parent expert whom Mondale brought to the hearings: "Jolly K.," the founder of Parents Anonymous (P.A.), a self-help organization for child abusers (mostly physical abusers) modeled on Alcoholics Anonymous. Six feet tall, a former prostitute with a bold, no-nonsense style, Jolly K. told the senators that she had repeatedly attacked and even tried to strangle her school-age daughter Faith. Unable to control herself, she had sought help from ten different protective-service agencies, where she was listened to but not really heard. None had been able to offer her more than a place on a waiting list for vaguely defined or undefined treatment. Finally, with the help of a psychiatrist she had assembled a group of mothers who shared her problem, and together they had created the kind of group psychotherapy they needed and talked their way through to self-control. This was the beginning of Parents Anonymous.

Since then Jolly K. had traveled the country, lecturing, starting up local groups, and meeting with journalists. In an interview, she candidly described how her own mother had abused her and dumped her into foster homes and institutions— that is, she identified her problem as an "intergenerational transmission of trauma." As a teenager, she had run away into a life of promiscuity, short-lived marriages, and three pregnancies. "I never loved Faith's father, even though I married him. So my perception was that my [other two children] were good, and Faith was bad, *like me* [italics added]. . . . By the time Faith was six or seven, I was into hard-core abuse. Calling her a pig, making her eat off the floor. Once I almost choked her into unconsciousness."

Jolly K. was clearly aware that she harbored a prejudice (although she did not call it such): Faith was a *bad* child, as she herself was a *bad* person, both members of a subgroup of children who are bad. Perfectly demonstrating the psychoanalytic theory that prejudices begin as projections, she had laid her own felt badness on her daughter and then tried to eliminate that badness by eliminating the girl, cutting her out of the family and away from her *good* siblings. (In the terms I use, her childism was of the eliminating sort, for which physical abuse was one means and emotional abuse another.) But the message Jolly K. delivered to the senators was not "We (all of us) must learn not to project our self-hatred onto our children in the form of a prejudice." Her message was also not "What I am describing is not just a matter of physical abuse; I emotionally abused my child as well, calling her names, humiliating her, terrorizing her, stereotyping her as a dirty barnyard animal." Jolly K.'s message, although explained simplistically—less simplistically, however, than the public confessions that became standard fare on daytime television in the 1990s—was that with counseling and support an abusing parent *can* give up abusing just as an alcoholic can give up drinking. The "intergenerational transmission of trauma" can be interrupted. She was quite right, and her testimony also fitted perfectly with Senator Mondale's laudable progressive purpose to get a bill that would make available to parents just what Jolly K. had searched for in vain: individual treatment and the possibility of keeping her child safe and her family intact. On her own initiative, Jolly K. had become a treated parent who had resources and a community in the event of a relapse.

By the close of the 1973 congressional hearings, child

abuse was judged by the majority of the legislators to be a problem that cut across classes and that could be addressed therapeutically. But they, in effect, vetoed their own good findings by also concluding that they did not need to address availability of treatment, the social or economic situations of abusive families, or even prevailing cultural norms, like acceptance of corporal punishment, that are manifestations of a societal prejudice against children. They did not have to look at child abuse as a form of *discrimination* against children or groups of children. "Family preservation" through counseling (not removal of children into foster care, as Kempe had initially recommended) was set up to become the prevailing prevention and treatment strategy, even though little was known about how it might be effective even with neurotic or character-disordered parents, much less with psychopathic ones.

And little was ever going to be known, because psychotherapy for abusers was not provided for in the 1974 act, despite its reliance on psychotherapy as the main mode of address to be provided for parents. Little was going to be known about treatment for children either, as funds were not allocated for their treatment either. The foster care system was set up to grow, even though that was not the legislators' intention. (By 2011, it was estimated that each year 800,000 American children spent some time in the foster care system, the majority in multiple placements. If the foster care residents were all ghettoized together into a city, the city's population would be comparable to that of San Francisco.) And the population of child abusers in prisons was also set up to grow, without any therapeutic programs being established either in prisons or as alternatives to prison. So once again, there was an implementation problem, just as there had been in the 1960s when reporting laws were passed without provisions for investigating what was reported or doing something about it. To this day, an abusing parent looking for or recommended to psychotherapy will most likely find himself or herself in Jolly K.'s situation. Her organization, Parents Anonymous, has 267 affiliate private organizations but receives almost no aid from federal or state governments; in the public domain, there are few programs. (The same situation exists for substance abuse: there are two large private organizations, A.A. and N.A., but little in the way of government-funded treatment programs. Help for parents has been thoroughly "privatized.")

There was another problem with the 1974 act: it was aimed only at physical abuse. No Jolly K. came forward to describe any other kind of child abuse. No reformed neglecter appeared, no reformed sexual abuser. Physical *neglect*, which social workers and protective service personnel had long recognized as a problem among the poor (though not exclusive to the poor by any means), had not even been a topic at the hearings. No one testified about what treatment services might help a parent stop being neglectful. Similarly, sexual abuse had not come up, so there was no threat to the then prevailing social silence and secrecy about sexual abuse and sexual crimes committed by parents or other adults. (Henry Kempe protested the omission of sexual abuse from the provisions of the 1974 act.) The name-calling and being forced to eat off the floor that Jolly K.'s daughter Faith had suffered, later to be called emotional abuse, was not part of the legislative formulation either. In effect, all controversy about the remedy—therapy for parents and family preservation—was kept at bay by the "ruling-out" exclusions. The legislation followed the pattern of the battered child research: ruling out of consideration exactly what needed the most attention— the whole proverbial elephant in the living room that might have been called "traumatization of children" or "disruption

of normal child development." No one—researchers, therapists, or legislators—realized that the material under discussion was not the whole story.

Mondale, however, forced by the desire of the confused
legislators to make a definition of "child abuse" part of the
Child Abuse Prevention and Treatment Act, did pen a definition for the Preamble. The very acts that had been excluded
from or silenced in the discussion and ruled out within the
bill itself were named in the Preamble, which announced the
1974 act as far more encompassing than it really was: "'Child
Abuse and Neglect' means the physical or mental injury, sexual abuse, negligent treatment, or maltreatment of any child
under the age of eighteen by a person who is responsible for
the child's welfare under circumstances which indicate the
child's health or welfare is harmed or threatened thereby."

With this act, which has been amended many times
since 1974, Child Protective Services (CPS) became the sole
safety net for children—the majority of whom go unprotected
by it. In comparably developed countries that have lower
rates of child abuse and neglect than those in the United
States, there is much less reliance on CPS because children
have a range of preventative and development-oriented services: universal healthcare, health services, and parent support services in homes after the birth of a child; maternal and
paternal leaves for infant care; developmental preschool programs; after-school programs; and economic welfare supports
of various kinds. But in America, children are governmen-
tally supported chiefly by protective services (and by public
schools for children over age six). Nothing can be done for
children until they have been reported on suspicion of abuse
or neglect; any child not referred to protective services (or
any child so referred but then judged not to need protection)
is not supported.

It is also ironic, to say the least, that legislators who objected to American children being "federalized" into developmental programs, because the authority of their parents would be undermined and their minds would be tinkered with, agreed to institute as the sole service universally available to children an *investigative* service, invasive of family life and privacy by definition. But in the logic of obsessional prejudice, the project makes sense. There is a huge collective projection: those who fear invasion and infiltration by socialists set up a situation in which *bad* families suspected of making their children bad will be invaded or infiltrated, *their* privacy breached. Not surprisingly, since 1974 the majority of families investigated have been impoverished, and the majority of those are African American, Hispanic, or Native American. As CPS and fostering grew and grew, however, the conservatives began to hate what they had created and rail against it, for it went way beyond the families of targeted groups and directly into the conservative middle class. If the children removed from all these families were gathered in one place, we would recognize the foster care system as a ghetto, a barrio, or a reservation so large that no child is safe from it. Although there are excellent individual foster families, the system is hell for children.

CHAPTER FOUR

The Politicization
of Child Abuse

BY THE END OF THE 1970S, WITH THE DEFEAT OF THE
progressive Comprehensive Child Development Act and the
field of Child Abuse and Neglect in disarray, the damage
being done to the nation's children was becoming evident to
many Americans. Money to fund Child Protective Services
was minimal. The child poverty rate was rising year by year,
and the nation was declining on international measures of
child well-being in almost every area. Daycare was scarce
and often of poor quality—unless you could afford a nanny
or send your child to a private program. The nation's divorce
rate was rising, too, but there was no help for the children of
these divorces, no resources outside their immediate or extended families. As the number of broken families was rising,
Ronald Reagan capitalized on the widespread anxiety in his
presidential campaign of 1979 with a platform that called for
reaffirming "family values" and reinforcing parents' rights
over children's. He specifically targeted the budget of National Center for Child Abuse and Neglect (NCCAN), which
had been created by the 1974 Child Abuse Prevention and
Treatment Act, because the Center's programs and research

seemed to him to represent excessive government intrusion into family life. But his platform offered no "family-centered approach" (in Nixon's phrase) to children's issues, only opposition to government "interference" and plans for privatizing social services.

In the literature from the late 1970s and early 1980s, I found one book that captured the realities of the deepening crisis for children of that period. The author was the widely respected journalist Vance Packard, who had written half a dozen best sellers whose titles conveyed his conviction that postwar America was a wasteland, devoid of progressive values or community life, filled with alienated and desperate people: *The Hidden Persuaders, The Status Seekers, The Waste Makers, The People Shapers, The Sexual Wilderness, A Nation of Strangers.* In 1983 his *Our Endangered Children* reached the best-seller list, too. But even readers who had been sympathetic to Packard's earlier books were shocked by his assertion that America nourished an "anti-child culture." This was not only a sociological claim but a psychological one: Americans' very way of thinking and feeling was anti-child. They viewed their children as objects of hatred, fear, and contempt, Packard noted, although he did not identify this attitude as a prejudice. Surveying the damage done to children's welfare and well-being since the early 1970s, he declared that in America, an "anti-child culture" had triumphed. As proof of his claim Packard detailed the way an anti-child political elite inspired by Richard Nixon and then led by Ronald Reagan had defeated or rolled back every concrete pro-child program generated since Head Start began in the 1960s.

Packard understood that the "anti-child culture"—the childist culture—was refusing children their rights to provision, protection, and participation as those rights were being formulated at the time for the Convention on the Rights of the Child. But no American in a powerful political position was able to work on the basis of this understanding and insist that the needs and rights of children must be paramount. Not even Senator Walter Mondale, who had turned his attention to a presidential run and then was sidelined after suffering a humiliating defeat by Reagan in 1984. The question Packard did not ask, however, was why and how a culture that had fostered pro-child progressivism in the early twentieth century, and had united behind a vision of a Great Society in the 1960s, had become anti-child soon afterward, and had ended up with no progressive leader to rally it. But the answer goes to the heart of the childism that parents use to justify child abuse and neglect.

The shift began in the 1960s and 1970s with the rise of social protest movements—civil rights, antiwar, feminist—that drew much of their support from young people. Fired by the spirit of change, these young people broadened their movement into what became known simply as the youth movement or, more combatively, the Counterculture. Many adults began to fear that their children had become politicized and were becoming more so, and that they would begin demanding the right to participate in the political system. Children were now protesting not one by one, as Charles Dickens's little heroes and heroines had, but as a group. Rebellious and ungrateful, these children and their advocates were repudiating "family values"—and chiefly the value of child ownership. There was even a short-lived but threatening Children's Liberation Movement in the early 1970s. Far from serving adults, "bad" children were seeking political, anti-family "liberation." White youths were following the example of the "Negro" children who had marched from Selma to Birmingham in 1964. Girls were refusing to accept the "feminine mystique" of their homemaker mothers. And these rebellious children were turning against their families with the help of state organizations, especially legal advocacy groups. Child Protective Services was thought by many fearful adults to be an organ of the state created specifically to disrupt families.

In the 1970s, these feared and hated young people (not so much younger children) were omnipresent in the media, especially the newly pervasive medium of television. Conservatives, particularly conservative Christians, viewed their protests as a "Children's Crusade," an allusion to two movements in about 1212 in which hoards of children—so legend had it—were caught up in a wild, undisciplined Crusade to take the Holy Land from the infidels that was quite unlike the adult military Crusades so admired by fundamentalist Christians. The 1960s youth rebellion seemed to the "silent majority" of Americans on the older side of what came to be called the generation gap to be a similar crusade of idealists run amok or hijacked by anarchists or "socialists" who were themselves the infidels.

The children's crusade was understood to be against family control, against the military, and for sexual freedom: "Make Love not War." The young were politicizing sex with their slogan "The Personal Is Political," generated by feminists, and the response of many adults was to push back with politicized projections: to attack the wild sexuality of the young with a kind of updated Victorianism. By the late 1970s, narcissistic childism focused on erasing the political identity of those in the youth movement was becoming more dominant than the obsessional Nixonian form. Reagan and his conservative constituencies tapped into the narcissistic trends as much as they shaped and molded them in the 1980s.

The anti–Vietnam War movement had begun as a free speech movement in the mid-1960s. Its young leaders insisted upon a real university education, in real universities, not the huge, impersonal, factory-like places that were growing up everywhere to accommodate the Baby Boom numbers. In these places, there was no "free speech," they argued. As it grew into an antiwar movement by the late 1960s, the free speech movement was correctly understood to be very different from and more political than the 1950s rock-'n'-roll youth subculture described by the eminent journalist Harrison Salisbury in *The Shook-Up Generation* (1958). That subculture had also been upsetting to adults, provoking a reaction so strong that a 1954 *Newsweek* story had posed the question "Do Americans hate their children?" But the late 1960s and early 1970s Counterculturists were more feared and hated precisely because they were *political*. Their critics lambasted them as intent on overthrowing authority, flouting "law and order," disregarding their parents, acting out sexually against traditional mores, stomping on traditional values, smashing institutions—particularly their own schools and colleges, which were seen by conservatives as bastions of "spare the rod and spoil the child" liberalism. The rebellious young, in other words, threatened particularly the narcissistic characters among their parents—those whose childism took the form of identity erasure. Although Nixonian obsessional childism certainly did not disappear as the Vietnam War ended, the Reagan-era anti-child culture was predominantly staffed by adults who exemplified what the historian Christopher Lasch diagnosed psychoanalytically in his 1979 study as "the culture of narcissism."

The unrelenting availability of images or stereotypes—projections—of children as objects of fear, hatred, and contempt that Packard described was essential to the development of childism in this era. Such images were widely interpreted along the fundamental "role-reversal" childist line by adults who were feeling beleaguered and without power (the "silent majority"). These adults began to worry that their fearful, hated, contemptible children would not take care of them or serve them; on the contrary, the *state* was demanding that measures be taken to provide for and protect these children *at parental expense,* using parental tax dollars, and at the price of loss of parental (and especially patriarchal) authority and rights. Adults began to see their children as a threat to the middle-class family, economic growth, and adult well-being. The children were perceived as unwilling to be parents to their parents. (Among parents undergoing the crisis of a divorce, on the rise during this period, who already felt injured and deprived of any kind of provision and protection themselves, role-reversal thinking came especially easily.)

The well-publicized conflict of generations during this period was, narcissistically, about identities—those the young wanted to assert and those adults wanted to erase. Many young women were viewed as a direct threat to traditional images of docile domesticity; many young men were perceived as "untraditional" by offended traditional males: long-haired "effete snobs" and "pointy-headed intellectuals," and probably homosexuals as well. Childism of the narcissistic sort and narcissistically based sexism coincided. Further, when the leadership of the youth rebellion began to include young blacks who sought separation from, rather than integration with, whites, and who sometimes advocated violence, racist responses mingled with the narcissistic childist and sexist responses. Images of young men proclaiming black power, rifles in hand, were everywhere—and in response, the white establishment began to pass laws that filled the nation's reformatories and prisons with young black men. Inner-city ghetto children, identified as the fatherless products of "the pathology of the Negro family" (a common phrase after the Moynihan Report of 1965 noted that single mothers were the norm in African American communities), were believed to be waiting to fill the ranks of threatening black youths. One of the key reasons for the intensity of the childism of the 1970s and 1980s was its simultaneous intertwining with both sexism (and homophobia) and racism.

A rein-them-in "law and order" attitude toward the young grew up among those Richard Nixon had called the silent majority, a phrase that soon was taken to mean that this majority had been *actively* silenced—shouted down and narcissistically wounded by the protesting young. By the late 1970s this mental attitude was being reinforced institutionally. The Supreme Court of the United States ruled in *Wright v. Ingraham* (1977) that school officials had a right to punish children corporally: this was a "traditional right" that had been exercised in America since colonial times, as the majority opinion pointed out several times. The Court majority noted further that this traditional *parents'* right was also an *educator's* right.

After the Justices heard testimony from two junior high school boys in Dade County, Florida, describing the paddling they had been given with two-by-fours that had left them so welted and bruised that they required emergency medical treatment (duly documented), the Court majority declared that the beatings did not violate the "cruel and unusual punishment" clause of the Eighth Amendment to the Constitution. These boys were not "battered children." The decision significantly reserved Eighth Amendment protection for *adults* involved in criminal processes or imprisoned. (Thus the protection does not apply to young people in prisons or to those detained under suspicion, like current residents of Guantánamo Bay, many of whom were under the age of eighteen when they were captured. The young in such places are not protected against torture.) Further, the Court ruled that the due process clause of the Fourteenth Amendment does not require that children be given notification of the charges against them or an informal hearing before the infliction of corporal punishment in a school. This ruling re-enforced the idea that school officials have the right to punish into obedience youths deemed insubordinate. Schools that had been developed since the early twentieth century on the model of a factory were encouraged to follow a new model: the military academy or the military prison.

The courts became one of the central sites of the childism aimed at keeping young people from participating in decisions regarding their well-being or the political process generally. But the same goal was pursued in the court of world opinion at the United Nations, where the drafting of the Convention on the Rights of the Child was under way from 1979 (the International Year of the Child) through 1989. The very idea of this Convention was lamented by American conservatives. But of the rights it outlined—the 3 Ps of provision, protection, and participation—the last was considered the most threatening, for it seemed to signal a worldwide political action by the young. The Convention did not extend the right to vote to persons under eighteen (as the American Children's Liberation exponents had advocated), but it did call for children to be consulted "according to their evolving abilities" in matters concerning them.

In addition to responding to the activities of rebellious youth, American childism was triggered by events of the 1970s perpetrated not by children or youths themselves but by the adults—like the Convention drafters—who championed them. In the late 1960s, the Supreme Court had focused on children's rights, particularly participation rights, which were viewed by conservatives as a license for rebellion. From their point of view, the liberal Warren Court epitomized the attack on parental authority. It seemed to be promoting the educational reformers among the Children's Liberationists who were inspired by the social critic Paul Goodman's well-known reflection on education and schooling *Growing Up Absurd* (1960).

While conservatives derided these educators as "kiddie libbers" (extremists like "women's libbers"), more reform-oriented developmentalist child advocates and children's-rights activists, such as the leaders of the Children's Defense Fund, faced a dilemma. They agreed that the Children's Liberationists were taking extreme positions, and they tried to distinguish their more moderate aims from those of the liberationists. But their response created a schism between the extremists and the reformers; neither camp was able to make much headway against the conservatives who were fueling the anti-child culture. That schism continues to divide the present generation of children's advocates, though the reformers are in the majority now, which is fortunate for today's children. Despite their good intentions, the Children's Liberation theorists, by focusing their attention on what they took to be discrimination against children as participators (for example, as voters) really neglected children's needs for provision and protection.

In the legal sphere, conservatives focused their wrath on President Johnson's appointment of his friend and adviser Abe Fortas to the Supreme Court in 1963. Fearing that many of his progressive Great Society initiatives would be ruled unconstitutional, Johnson had created a strong liberal network in the Court's majority: Fortas was a former student and friend of the liberal Justice William O. Douglas. But Fortas was also interested in children's issues, as soon became clear when an unusual series of cases came before the Court.

By the time Fortas resigned from the Court in 1969, he had made what is arguably the most influential judicial contribution to children's rights in American history. And he had given the obsessionals among conservatives evidence of a conspiracy inside the federal government—led by a Jew—that was fomenting child revolution. The narcissists saw children being empowered to speak up by the unpatriotic infiltrators who had penetrated and infected the Court.

Fortas wrote the majority decisions in two cases that brought the juvenile courts to Supreme Court attention for the first time since they were established at the end of the nineteenth century. Of the two cases, *Kent v. United States* (1966) and *In re Gault* (1967), the most consequential was the second, which concerned a fifteen-year-old boy in Arizona who had been sentenced to six years in a state-run industrial school for making one allegedly obscene phone call to an adult female neighbor—an offense that would have gotten him a fifty-dollar fine or at most two months in jail had he been an adult. The majority opinion extended Fourteenth Amendment guarantees of the right to sufficient notice of a trial, the right to counsel, the right to confrontation of witnesses, and the right against self-incrimination to juvenile court proceedings. (The not very hidden agenda of the 1977 *Wright v. Ingraham* decision was to block such procedural rights within a school when it operates de facto like a juvenile court or a prison.) *In re Gault* is now routinely invoked whenever any question comes up about a child's right to participate (or be properly represented) in issues—including custody and abuse—that concern him or her.

Two years after *In re Gault*, Fortas wrote the majority opinion in another controversial case, *Tinker v. Des Moines School District* (1969), which explicitly connected his general advocacy for children to the political youth rebellion. His opinion extended First Amendment protection to three teen-agers who had been suspended from school for wearing black armbands to protest against the Vietnam War. "Neither students nor teachers shed their constitutional rights to freedom of speech or expression at the schoolhouse gate," Fortas wrote, and conservatives interpreted his opinion as an open invitation to subversives and Communist agents to use students as their pawns.

Both the reform of the juvenile courts and the extension of free speech rights to the young provoked strong opposition from those who wanted more adult control over their children—those who wanted the young to be, in effect, seen and not heard, at least not heard *politically,* not able to speak for themselves, to question or protest against adult authority. The subsequent Burger and Rehnquist Courts, which did not have clear liberal majorities, steadily abandoned the Warren Court's exemplary record of deciding in favor of children's claims and thus assuring children equal protection, due process, privacy, free expression, and free exercise of religion. The later Courts frequently found that children were not capable of exercising legal rights or making decisions on their own behalf, even though rulings in two important cases did take children's views into consideration. One concerned a twelve-year-old who successfully argued that he should be released from his birth family's claims on him so that he could be legally adopted by his long-time foster family. In this decision, the boy's judgment about who his "psychological parents" were was properly acknowledged, as Anna Freud and her co-authors from Yale had argued that it should be in *In the Best Interests of the Child.*

What was shaping up in the late 1970s, while the anti-child cohort fed on images of children in revolt backed up by political and legal advocates, was the phenomenon beginning to be known by the 1980s as the culture wars. In these wars, which are still going on, progressives were locked in ideological struggle with conservatives, feminists were meeting an anti-feminist backlash (described by Susan Faludi in her important 1991 study *Backlash: The Undeclared War on American Women*), and the civil rights movement was stalled by a counter-movement trying to undermine the achievements of the 1960s. But underlying these battles among adults was the little talked about but acutely felt struggle between children and adults—and not just conservative adults. A conflict of the generations.

Part of that conflict concerned an issue that was widely recognized yet almost never discussed. That issue was child sexual abuse, viewed as a specific kind of child abuse and neglect. Both sexually abused children and adults who had been sexually abused as children emerged in the 1980s, with help from feminists, to protest politically against their childist abusers, who were usually part of their own families, often sleeping in the bedroom next door. Anna's taking her stepbrother to court when she was nineteen was part of that movement. In response, the narcissistic form of childism that had begun to prevail in the 1980s was further mobilized: childist adults gathered together to denounce these children as liars or false accusers and to make sure that the children's stories did not receive political support. There was to be no free speech about sexual abuse.

As the 1980s unfolded, the abusers being confronted by their children were now members of the very Baby Boom generation that, during their teenage and young adult years in the early 1970s, had been the target of Nixonian obsessional childism. As they came into adulthood, the Boomers had been ridiculed and repudiated by a culture that was growing more and more narcissistic. And as parents of young children many of them became childist themselves, expecting their own children to take care of them, to admire them unquestioningly, to serve their own forms of learned narcissism. This intergenerational transmission of trauma played out most acutely in the domain of sexuality. For the feminists were right: the personal *is* political, when people make it so. In the 1980s a full-scale culture war was waged between the "family values" camp and those who still took their bearings from the progressive tradition and the Great Society children's advocacy. But the largely unspoken contested territory was child sexual abuse. We still live with that war—it is like a civil war being fought over the question of child slavery, specifically child sexual slavery.

By the time the 1974 Child Abuse Prevention and Treatment Act (CAPTA) was passed, both Child Abuse and Neglect advocates like Dr. Kempe and members of Congress generally recognized that the "Child Abuse" in CAN's title should also refer to sexual abuse, not just to physical abuse, and the "Neglect" should cover many types of neglect. So, as I noted before, these missing acts were included in the definition Senator Mondale had crafted for CAPTA's Preamble: "'Child Abuse and Neglect' means the physical or mental injury, sexual abuse, negligent treatment, or maltreatment of any child under the age of eighteen by a person who is responsible for the child's welfare under circumstances which indicate the child's health or welfare is harmed or threatened thereby." But that definition obscured the truth that neglect had been almost completely neglected in the development of CAN and that sexual abuse had been willfully misunderstood and actively denied both within the field and within the general culture.

Further, the thought that many—even most—maltreated children are maltreated in many ways, by many types of acts of physical abuse, neglect, and sexual abuse, had become unthinkable. It was both "too horrible to be true" (to use Anna's lawyer's phrase) and too disruptive of a classification system that had become fixed. The field of CAN and the federal and state Child Protective Services had been set up on the basis of an abuse-acts typology—physical abuse, neglect, sexual abuse (and later emotional abuse)—that made it impossible for workers in the field to understand most maltreated children, let alone extremely and multiply abused children like Anna.

The neglect of neglect in CAN is relatively easy to understand in comparison to the denial of sexual abuse. But it is an important story in itself and crucial to understanding sexual abuse because one of the key characteristics of sexual abuse is that its victims have *always* been neglected by at least one adult before and/or while they were being sexually abused (by that adult or by another). All sexually abused children are in one way or another *unattended* children, particularly in their own homes.

Pediatricians did not study neglect for a simple reason: physically neglected children seldom ended up in pediatricians' offices or pediatric emergency rooms. Neglected children are to be found in their homes, with their neglecters, who neglect them on a daily basis, chronically, without pause, but (usually) without episodes of violence that require urgent hospital care. The neglected wither away, like children laboring in a factory, a sweatshop, or a refugee or concentration camp. If anyone sees them in their homes, it will not be a pediatrician but a social worker, who will need to have received a report of neglect and obtained a legal order to enter the home.

In the 1970s, a neglected child who did make it to a

hospital, nearly dead, would have been treated there by a pediatrician who would have judged the child as similar to a battered child. This attitude appears in another widely referenced article published in the *Journal of the American Medical Association,* "Homicide by Starvation: The Nutritional *Variant* [italics added] of 'The Battered Child,'" which appeared in 1963, the year after Kempe's article. The author, Lester Adelson, M.D., argued that the distinctions between battered and neglected children are not essential to a definition of neglect.

Discussing five cases of infants less than nine months old who had been brought to his Cleveland hospital dead or dying, Dr. Adelson noted that the starved babies had had no previous medical attention, whereas battered children are typically brought to the hospital many times—frequently to several different hospitals—with multiple injuries. Just like battering parents, however, neglecting parents lie and rationalize, insisting that their babies have a history of being "poor eaters" or that they have fallen ill only in the past few days, for some mysterious reason. But when the child is not already dead, simply offering it adequate food and water can reveal the truth: a baby eating ravenously is not a poor eater or too sick to eat. The child is the living proof of the neglect, and of the parents' lies; just like an X-ray, the proof of the child's appetite would then allow a prosecutor to take a neglecter to court or a child into foster care. The equivalent of a radiologist saying, "This is trauma," was an E.R. doctor saying, "The child was starved."

Parental motivations and the child's home situation, however, were completely left out of Adelson's account, which focuses on how to classify the result. Once again the pre-CAN, pre–battered child social work literature is more instructive than work published by these experts, for it shows what Adelson could not see. Leontine Young's *Wednesday's Children*, the study with the nuanced portrait of a physical abuser, also contains a portrait of the Lake family of neglecters: Mrs. Lake, twenty-six, and Mr. Lake, twenty-seven, who live in a squalid three-room apartment with their five ill-fed children, the oldest only seven and already parenting the other four. Mrs. Lake spends day after day on the couch, inert, unable even to go out and use for food the little money her husband brings home after his daily trip to the bar. Refusing to clean the apartment or dress the children, she is lost in a fog of complaints, including the standard role-reversal lament: "If only they wouldn't fight so much. Then I get sick of them. They never pay any attention to me." When Mr. Lake came home from work and the bar, Mrs. Lake would complain to him. Then he would accuse her of doing nothing for him, of taking his hard-earned money and spending it drinking at her own bar, to which she goes whenever she finds the energy to leave the house. The Lakes mirror each other in their sense of victimization: they accuse each other of the same acts of neglect, indifferent to the fact that they are inflicting on their children the same thing they feel has been inflicted on them all their lives and that they also inflict on each other. They don't want their children, whom they view as pests and intruders infiltrating their home.

Astute as she was in comparison to Lester Adelson, who was trapped in the emerging CAN act-type classification, in her summary statement Young nonetheless helped muddy the inquiry into the motivations for neglect:

> This picture, then, is neglect. *There is no visible parental attempt to hurt the children, very probably no active wish to do so* [italics added]. There is rather an immersion in self-need so total that everyone and everything outside it

are only dimly perceived like the blur of figures on shore to the swimmer under water. The children with their own needs intrude upon that immersion as irritants. They require physical care, guidance and control, attention and affection, patience and forethought—all the qualities the parents are futilely demanding from each other or from a denying world.

Young did understand the basic role-reversal feature of all maltreatment and all childism: the Lakes expected their children to be their caretakers. But though she recognized this expectation she stopped short of investigating it; rather, she stated: "There is no visible parental attempt to hurt the children, very probably no active wish to do so." On the basis of this kind of judgment, which was repeated in almost all social work studies of neglect both before and after Kempe's and Adelson's work, physical neglect was distinguished from physical abuse. Physical abuse involves acts of commission, neglect involves acts of omission. At first *omission* meant not fulfilling a child's basic needs for food, shelter, and safety; later, refusing medical attention, education, emotional support, and understanding were added to the list of neglecting acts. Assessing intention always remained problematic.

The commission/omission distinction persists to this day, even though in the popular culture many realize that such a distinction can be blinding. The popular concept of "passive-aggressive behavior" has appeared to blur the categories. One need not be a social worker or a clinician to sense that not doing something can be an aggressive act and can involve an active, conscious intention to harm. But in CAN the idea that parents might actively want to harm their children by neglecting or eliminating them or erasing them was itself neglected. When Anna said that her stepmother never fed her properly, wanted to kill her, and did nothing to stop her stepbrother from raping her or her other stepsiblings from enslaving her, she was making it clear that *omission* did not describe the sins of the chief neglecter in her hell.

One full-scale study in the CAN literature did explore the idea that there is a character type that is prone to use physical neglect intentionally. Financed by the Children's Bureau, Norman Polansky, a professor at the University of Georgia's School of Social Work and an experienced, psychoanalytically oriented clinician, conducted this study in southern Appalachia and published it as *Roots of Futility* (1972). Later he replicated the study in an urban setting, Philadelphia, and summarized all the work in *Damaged Parents: An Anatomy of Child Neglect* (1981), which is still, in my judgment, the most thorough and in-depth study of neglect (that is, *physical* neglect) among the poor.

Polansky and his co-workers were able both to confirm that physically neglecting families are more common among the poor than among the middle and upper classes, and to demonstrate that a specific character disorder distinguishes poor mothers who neglect their children from poor mothers who do not. (The distinct character-disorder type was not established for the fathers, who had been included only in the Philadelphia research.) "Poverty makes it all the more difficult for such a [character-disordered] mother to cope; in fact, she is less able to cope than other mothers in the same miserable circumstances." That is, Polansky argued that poverty does not cause neglect; rather, neglecters are more likely to neglect when they live in poverty. The public health or social policy implication was obvious: programs to reduce poverty will reduce the incidence of neglecters who neglect. But the character disorder needs therapeutic attention.

Realizing how important it is to attach the name of a child's suffering not to the child but to the cause of the suffering—the parent who needs therapy—Polansky spoke of "the apathy-futility syndrome." Its most salient characteristic was developmental immaturity of an obsessional sort. The women Polansky studied were obsessionally slovenly and self-neglecting, locked into repetitive, ritualistic depression. They had the obsessional idea that nothing was worth doing. "What's the use of eating supper; you'll only be hungry before breakfast," one mother said. Emotionally numb, cut off from their feelings, and without hope, they were verbally inaccessible, seeming to be mute even inside themselves, carrying on none of the interior dialogue that is needed to solve problems, make judgments, or hold opinions—or, the researchers might have added, bear in mind (the technical psychoanalytic terms is *mentalize*) their children's emotional and physical needs. Without skills, including social skills, they were deeply fearful of failure and obsessionally organized their lives so that they did not need even to try to do anything. The mothers had not produced children because they wanted children; they had children because they had become pregnant (sometimes by rape) as teenagers or because they were trying to hang on to their husbands or because they lacked the motivation (or permission) to use contraceptives or because they needed children to care for their households and for themselves.

Importantly, Polansky and his colleagues observed, by observing their own reactions, that "the apathy-futility syndrome" induced feelings of apathy and futility even in the people who were trying to study or help these negligent mothers. The mothers' depression seemed to be contagious (among their children, too, the study might have noted). This observation was one of the first in the clinical literature to indicate the importance of clinicians' paying attention to what Freudians would call countertransference. For diagnosing and treating child abuse and neglect, what the therapist or re-searcher feels and feels prompted to do in an assessment or treatment situation is one of the most direct routes to discov-ering what the children have experienced and also what the perpetrators experienced, both in the present and in their own childhoods. Clinicians can feel themselves being drawn into experiencing a version of what the child or the perpetra-tor experienced, or both. There is an intergenerational trans-mission of trauma from parent to child to therapist.

While researchers considering physical abusers—male and female—have never been able to agree on a single *physi-cal* abuser type (not even the hysterical impulsive type de-scribed by Kempe's group), the developmentally immature apathy-futility neglecting obsessional character was widely recognized among social workers. And it would have been recognized among the children of such a person, like the child who told me about her mother: "She played with some dolls she had had since she was a kid, never with us. She said the dolls were her *good* children who never spoke and never made any demands. If she felt angry with the dolls she could just throw them out the window. Whenever she did that, I felt more scared of her than usual." In the terms I use, that is neglect in the service of a desire to eliminate.

Although Polansky's description was subsequently af-firmed in numerous studies, his apathy-futility type never had any effect on treatment or prevention, particularly after the 1970s, when conducting characterological or motivational studies of maltreaters fell out of favor in CAN. There were no programs specifically for lower-class physically neglecting parents for which this description, with its implications that in addition to long-term psychotherapeutic treatment these parents need economic help, would have been so useful. The reason for this policy breakdown is probably that physical neglect was and still is a phenomenon concentrated in (although not exclusive to) the poor, and programs of long-term psychotherapy have never been created in America for poor people, even when some degree of welfare has been made available. America has never had the universal health care or mental health care that would help bring a Mrs. Lake into treatment. And as I have noted, the psychotherapy called for in the 1974 Child Abuse Prevention and Treatment Act never materialized, even for those in the middle class.

It would have been useful if the in-depth interview methods Polansky developed for his study, which should be read as a study of impoverished physical neglecters only, had been extended to emotional neglecters, many of whom are middle class, and to other forms of neglect such as medical or educational neglect. And because it concentrated on intact families, Polansky's study did not consider one of the main types of male neglect across classes: desertion of the family and failure to be responsible for child support. To this day failure to provide child support is not considered a form of neglect because the man has removed himself from his family, where neglect, according to the literature, by definition takes place. Clinicians working with middle- and upper-class families are, by contrast, well aware that apathy-futility can be the defining characteristic of these unimpoverished people. But they will also note that apathetic-futile middle-class parents may be either obsessively slovenly and disorganized or, more frequently, obsessively organized and rigid in the way that Edgar Merrill and his Massachusetts group described in the early 1960s. At the beginning of the twentieth century, Freud had given the name "housewife psychosis" to women (like the mother of his famous patient Dora) who obsessively dedicate themselves to housework and neglect their children. Today we are familiar with the mother who wears herself out obsessively running her children around to lessons and activities, and overwhelms them with talent-enhancing toys, but cannot address her children's real needs because she is concerned only with her own vision of how her children ought to develop. In early 2011, Amy Chua's *Battle Hymn of the Tiger Mother* provoked a national argument over its contention that children should be kept incessantly busy to enable them to achieve peak performance levels—a full-scale obsessional-narcissistic program. Such children do not usually starve in the literal, physical sense, but they are emotionally starved. Yet even when the category "emotional neglect" finally entered the CAN literature in the late 1980s, it did not include a comparative empirical study of those who physically neglect and those who emotionally neglect.

The insight—so clear in Polansky's work but also in Young's—that people can physically neglect their children out of an "apathy-futility syndrome" was accepted in the child-maltreatment literature in the 1970s, but it was not pursued theoretically. Polansky's study seems to me to have shown that apathy-futility neglect consistently serves one purpose: eliminating or eradicating the child irritant, the source of headaches, the child needing and expecting love, the child viewed as draining away limited material and emotional resources and as refusing to parent the neglecter. But Polansky's work had no effect on how neglect was classified, and the data collection in CAN continued on its now standard act-oriented basis. By the time Polansky's book was published in 1981, the CAN statistics showed that the portion of neglected children among all children reported as maltreated was over 50 percent. It is closer to 60 percent thirty years later, as the poverty rate has increased. There are undoubtedly many more neglected children than are seen by neglect reporters or the social workers who investigate the reports. Those who are reported and investigated as victims of acts of omission and of apathy-futility still tend to be concentrated in high-poverty areas and impoverished families, although, as noted, neglect is not uncommon in families with resources. I think it probable that actively neglected children—unwanted children who are actively persecuted with deprivation—are the most underreported group because their neglect does not fit into the "omission" definition.

Also skewing the data, many children are likely to be reported as sexually abused, rather than neglected. In the late 1970s, as neglect was being defined—much too narrowly—in terms of physical acts of omission, the reporting numbers for sexual abuse began to rise shockingly. Commentators were at a loss to determine whether this was because the actual incidence of sexual abuse was increasing or because the reporting of sexual abuse was becoming more widespread. It may never be possible to answer that question, but the question obscures the fact that by the time this increase was noticed, the CAN classification was producing major distortions in the reporting data. The dramatic spike in sexual abuse reporting reflects, in part, the placement of many reported children into the sexual abuse category who might better have been placed in the neglect category—and who would have been better understood and treated if they had been considered multiply abused. The social background of the spike in reporting was the growing child-poverty rate, and the growing number of unattended children: "latchkey" children, school dropouts, runaways, children lost in the shuffle of divorces and merged families.

One of the key obstacles to understanding the increase in sexual abuse reporting in the 1970s was the way in which CAN researchers classified abuse. But the other key factor was that no one, including CAN researchers, had previously acknowledged the existence of child sexual abuse, and now Americans were finally beginning to overcome their reluctance to do so. Writing in 1984, the sociologist David Finkelhor, one of the most influential researchers and theoreticians in the CAN subfield of child sexual abuse, noted that ten years earlier—that is, when the Mondale hearings into physical child abuse were under way—child sexual abuse had been thought to be "a rather uncommon problem" both in America and worldwide. Incest was assumed to take place in "one in a million" families (as the 1970 edition of the *American Textbook of Psychiatry* announced with great certainty). But by the late 1970s, one out of three adult women, including women who had been children in the 1940s and 1950s, revealed in random questionnaire surveys that they had been the victims of unwanted sexual contact before the age of fourteen. (The sexologist Alfred Kinsey's research, done in the early 1950s, had given a figure of about 10 percent—but that research was conducted at a time when it was much more difficult for women to speak about sexual abuse.) Books for the general public about sexual abuse were appearing, including a few widely read sexual abuse memoirs, most notably Louise Armstrong's *Kiss Daddy Goodnight* (1978). The sexual abuse memoir appeared at the same time as the physical abuse memoir, a genre that reached the best-seller lists with *Mommie Dearest* (1978), written by the daughter of Joan Crawford. By the mid-1980s sexual abuse memoirs had become common, and television and magazine accounts were numerous. The writers of these memoirs were protestors; they were not quiet victims, hiding their sense of guilt, but openly angry women demanding accountability and change. Women who reported that they had once been sexually abused prepared the way for girls to say they were currently being abused.

Preconceptions and myths about sexual abuse began

to fall away, allowing more of its many motivational dimensions and many character types to be discovered by researchers. The crucial myth was that most child rape is committed by strangers, the view of the child abuser as infiltrator that had dominated popular thinking in the 1950s. CAN experts began to realize that, on the contrary, child rape is a family problem, occurring in homes or in church or in school where the adults are known to the children and in loco parentis. This realization allowed a distinction to be made between sexual abuse of an individual child and sex trafficking, sex tourism, and child pornography, which involve multiple victims. These multi-victim criminal acts are commonly committed by strangers, and they are socially and economically institutionalized, usually outside of homes, serving many purposes. Such institutionalized acts increase with economic expansion, whether called expansionary capitalism or globalization, and they commonly intersect with racism and colonialism as well as sexism. Individual sexual abuse, by contrast, increases with intergenerational conflict, intergenerational transmission of trauma, and conflict inside the family, including domestic violence, particularly between spouses.

During the 1980s, it gradually became apparent to child health and mental health providers and researchers that most individual child sexual abuse by family members and relatives goes on for a long period of time, often many years; it is not usually an isolated or single episode. Suffering from shame and fear, most child victims (like Anna) never reveal the abuse or reveal it only years later, as adults. Sexual abuse reporting is thus even less of a guide to the problem than reporting of physical abuse and neglect. The underreporting reinforces the denial of the problem. Victims of child sexual abuse appear in emergency rooms less frequently than victims of physical abuse, and this, too, contributes to under-

reporting and denial. In contrast particularly to physical neglect, sexual abuse is common among all classes under all
social circumstances. Unlike most neglecters, sexual abuse
perpetrators often have the resources and the access to experts and lawyers to contest accusations of child sexual
abuse, as well as to defend themselves by invoking their positions in their communities and their carefully cultivated rep-
utations. Discovery of child sexual abuse can quickly turn
into a confrontation between a child and the abuser. There is
far more legislation and case law concerning sexual abuse
than there is concerning any other reporting category.

This last characteristic of child sexual abuse helps explain its most consequential difference from physical abuse
and physical and emotional neglect. Child and adolescent
sexual abuse victims are the only victims of a type of maltreatment who have to prove that they did not *provoke* their
abuse by being seductive or that they did not lie when they
reported it. Often they cannot produce any witnesses to their
abuse. Because the abuse is *sexual,* its victims are subject to
the same kind of sexism that results in blaming the victim or
blaming the person who blames the (usually) male perpetrator. And sexual abuse is thus the one type of maltreatment
whose discovery has met with a politicized backlash, a multi-
faceted movement aimed at undoing that discovery and dis-
proving its truth. Victims and their advocates have to battle
politically and legally to protect the child and uncover the
truth.

Child sexual abuse has become a site of contestation
between children and adults; a political and legal battlefield,
it stands at the crossroads of generational conflict and transmission of trauma. Understanding adult motivations and their
legitimating belief systems (childism) is of great importance
in helping children who are reported as physically abused or

neglected, but it is critical to helping children reported as sexually abused because those children will be caught up not only in the drama of having their families investigated and probably prosecuted but in a vast social-political drama of adult-child relationships. How to deal with a family in which sexual abuse has taken place becomes a key social and political question.

I believe that this situation needs to be seen against the background of a general rule about childism: sexual abuse serves the childisms of hysterical role manipulation and narcissistic identity erasure, but it seldom serves the childism of obsessional elimination, while acts of physical and emotional neglect often do. Sexual victims are kept in the house, not eliminated; their service is required, their availability is bound up with their abuser's desire and fantasies. Sexual abusers manipulate sexual roles and confuse the child victims, making them doubt their own identity, and this is part of the abusers' purpose, a source of their pleasure and their satisfaction. Sexual abusers may also erase the child's self, including his or her capacity to tell the truth of the experience, so that they can control the story. The two motivations, the first hysterical, the second narcissistic, often occur within the same person, just as hysterical and narcissistic milieus often mingle in the same household or the same society.

The studies by CAN researchers did not employ this childism-based conceptualization. But as increased reporting of child sexual abuse began, they did search for a single sexually abusing type and family type, and they did agree on one thing. All sexually abusing families share a common characteristic: for sexual abuse to become the main type of abuse in a family—no matter which form of childism it serves—there has to be a family system organized around and affected by the perpetrator. The system protects an open secret. Collusion is involved—often of the sort that develops when addicts manipulate their families into supporting their alcoholism, drug taking, or gambling.

The tyrant at the center of an in-house collusion system is usually male. Using their reporting categories, CAN researchers established that whereas physical abuse was committed as frequently by women as by men, and neglect was committed more frequently by women than by men, sexual abuse was much more commonly committed by men than by women—perhaps 90 percent of perpetrators were male. In the late 1970s and early 1980s, children reported for sexual abuse were predominantly female (75 percent of all cases), and older (the average age was 8.1) than physically battered and neglected children. (Later more male victims were reported, and more young children.) Male sexual abusers were far more commonly heterosexual than homosexual. Despite this last finding, the idea that male homosexual abuse was the most common sort of sexual abuse persisted, and still persists, as a part of societal homophobia, which has been aggravated by church-based homophobic campaigns like the one led in 1977 by Anita Bryant, a born-again pop singer who opposed state anti-discrimination legislation designed to protect homosexuals.

In the late 1970s, in a consideration of the fast-growing but unorganized field of child sex abuse study, the sociologist David Finkelhor asked extremely important questions about why sexual abuse had risen "from virtual obscurity to extremely high visibility" in so short a period, leaving shocked researchers scrambling to catch up. His answer tells a great deal about sexual abuse and its long history as an open secret. According to Finkelhor, publicity or image-creation of two kinds precipitated this sudden visibility: that which came from within the field of Child Abuse and Neglect, where there had been such success in publicizing physical abuse and winning swift (if confused) legal attention to it; and that which came from the feminist movement. There was much conflict between the two camps.

In the CAN camp, Henry Kempe again courageously took the lead, stepping forward with a speech titled "Sexual Abuse: Another Hidden Pediatric Problem" at the 1977 annual meeting of the American Academy of Pediatrics. Kempe told his audience of more than a thousand pediatricians that "between 1967 and 1972 the number of sexually abused children increased tenfold in our hospital" and that within that group the number of children under the age of five who were sexually abused increased from 5 percent of the total to 25 percent. Although he approached sexual abuse as a "pediatric problem" comparable to and on the model of "the battered child syndrome," Kempe now acknowledged that he was also dealing with a social problem—the changing nature of the American family—which was something he had not considered in 1962. While he condensed into one powerful speech most of what was then known among pediatricians about child sexual abuse, he also sketched what has become an ongoing redefinition of the American family that has had profound consequences, some of them specifically impacting the incidence of sexual abuse. He noted some (though not all) of the social factors exposing the once hidden inner life of families (and, I would argue, the forms of hysterical, obsessional, and narcissistic childism predominating in them).

The divorce rate was spiraling upward, and patriarchal control of family affairs and women and children was threatened, turning many men tyrannical in defense. The number of children being raised by single mothers or in families where there were adults who were not biological parents or siblings who were not biologically related was increasing. The percentage of children dependent on someone not related to them for in-house daycare was growing along with the number of working women. Without the kinds of programs that had been called for in the vetoed Comprehensive Child Development Act of 1971, reliable, affordable daycare outside of the home remained hard to find even as the ranks of women going into the workforce swelled. Less protection for children—especially small children—translated immediately into more abuse, especially of preschool children. And the disruption, the mixing, and the merging of families diminished the effectiveness of traditional forms of the incest taboo as well as of familiar forms of social sexual repression and control of drugs and alcohol, substances that sexual abusers often abuse to eliminate, manipulate, or erase themselves as well as their children.

After he had outlined the social context for his discussion of child sexual abuse, Kempe turned to the standard psychiatric classification of child sexual abuse into three subtypes: pedophilia, rape and molestation, and incest. His discussions were clinically sound, but his classification was not only unilluminating, it was (unintentionally) obfuscating and basically incoherent. It does not take clinical training to note that pedophiles (people who have a preference for sex with children) can rape or commit incest or both; rapists can be pedophiles (or not); incest perpetrators can be pedophiles (or not), and so forth. The three subtypes reference acts, not actors or their motivations. They have no reference to a child's experience—for example, to the experience of a child who is raped by a pedophile father, thus experiencing all three subtypes of abuse at once. Relying on this subtypes of sexual abuse classification left CAN researchers out of touch with the complexity of sexual abuse and of maltreatment in general, and certainly out of touch with abusers and their motivations and prejudices.

On the other hand, Kempe did rightly and importantly emphasize how crucial it is to believe what children say about what they have experienced. He was obviously well aware of the then standard line within psychiatry and psychoanalysis in which stories of seduction are attributed to the children's fantasies: "Children do not fabricate stories of detailed sexual activities unless they have witnessed them, and they have, indeed, been witnesses to their abuse," he said. Kempe was aiming at one of the most important reasons for denial of child sexual abuse: psychiatrists and psychoanalysts had a long history of interpreting Freud's work on hysteria as claiming that when a girl or woman says she has been sexually abused, particularly by her father, she is presenting her Oedipal fantasy, not describing an actual experience.

With the notable exception of child analysts, who were as alert as social workers, most psychiatrists and psychoanalysts of adults were much slower than Kempe to see that childhood sexual abuse is usually all too real. Kempe himself had been mentored by the child analyst Rene Spitz, a trainee of Sándor Ferenczi in prewar Budapest, where there was much more awareness of sexual and other kinds of traumas than in the other European cities where Freudian psychoanalysis developed. Ferenczi thought that Freud had overemphasized the importance of children's fantasies, particularly Oedipal fantasies, in the stories patients tell in analysis. He had started in the late 1920s to write about "the unwanted child" (with a depressed mother of either the apathy-futility sort or the more active sort) and then about sexually abused children and adult survivors of childhood sexual abuse. Ferenczi's work was taken seriously by child analysts, who thought it was crucial to pay attention to *both* unconscious fantasy *and* external or environmental causes like traumas. Rene Spitz, for example, wrote a classic paper on "hospitalism" that deals with how a hospital setting in which a child feels unwanted or not warmly loved can cause that child to wither ("fail to thrive") and even die of "anaclitic depression" (the depression of a child who has no one to cling to and then becomes unable to cling). Anna Freud's Cleveland-based colleague Selma Fraiburg carried this balanced approach into the study of intergenerational transmission of trauma, including sexual trauma.

By the 1960s, what overemphasis there was among American child analysts on fantasy at the expense of concern for trauma had nearly been eliminated. But it had not been done away with among adult analysts, many of whom had become more Freudian than Freud on the topic. Their ultra-orthodoxy had made it difficult for the adult women they saw to speak of their experiences. The first generation of feminists to be concerned with child sexual abuse was hostile to this rigidified Freudian psychoanalysis and protested it politically. In effect, these women viewed it as itself a kind of sexual abuse, of the identity-erasing or silencing narcissistic form.

While he criticized the overemphasis in psychoanalytic theory on children's Oedipal fantasies, Kempe did so within a psychoanalytic framework, as is apparent in the longest segment of his 1978 speech, where he emphasized the role of the mother in father-daughter incest:

> Writers have, for the most part, stressed unduly the seductive nature of young girls involved sexually with fathers and brothers as opposed to the more important participatory role played by mothers. Our experience suggests that the seduction that some girls tend to experiment with to a cer-

tain degree and usually safely, within the family, is usually normal and does not explain incest, which is not initiated by the child but by the adult male, with the mother's complicity. Stories by mothers that they "could not be more surprised" can generally be discounted[;] we have simply not seen an innocent mother in cases of long-standing incest. Still, the mother escapes the punishment her husband will likely suffer.

Why do mothers play such an important role in incest between father and daughter? Often, a very dependent mother is frantic to hold her man to the family for her needs and the financial support he provides. The sexual role of the daughter is one way of providing him a younger, more attractive bond within the family than she can provide. This is particularly true if she is frigid, rejected sexually, or is herself promiscuous. . . . The vast majority of incest situations find the family caught up in a life-style from which they find no easy way out and in which discovery must at all costs be avoided. In order to preserve the family, even after discovery has occurred, admission is often followed by denial and the immediate family tends to condemn the victim if she is the cause of discovery [that is, if she reveals the incest publicly or objects to it]. She is then bereft of all support and has few choices.

Later in his speech, Kempe returned to the theme of the mother-daughter relationship in incest cases, developing his interpretation (which in my opinion replaced overemphasis on fantasy with overemphasis on maternal complicity). He described symptoms that often appear in an incestuously abused girl as she comes into adolescence: chronic depression, self-castigation and low self-esteem, persistent physical ailments like headaches, anorexia, social isolation, increasing rebelliousness and running away, often into prostitution. Not infrequently, she contracts a sexually transmitted disease. A troubled mother-daughter relationship is very common, he said; "Girls involved in incest often will eventually forgive their fathers but rarely will they forgive their mothers who failed to protect them."

In the incest model that Kempe offered, the mother is *always* the colluder or the one who does not see or does not believe. He was unusual at the time for his recognition that the child's experiences of being believed or not, and of being protected or not, are critical and *part of the abuse experience*. In terms of acts, the unprotected child is neglected or unattended. However, Kempe also assumed, I think incorrectly, that incest is distinguished from pedophilia and child molestation or rape by being triangular—that is, by involving a third-party colluder, the mother, with "the more important participatory role" in relation to the girl's symptom formation.

Kempe's assumption was not questioned by pediatricians, who had had little experience with the types of third-party collusion routinely accorded molesters and pedophiles not committing incest. To cite an example that is familiar to us now: sexually abusing Catholic priests relied on collusion from church officials, who either ignored the abuse or moved the priests to new parishes, where the abuse could continue against other children. Kempe made no mention of the frequency with which sexual abusers of all sorts (not just incestuous abusers) explicitly count on (and are excited by, inflated by) collusion, as they count on the child's remaining silent out of fear, guilt, or bewilderment. Often the colluders (who might in some instances be neglecters) are the mothers, but collusion from the mother is not, as Kempe claimed, obvious in every case, and it is not always more important in the incest situation for the symptom formation than the father's actions. Similarly, his claim that incest victims tend eventually to forgive their fathers but not their colluding mothers reflects, in my estimation, the sexism of the majority of pediatricians at that time, whose ability to understand a girl's experience or that of her mother was profoundly compromised. To note just one missing ingredient of Kempe's social analysis: the spiraling divorce rate meant that many more children saw their fathers only during visitations to the father's home, where the mothers were unable to supervise or observe. More generally, Kempe missed in his social analysis how crucial to incest is the father's assertion of his ownership of the child and his patriarchal "rights" or privileges. He missed the entanglement of sexism with childism that is characteristic of historical moments when families break down and the patriarch turns sexually tyrannical—tragically turning against "his" children as well as "his" women. (In subgroups where the abusers were addicts, Vietnam War veterans with posttraumatic stress disorder, or former prison inmates who had been traumatized in prison, the intergenerational transmission of violence was often key.)

It was Kempe's sexism and the sexism of the majority of pediatricians at the time that brought them, and CAN, into conflict with the feminist movement and feminist researchers. In the early 1970s, the most important feminist writer on child sexual abuse was Florence Rush, whose collection of nearly a decade of speeches and pamphlets was published in 1980 under the title *The Best Kept Secret: Sexual Abuse of Children.*

When she joined New York Radical Feminists and attended one of the group's conferences in 1971, Rush, then in her fifties and the mother of three, was a social worker employed by a residence for dependent and neglected girls. The Radical Feminists conference had been organized to follow up an emotional open forum—the first of many "speak outs"—in which women had testified to their experiences of being raped as adults. Rush gave a stirring talk on the sexual abuse (including rape) of children, and from then on abuse of children was always included in the agenda of feminist anti-violence and anti-rape activism. Soon researchers like the social psychologist Diana Russell were giving an emphasis on sexism and data about it as an organizing concept to the activists. Russell collected her papers from her years of work in *Sexual Exploitation: Rape, Sexual Abuse of Children and Sexual Harassment* (1984) and *The Sexual Trauma* (1986).

Feminist activists writing about child abuse set it in the same social context that Kempe saw, but they evaluated the context and the abuse differently, and they questioned the psychodynamic emphasis on the mother's collusion and the underemphasis on sexism. There was a clear political agenda in the feminist critique: to expose child sexual abuse as part of domestic violence against women generally—that is, as a type of sexism and sexist violence. But this subsumption of child sexual abuse into the category "domestic violence" meant that feminists' appreciation of the specificities of child sexual abuse was limited; and no concept of childism emerged from their concept of sexism.

Similarities between what children suffer and what women suffer in violent households were tacitly asserted (and differences ignored) when the unfortunate term "battered woman syndrome," modeled on the equally unfortunate "battered child syndrome," came into use. Susan Brownmiller's 1975 best seller *Against Our Will: Men, Women, and Rape* encouraged the perception that child sexual abuse was a phenomenon identical with the rape and battering of women. She emphasized (wrongly) that child sexual abuse, like adult rape, tends to be committed by nonfamily members and strangers. She also stressed that it is encouraged—even promoted—by the entertainment media and especially by child pornography, but, again wrongly, she saw child pornography as fundamentally the same as adult pornography, thus missing its essence: the manipulation of children into playing adult roles or perverse caricatures of adult roles.

The feminists' approach to the study of child sexual abuse created a paradox. Although the feminist activists brought a needed emphasis on social context, and sexism, they did not distinguish the features of child sexual abuse that are specific to children, and thus they did not distinguish the specific prejudice (childism) involved, which is related to, and may overlap with, sexism but which also differs from sexism in important ways. Most feminists followed Brownmiller and others in arguing that sexual abuse of women and girls alike is entirely a function of the status of women and girls in patriarchal societies. Rape is an assertion of status and power through violence, Brownmiller had claimed, and rapists are concerned with domination more than with sex per se, so rape generally leads to more violence than is involved in the sexual act itself. Again, this over-general description of "rapists" obscured the fact that although many—certainly not all—adult rapes (particularly by strangers) do involve more violence than the violence of the rape act itself, most child rapes do not. Child rapists, like Anna's stepbrother, being predominantly family members or people who are well known to the child, do not usually need to employ coercive violence before or silencing violence after the act because they have already persuaded the child through cajolery, threats of harm to others, repetitive rituals, or lies (often to the effect that the rape is a game, a special treat, or a manifestation of God's love). Verbal manipulation is more effective with children and is safer from detection than violence, which risks exposing the in-house open secret publicly and can lead to the loss of the child's continuous service. (Anna's stepbrother continued his rape and molestation of her for five years, enjoying her continuous service, until he and her father became afraid that his open secret would get out—that is, that Anna would talk.)

Like most feminists who considered child sexual abuse, Rush and Brownmiller agreed with Kempe that overemphasis on a child's fantasy or complicity was blaming the victim, but they argued that blaming the mother for colluding was also blaming the victim. They rightly felt that a sexist stereotype was being created, to which Louise Armstrong gave the name "the incest mother." From this feminist point of view, the family-preservation policy that had come into favor within CAN when the battered child syndrome and physical abuse were at issue should not be applied in sexual abuse cases. "Family preservation" did not protect women or children because it put both in danger of further abuse, and it ignored the mothers' desire to rescue their daughters from the family. The approach favored by a majority of feminists, called victim advocacy, assumed that in most cases women and children should be helped to establish themselves outside of the family context while the abuser was prosecuted. Battered women and battered children needed state-supported shelters not "family preservation."

Many CAN policy makers, by contrast, argued that family preservation would lead to less denial within the family of sexual abuse and less likelihood of retaliation against the child, while at the same time it would encourage victims or nonabusing family members to report abuse and seek treatment. Particularly if "the sexually abusive family" could ever be identified as a type, such a family might be approached and helped before the abuse took place, thus preserving the family. The controversy between CAN researchers and victim-advocate feminists grew increasingly acrimonious during the 1980s. Both sides became entrenched in their respective approaches, to the extent that when a backlash against the very idea of childhood sexual abuse gained momentum in the 1990s, the two camps were unable to join against their common social enemy: the childists who were working to suppress children's normal developmental needs and rights, block child-development programs as a threat to "family values," and combat what they perceived as the insubordination and rebellion of children in general.

The very political CAN-feminist controversy helped obscure the basic principle that each child caught in an abuse situation or a contested custody situation should be assessed *individually* and that a recommendation concerning the child's care should be made on the basis of that particular child's experiences and relationships. Although Anna Freud's *In the Best Interests of the Child* and some other studies did articulate this principle vigorously, it was not consistently applied within Child Protective Services or by courts, for it requires that the assessor have patience, empathic listening skills, and freedom from polemical and institutional pressure.

As Finkelhor pointed out, the professions that should have been most concerned over the rise in reports of child sexual abuse and most determined to assure individual children a careful assessment were psychiatry and psychology. Much sexual abuse involves no discernible physical trauma that requires pediatric medical treatment (although this is not true of the rape of small children, which is always physically damaging, and it is not true of *anorexia nervosa* secondary to sexual abuse, which can be lethal). All sexual abuse does, however, involve a degree of neglect and emotional trauma (greater in proportion to the lack of protection and the lack of protective cultural norms). But practitioners in psychiatry and psychology, still laboring to free themselves of Freudian distortion, were slow to react to the rise in child sexual abuse reporting, slow to theorize about the problem, and slow to engage in empirical research. One consequence of their inaction was that in the 1970s, far less research and programmatic attention were given to child sexual abuse than pediatricians had been able to muster for child physical abuse. Nor was there a legislative initiative to address the problem, as there had been in the 1960s and early 1970s for battered children.

As I noted at the beginning of this chapter, during the eight years of Ronald Reagan's presidency the legislative concern for America's "endangered children" weakened, and their situation became progressively worse. Following Reagan's lead, Congress began a process of deregulating the manufacturing and service industries—in effect, subsidizing corporations and international consortiums engaged in the kind of capitalism that came to be known as globalization. Child labor and child sexual trafficking increased globally, as did the child poverty rate everywhere except in the more social-democratic states of Western Europe and the British Commonwealth. In America, Congress was supporting privatization of government services of all sorts, including children's services and—crucially—daycare and schools. A small proportion of the population began to accumulate extraordinary wealth, while the numbers making up the poorer classes grew exponentially. Impoverished urban neighborhoods began to decay, and what had been known as pauperism at the end of the nineteenth century was once again undermining families and leaving children to live on the streets, joining the growing population of the homeless. Dilapidated inner-city schools were effectively resegregated. Violence of all sorts increased, and America began an era of frantic prison-building and incarceration—including the incarceration of youths and even children, especially African Americans. As the inner-city ghettos grew, the prison ghettos grew. Prison became a cruel kind of foster care.

In the early 1990s, researchers looking into the origin and nature of violence joined with developmentalist child-study researchers to consider the topic of youth violence. One of the most important of these was James Gilligan, a psychoanalytically oriented psychiatrist who worked in the main Massachusetts psychiatric prison, Bridgewater, and wrote about what he had learned in essays and then a book, *Violence: Our Deadly Epidemic and Its Causes* (1996). Gilligan stressed the fact that in Bridgewater the majority of the prisoners were adult men who had been abused (often sexually) as children, many violently. But whether their experiences met the CAN criteria for abuse or not, all the prisoners had one common experience: they had all been shamed and humiliated, and they all felt that their manhood had been threatened. Their violent crimes were efforts to overcome that shame and humiliation by inflicting it on others (including children) or by attacking anyone who seemed bent on shaming or humiliating them again. With their crimes, the prisoners had tried to force people or institutions to give them respect as a "cure" for the disrespect (dissing) they had endured: "Shame is the pathogen that causes violence just as specifically as the tubercle bacillus causes tuberculosis, except that in the case of violence it is an emotion, not a microbe." In *Preventing Violence* (2001), Gilligan summarized his thirty years of work and his pleas that social-democratic policies be established, including adequate welfare and aid to families and children, reformed public education, gun regulation, and laws against corporal punishment, as a way to reduce the atmosphere of violence that allowed the pathogen of shame to flourish as surely as lack of hygiene, clean air and water, and sewers had allowed the tubercle bacillus to flourish. Violence was an epidemic, he argued, and should be dealt with as a public health issue.

Gilligan employed the public health model developed by Kempe and his team, but he moved a huge step beyond Kempe: he acknowledged that he was not looking at a microbe but at an emotion within men—shame and humiliation—induced and transmitted by shamed and humiliated abusers. He did not start from a typology of violent acts but began with a search for the motivation of those acts. Shamed and humiliated men need to shame and humiliate, as later do their shamed and humiliated sons. Kempe had looked for the pathogen of "the battered child syndrome" and found it in the aggressive, hysterical abuser, without illuminating the causes of the abuser's abuse, much less how the abuse was rationalized or justified. He had looked abstractly at a single character type and a vague "aggression," while paying no attention to how character types, in the plural, shape and mold motivations—not creating them but giving them various forms. Gilligan's work, coming neither from CAN nor from feminist theory (where it was ignored because it only concerned males), was an important move in the direction of showing how violence can spread through an entire society like a contagion via intergenerational transmission of trauma. Further, he suggested the kinds of social policies and political commitments that were and still are needed in order to prevent violence against children, the source, as he showed, of much adult violence.

But although Gilligan's work pointed to this new direction, few recognized it in the 1980s and 1990s, when politically leftist Baby Boomers were confronting the social deterioration wrought during the Reagan years. Despite their concern about the prejudices of racism and sexism, these former activists ignored the prejudice of childism or the experiences of children. Their failure was an intellectual one, but of course it had more complex roots. Central was the fact that during the Reagan era Baby Boomers, liberals and conservatives alike, were enjoying the benefits of a rapid-growth economy organized to favor their needs, rather than those of the next generation, at the time they were establishing careers and raising their children. Reagan's deregulation and tax-cut agenda, along with the easy availability of credit and the lack of social emphasis on saving for the future, made it possible for many in the Baby Boom generation to enjoy a lifestyle that was materially beyond anything known to Americans since the late-nineteenth-century Gilded Age.

The political culture supported this shift in every way. Transfers of wealth into Boomer hands were legislated: for example, Social Security was organized so that their children would, as they became workers, start supporting their parents' retirements. Among the types of pension and social security systems existing in the world, America's Social Security system is unique in resting so squarely on the shoulders of the next generation. There is no such thing as Social Security for most children and there never has been since the Social Security Act of 1935, which emphasized the plight of seniors (and practically eliminated senior poverty). The childism flourishing in the country and present in so many Baby Boom households made it hard for Boomers to see themselves as constituting problems for their own children. Weren't they creating the most child-centric culture in the history of the world?

Concomitantly, however, updates on the condition of "our endangered children" continued to appear throughout the 1990s, only to come up against the narcissism and indifference that permeated the Baby Boom generation. One of the most thorough studies of the problem was *Today's Chil-*

dren: Creating a Future for a Generation in Crisis (1992), which detailed how the children belonging to the generation born around 1970 were being affected by their parents' opposition to the Great Society pro-child initiatives. And this book was frank about the ways wealthy liberal Baby Boomers were colluding with their conservative counterparts: failing to support public schools because they were sending their children to private schools (and, later, privately run charter schools); failing to support public daycare because they could afford nannies; failing to support universal healthcare because they had private insurance; failing to reform Social Security because they had adequate private retirement accounts.

The author of *Today's Children*, Dr. David Hamburg, a physician and president of the Carnegie Corporation in New York—a major sponsor of research on children's welfare—was perfectly positioned to present the big picture. With a cascade of statistics and policy analyses, he described a country with the highest infant mortality rates of any in the developed world, a country without a healthcare system that guaranteed prenatal and postnatal maternal care, a country that lacked an early-childhood program for daycare and preschool education. He portrayed America's public junior high and high schools as collapsing organizationally and producing a dropout rate higher than that of any comparable country (while an elite segment of the middle and upper classes went on to colleges and universities that were growing more and more expensive). Like James Gilligan, Hamburg wrote about prisons housing increasing numbers of juveniles, and pointed out that these prisons were becoming a fast-growing corporate enterprise, comparable to the financial and defense industries in their lack of oversight regulation. Considering the inadequacy of child-welfare funding and aid to impoverished families, Hamburg showed that it had led to pervasive family breakdown, and he presented tables of teenage pregnancy rates and male youth violence rates that were far greater than those in the European social democracies.

Hamburg was well aware of the nation's growing problem with child abuse and neglect, although he seemed unaware of the classification problems within the field of Child Abuse and Neglect. In fact, he contributed to those problems by assuming that child abuse and neglect are first and foremost physical abuse. Because he assumed that physical abuse is the template of all abuse, he reported physical abuse statistics as statistics for maltreatment in general: "Although statistics on death from maltreatment cannot be precise, between 1,200 and 5,000 children die from abuse each year. Six to ten times as many children survive abuse with serious injuries." But even though he offered no analysis of maltreatment forms (or any suggestion about their relation to prejudice), Hamburg described clearly the importance of intergenerational trauma to child abuse: "In addition, abused children tend to suffer severe psychological problems later in life, and they all too commonly perpetrate this violent behavior toward their own children. Although reports of child abuse and neglect have increased almost 200 percent in the past ten years [1982–1992], these problems have not received high priority from the scientific, educational or health communities."

It is striking that in this study and a long shelf of others focused on what happened to America's families and children after 1970, there was so little ideological analysis, so little attempt to ask what ideas—what prejudices—were guiding not just the maltreatment of children but the failure to address it. Without this level of analysis, no momentum was generated for demanding a new comprehensive child development act or, generally, for preventing the growing crisis for children and their families. It certainly is the case that changes in family structure had left many children underprovisioned and underprotected or neglected, and that state and federal governments were doing little to address their needs. But these studies, crucial as they were and still are, do not explore the contemporary stereotypes and images of children that attracted, even activated, a societal prejudice against children. Like Packard's *Our Endangered Children* a decade earlier, these 1990s books contained no discussion of childism that could foster the kind of political awareness that had infused the civil rights and feminist movements. Even the Clinton administration, ushered into office in 1992 on waves of rhetoric about putting children first and well advised by children's advocates, including Hamburg himself and Marian Wright Edelman of the Children's Defense Fund, soon abandoned its pro-child agenda and set about dismantling rather than reforming the welfare system, caving in to "family values" proponents in Congress and across the country by promoting a "workfare" program aimed at deficit reduction. Hillary Clinton, who had written several important articles on children's rights in the 1970s while she was at Yale Law School—where she was mentored by Albert Solnit and Joseph Goldstein, co-authors with Anna Freud of *In the Best Interests of the Child*—was pilloried as a "kiddie libber" by conservatives and rendered ineffectual after she failed to get a healthcare reform bill before Congress.

This focus on a "generation in crisis" was the context in which the now enormous literature on child sexual abuse grew up, fed by research within the field of Child Abuse and Neglect, by feminist studies, by the personal memoir tradition and the television talk shows, and by the slowly increasing attention to the issue within the fields of psychoanalysis and psychiatry, particularly from child analysts. It was a complex literature, which had from its inception a number of features that distinguished it from the earlier literatures on physical abuse and physical neglect. But the most important thing to be said about it is that it was—and remains—a thoroughly politicized literature. Almost everyone who contributed to the sexual abuse literature had a political purpose that omitted or discounted some part of the story. The problem endemic to all previous studies of child maltreatment recurred: the motivations and beliefs of the adults being reported and investigated as sexual abusers were not present. Volumes of studies of sexually abused children and volumes of studies of the behavior (rather than the motivations) of sexually abusing adults appeared, but only rarely were the relationships between children and adults seen as serving adult purposes and adult beliefs or prejudices.

The 1990s atmosphere of narcissism and polemic also permeated the child sexual abuse literature and made it polemical. The literature itself was like an abused child, internalizing childism. Everyone was dealing explicitly with politically divisive questions about how much and what kind of intervention, mostly aimed at men, were necessary to protect children within families. Child sexual abuse represented a direct challenge to the fortress of the family and to the "family values" ideologists, but it also constantly challenged claims to "the truth" that came from all political directions, including that of theorists who were primarily focused on sexism and its harms, which were thought to fall similarly on women and children. A narcissistic culture is one in which claims to possession or ownership of "the truth" go along with claims to ownership of children and ownership of the future that children represent. And a narcissistic culture is one in which denial and lying become so accepted that all statements—including children's descriptions of their abuse— are said to be lies. Like the adults around them, children can learn in such a culture to say as a matter of self-protection—protection of their identities—what they think others want to hear.

As a guide to this history of how "Who has the truth?" became the central question of the child sexual abuse literature, let me note a widely influential, often popularized and republished *Child Abuse and Neglect* journal article called "The Child Sexual Abuse Accommodation Syndrome" (1983). The author, a child psychologist named Roland Summit, argued (rightly) that children who have accommodated themselves to their abusers' demands for many years are often able to tell their stories only in bits and pieces, fits and starts, variations and recantations and exaggerations. They become as confused as hostages who accommodate themselves to the people who have taken them hostage. But, Summit went on to insist, these children *never* lie or fantasize about sexual abuse when they are asked about it in investigations, not even if they are interviewed over and over, not even if they are trying to accommodate themselves to their *interviewers'* suggestions.

Unlike Kempe's sensible statement that "children are witnesses to their own abuse," Summit's phrase, "children never lie," was both polemical and counterproductive. What is at issue in children's stories (and later court testimony) is not whether children *intentionally mislead* (which is how *lie* should be defined) but whether they can be influenced by their own reactive fantasies, by their fear of interviewers and of what interviewers can do to them or to their parents, and by the agenda-ridden conditions under which they are questioned. Assuming the neutrality of interviewers and the safety of interview situations for children, Summit missed the key questions: Do children in interview contexts misremember, distort, embellish, or fabricate not in order to mislead but in order to accommodate themselves to their own reactions, to their questioners, to their therapists, or to their parents? Could they be speaking out of fear or shame and humiliation? Could they distort out of internalized childism?

There was little interest in such questions in the 1980s child sexual abuse battles. For many feminists advocating for victims of domestic violence and rape, the "children never lie" position seemed like an obviously corrective, child-supportive position. Summit was hailed as a hero of truth-telling, and he became famous in victim-advocacy feminist organizations as an expert witness at abuse and custody trials. Other contributors who advanced the "children never lie" sound-bite were similarly influential. When a Swiss psychoanalyst named Alice Miller turned against psychoanalysis, accusing Freud of denying the incidence of child abuse in fin de siècle Viennese families through his emphasis on Oedipal fantasy, she became a heroine for many feminists doing victim-advocacy work with children. English translations of her books, from *Prisoners of Childhood* (1981) through *Thou Shalt Not Be Aware* (1984) and *Banished Knowledge* (1990), which all contained valuable reflections on how traumatic it is for children when they are not believed, became manifestos for the "children never lie" position. At Miller's extreme of the Freudian distinction between unconscious fantasy and real trauma, unconscious fantasy disappeared from consideration. Internalized childism could not be a topic.

This whole trend of feminist analysis—with its mixture of important critiquing of sexist agendas and ill-informed embracing of distorting "truths" thought to be child-supportive—became even more complicated in the 1980s when multiple-victim abuse began to be reported more frequently. Soon even more complicated reports of multiple-abuser abuse started to appear. When there were both multiple abusers and multiple victims—a vast tangle of stories—none of the existing camps of would-be protectors, armed with their preexisting ideas and categories, were prepared to listen. If the act-oriented CAN typology of sexual abuses as pedophilia, molestation or rape, or incest was incoherent for one abuser with one victim, it was even more useless for abusers who worked in teams or cults or who went from one child to the next in a household or a church or a sports team or—particularly—a daycare center.

Further complicating the situation was the appearance of another group of experts: criminologists. Because they worked in the places—prisons—where many multiple-victim abusers were available for study, criminologists generated the most literature on multiple-victim abusers. Their books became a source of horrified fascination in a decade marked by spectacular serial killings and lurid portraits of serial killers. Millions saw the horror film *The Silence of the Lambs* (1991), in which the serial killer was also a cannibal. Permeating the popular culture were images of satanic abusers who could deceive the police and trained investigators with their uncanny abilities in scene-setting and role manipulation— Dr. Hannibal Lector was a psychiatrist! Many real-life police personnel and criminologists responded by trying to become undeceivable, in perfect possession of the truth, with, as it were, better X-ray vision than the perpetrators.

The multiple-victim research subjects studied by criminologists in prisons were not usually parents who had abused more than one of their children at home. Most had abused children in many different families, although usually in families known to them, in their neighborhoods, the athletic teams they coached, their extended families, their churches. (Priests seldom ended up in prison because church officials were, as I noted before, not required by law to report them and protected them by moving them to a new parish, away from the site of their abuse, where they would often begin abusing again.) It astonished criminology prison researchers to discover that the nonrelative offenders they studied had, typically, so many victims—sometimes hundreds. But they did not interview the victims, so what those hundreds of children might have taught them was lost.

Many 1980s criminologists suspected that they were dealing with people who were quite different from the majority of parental sexual abusers. They revamped the old concept of the psychopath (or sociopath) to arrive at the important hypothesis that sociopaths are people who have never followed a normal human developmental course, never been parented, only been (so I would describe it) subject to efforts at eliminating them, manipulating them, or erasing them—without even a small island of safety or care. Sociopaths may in various ways be pushed or manipulated or erased while on their life course, but the important point is that their suffering begins early in life. They do not become human as babies—and so, since ancient times sociopaths have been portrayed as monsters, aliens, without even a society of monsters in which to grow up, like the society of the Cyclopes described by Homer. They are not "feral children"—to use Anna's phrase about herself—but complete isolates.

But there were also sensationalist criminologists who assumed that the multiple-victim abusers they saw in prisons should be considered the *paradigmatic* abusers. For them, "the typical sexual abuser"—that person whom CAN researchers had looked for in vain for years—was before their eyes at last, and he was the *multiple* abuser. Parental abusers of a single child would show the same characteristics, it was assumed, as sociopaths. And out of that (quite incorrect, in my view) assumption came a literature that was terrifying—and, as it turned out, panic-inducing when it reached the general reading public.

Anna C. Salter, for example, a psychologist working with the Wisconsin Department of Corrections, interviewed and treated hundreds of sex offenders. After publishing a relatively nonpolemical book, *Treating Child Sex Offenders and Victims* (1988), for a specialized clinical audience, she produced a tough-minded, witty, commercially successful book for a wider audience with the memorable one-word title *Predators*. Her long subtitle (featuring the misguided pedophile/rapist distinction) was full of drama: *Pedophiles, Rapists, and Other Sex Offenders; Who They Are, How They Operate, and How We Can Protect Ourselves and Our Children* (2003).

In this book, which summarized the lectures she had given around the country and worldwide in the 1980s and 1990s, Dr. Salter was on a mission to show that sex crimes are far more common than people think, and that very few of the criminals are ever detected, much less apprehended and convicted. *Everyone* is vulnerable because the methods of sex offenders—or of the character-type "the sex offender"—are not understood; indeed, most people are completely ignorant of or deluded about "who they are" and do not realize that they are *all alike*, and they are *everywhere*—like secret agents in an unsuspecting society. Sex offenders, she argued, are most frequently the upstanding, morally correct, rigid, calculating, good citizens who live next door. *Predators* was a kind of Most Wanted poster for this single character-type: the male infiltrator who lives a double life, has a cold-blooded motivation to deceive as well as to abuse, and has multiple victims. The decades-long search for "the sexual abuser" had produced "the multiple-victim sexual abuser" as an uncanny, obsessional collector of victims, busy destroying our society. This was the FBI director J. Edgar Hoover's 1950s nightmare—

"How Safe Is Your Daughter?" he had asked in a popular article—magnified exponentially. *All* our daughters were suddenly at risk.

The thesis of *Predator* became part of the politicization of child sex abuse research that was beginning to induce a national panic over the problem. Along with the "children never lie" theorists, the "predators are *everywhere*" proponents supplied the terror-inducing ingredients. Less-polemical scientists were hard pressed to stand against the incipient panic because it was organized around the one thing all those involved in the discovery of child sexual abuse in the 1970s and 1980s could say with certainty: more secrecy surrounds child sexual abuse than any other type of abuse, so its discovery—generally, and in every individual case—is difficult and conflicted and productive of uncertainty and fear. On the defensive, pediatricians stepped up their reliance on physical examinations, even though these are difficult to conduct, not least because of the potentially retraumatizing invasion of the child's body and privacy that the exams involve.

In the late 1980s, American pediatricians hoped that the culposcope, an instrument that illuminates, magnifies, and photographs the external genito-urinary and anal areas, would uncover sexual abuse of children the same way X-rays had revealed physical battering abuse. It did not. But the culposcope experimentation became part of a reaction within pediatric communities as well as within CAN against the way the study of sex offenders was being conducted; reeling out of control, it was producing scandals, some precipitated by pediatricians looking for sure-fire ways to identify and prosecute abusers.

In 1987 two pediatricians in northern England (one female, one male) set off a huge scandal, the "Cleveland Affair," by subscribing to the theory—now thoroughly discredited—

that "reflex anal dilatation" (RAD) could supply conclusive evidence of anal sexual abuse. In a period of five months, the two doctors referred 121 children to social workers and police, and these children were immediately removed from their homes—often in the middle of the night—by means of traumatizing police raids. Many of the children were kept for months (and a few for years) in hospitals, children's homes, or foster care. When the cases went to court, all but twenty-five were dismissed because there was no evidence but the RAD-based pediatric diagnosis, which was questioned by experts both during the trials and later in a government inquiry into the affair. The origin and accumulation of the Blue Beardian fantasy that the whole community was filled with sexual abusers (they are everywhere) with innumerable victims were not questioned. The mostly working-class parents who had been falsely accused were outraged, and they staged a number of protests, eventually drawing the media to their side and casting a long-lasting shadow over the child-protective social services. RAD was officially discredited, but the two zealous pediatricians went on practicing, holding to their belief in its accuracy as well as to their belief that there were child sexual abusers all around them whom it was their duty to expose.

Because the majority of sexual abuse acts leave no physical traces (molestation seldom does, for example), those involved in protecting children have usually supported a variety of efforts to make their fields more "scientific." But this has seldom meant paying more attention to the children or, for that matter, to the motivations of the people accused of doing the abusing. Technology has exercised the greatest allure. Penile plethysmography, for example, which tracks penile erectile response to various stimuli, was advocated, but it eventually proved unreliable in identifying male pedophiles or men particularly aroused by children. It also proved unreliable in determining whether "reconditioning" or the use of drugs like Depo-provera could reduce a male sex offender's child-focused libido as the scientists in the film *A Clockwork Orange* had hoped their "aversion therapy" would reduce the incidence of juvenile delinquency. Psychological testing and polygraphing of males and females, too, were never conclusive. Neither by technological means nor by interviewing and treating sex offenders did "the child sexual abuser" get discovered.

Sexual abuse is the type of abuse that depends most for its discovery on the verbal testimony of the victim, and the victim alone, so it is not surprising that in this area of study questions about the reliability of children's testimony have been more important than motivational questions or definitional questions about what acts constitute abuse and what penalties should be legislated. The problems with children's testimony were already front and center in the late 1980s, when a full-scale panic over child sexual abuse swept America.

CHAPTER FIVE

Mass Hysteria and Child Sexual Abuse

IN THE 1980S, CHILD SEXUAL ABUSE STUDY DID MOVE forward, despite its complexities and the ruptures these produced inside the field of Child Abuse and Neglect, as well as between CAN researchers and feminist theorists and later among criminologists. The American public became more aware of the problem thanks to the efforts of the researchers and advocates who contributed to the study, but they also became more confused. At the same time, a situation was brewing that would soon erupt in mass hysteria and turn that halting, confusing progress back on itself. No comparable phenomenon had arisen to affect research into physical abuse or neglect. But for the next two decades, this social phenomenon would change—and in many respects reverse—the course of the research into sexual abuse, especially in North America and Great Britain, where resurgent social, political, and particularly religious conservatism fueled the hysteria. Both the public and researchers and clinicians began viewing child sexual abuse in a new, regressive light; and another surge of conservatism between 2000 and 2010 has kept this trend going. Child sexual abuse came to be the central front of a cultural civil war in America in which the nation's collective sense of reality and truth, and even its commitment to equality among citizens, was threatened.

In late 1983 shocking headlines began to appear, particularly in the newspapers of small, ethnically homogeneous cities, concerning young children who were forced by their daycare workers to join in sexual orgies. The orgies not only involved the children and adults; they included forced sexual acts with corpses in which children were afterward forced to eat the flesh of the dismembered bodies. Within a few years, hundreds of investigations into disturbingly similar claims were under way in almost every state of the nation, many of them leading to criminal prosecutions. Accusations proliferated, not just of multiple-abuser child sexual abuse, but of ritual sex involving children, child sacrifice, mutilations of young children, and satanic cults. Soon, two new categories of CAN were given their obligatory abbreviations: MV/MO (multiple victim/multiple offender abuse) and SRA (satanic ritual abuse).

Starting in 1984, national magazines such as *Time* and *Newsweek*, as well as television news programs, began to present stories that compared SRA cases from around the country and identified an alleged trend. A huge public outcry arose before any of the reported cases was even heard in court, and the trials often lasted for many months, sometimes years. Parents across the country became afraid to send their children to daycare centers and preschools, while those who had denounced out-of-home childcare as antithetical to "family values" seized on the stories as proof that daycare centers and preschools were staffed by child abusers out to harm and corrupt the nation's children.

People attached to various kinds of child protective services, as well as police departments and attorneys general, were suddenly swamped with reports of bizarre sexual practices involving children. These experts had no experience in investigating such reports and lacked the historical knowledge of past "moral panics" to help them understand what was happening. More than a decade would pass before historical studies like Philip Jenkins's *Moral Panic: Changing Constructions of the Child Molester in Modern America* (1998) helped identify the phenomenon, and two decades before its broader context could be considered, as in David Frankfurter's *Evil Incarnate: Rumors of Demonic Conspiracy and Satanic Abuse in History* (2006). CAN researchers were unprepared to recognize the cross-cultural and transhistorical phenomenon that the French social critic Gustave Le Bon, a contemporary of Freud's, had been the first to name "mass hysteria." That there could be "mass obsessionality," like the anti-Communist fears of the 1950s, or "mass narcissism," as was happening in the 1980s panic, apparently did not occur to anyone, although phrases like "law and order mentality" and "culture of narcissism" did enter the national language.

The sudden explosion of MV/MO and particularly SRA cases in the mid-1980s was initially very difficult for researchers to evaluate because, like a rumor spun out of a partial truth or a fact taken out of context, it had been preceded by cases in the CAN annals that lent some credence to the accusations. There were cases—reported and investigated before 1983—that involved multiple abusers and some level of organization of those abusers within a family, a club or gang, a fraternity, a cult, a sex ring, a trafficking operation, or a pornography ring. Commercial, institutionalized sex slavery and child sex slavery had become recognized features of global capitalism, and they often involved violent, even terrorist practices. From both child and adult patients, clinicians had heard of domestic abuse situations in which children were passed around from one family member to another. (Anna's case is one such; she experienced her family as being "like a cult.") Instances of ritualized abuse, even in preschools, were on record, as were a few cases involving satanic ritual "churches." But to my knowledge no psychological studies of satanic ritual groups were made before the 1980s; studies on the phenomenon were largely conducted while the panic was going on, facing researchers with the formidable challenge of sorting out what was distortion and what real. The challenge of figuring out what was "the truth."

The MV/MO cases that began to appear around 1983 all involved a similar cast of characters: an adult (usually only one) who set the scene by reporting that children were being abused; the adult authorities—police and prosecutors—who went after the alleged abusers, often with the zealous righteousness of the earlier "child-savers," and used (and often misused) the child witnesses; the men and women of the press, who seized on the developing story and employed gossip, rumor, and intrigue to sensationalize and commercialize it before any of the cases came to trial (in one early case in Jordan, Minnesota, the zealous prosecutor was hailed by *People* magazine as a "national hero"); and finally, the CAN experts, who appeared in the role of guides—intelligence officers in the battle for the truth. In other words, a number of disparate adults with different agendas constructed their own version of the abuse and their own images of the children. Projecting their own fantasies and fears onto the children, they drew the children into their battles with one another about what constituted "the truth."

It is important to realize, however, that these battles were not over whether abuse occurred inside homes; they were part of a *political* war over whether the adults and institutions who dealt with other people's children were undermining the family and destroying small children or turning them into agents of subversion. The children themselves became the weapons, wielded by almost every adult involved. In the 1990s, each SRA case became a microcosm of what was happening in the American culture war. And as in all wars, truth was the first casualty.

National media attention focused on California late in 1983. Various members of the McMartin family, who owned and staffed a Manhattan Beach preschool, had been accused of child abuse. Responding to the complaint of a single parent named Judy Johnson, the Los Angeles Police Department launched an investigation. But the police did not send investigators to the school; rather they wrote to the other parents notifying them that Ray Buckey, the owner's adult grandson, was under suspicion of abuse and asking them to report any indications they might find that their children had been abused by him. The letter sent by the LAPD explicitly suggested that parents ask their four- and five-year-old children about oral sex, fondling, sodomy, nude photography, and bondage. With this terrifying letter, the police put a match to the bonfire.

A social worker, later revealed by the press to be unlicensed, was hired to interview the few children who told their parents that "Mr. Ray" had done something to them. From the start, the interviews were videotaped (a procedure widely adopted in the 1980s to spare children multiple interviews or the ordeal of testifying in open court). As had happened in investigations elsewhere, the children who were first questioned reported inappropriate touching. Then, as the number of parents bringing in their children grew, the stories became more frightening, the questioning more suggestive, and the interview sessions longer (up to two hours for a preschool child). Children spoke of having been drugged, penetrated with objects; they told about various "games" (each with a particular name) that they had been required to play and described pets at school that had been killed in front of them. Many children offered ominously similar details.

Parents began to bring in older children who had earlier been enrolled at the preschool, and now the first reports of SRA surfaced. With much greater verbal skills, the older children variously described how they had been forced to drink animals' blood at a nearby church, how they had been abused by teachers dressed in black robes and carrying candles, and how bodies had been exhumed at a cemetery and cut into pieces. Soon children attending five other preschools in the surrounding community were being interviewed, and they told stories similar to the ones told by the McMartin students. An interschool satanist conspiracy seemed to be in operation.

Judy Johnson, who turned out to have a psychiatric history, continued to make reports to the police, and these became increasingly bizarre: her son was made to watch the beheading of a baby, teachers at the school had placed a symbolic star on his bottom. Eventually, nearly 400 children were interviewed, some 380 of whom (figures vary from report to report) said they had been abused in some way. In March 1984, seven indictments were handed down by a Los Angeles grand jury, and six months later a trial began—the longest and most costly criminal trial in American history, which ended, seven years and over $15 million dollars later, in the release of the final two defendants, Ray Buckey and his sister, after a deadlocked trial and a retrial. (Five of the defendants were dropped during the course of the case for lack of *any* physical evidence against them.)

The initial driving force in this case was not, as in the Jordan, Minnesota, case, the prosecutor, but rather the lead interviewer. This had serious consequences for the entire field of Child Abuse and Neglect, which became split over whether the interviewer had manipulated the children's responses or discovered the truth about their abuse through her imaginative interview techniques. Every child-protection dimension of this case caused controversy: the interview techniques; the interpretive use made of the interviews; the workshops on SRA that the interviewer began to give (with a plethora of newly self-proclaimed experts in SRA following in her lucrative footsteps); the way the police department treated the issue of physical evidence; the laws that permitted the accused to linger in jail for years without bail before they were eventually acquitted.

The interviewer was Kee MacFarlane, who had lost her job at the National Center for Child Abuse and Neglect when the Center's budget was cut in the first year of Ronald Reagan's presidency. Now a social worker and an interviewer, she was practicing in Los Angeles when she was hired for the McMartin case. She deployed her own technique, using puppets and dolls (of both adults and children) with prominent, abnormally large genitalia to encourage child interviewees to point out on the dolls what they had experienced or witnessed. Her video archive was available for later review, and the McMartin defense ultimately turned on the fact that the majority of the CAN experts who reviewed the tapes found MacFarlane's hyper-sexualized dolls and her interview technique suggestive, even psychologically abusive. The CAN experts for the defense argued that MacFarlane had not only encouraged but shaped the children's fantasies and had encouraged their accommodation to her agenda, to the point of bribing them with approval and praise for giving the "right" answers.

What Kee MacFarlane got her child interviewees to

talk about most was not molestation of their own bodies but things they had supposedly *witnessed* and had words for—black-robed figures, ritual scenarios, blood drinking, dismembered infants, abductions, all alleged to have happened in particular places, notably secret underground tunnels at the preschool. The LAPD could not find these secret places (despite having the preschool's entire yard dug up by an archaeological team financed by the Hollywood actress and self-described psychic Shirley MacLaine). No physical evidence was found to corroborate the children's descriptions.

But MacFarlane was not deterred; she knew why the police had been stymied. Called before a congressional hearing in 1984, she gave the legislators quite a different order of problem to think about from the one Jolly K. of Parents Anonymous had presented in 1973. The physical abuse of one child inside the home by a parent that Jolly K. had described suddenly seemed a manageable matter compared with the multi-victim, multi-abuser epidemic MacFarlane outlined.

As a lone expert with a small staff, MacFarlane explained, she was dealing with an "avalanche" of revelations about group child abuse by nonparent groups, a disaster similar to an earthquake or a fire for which federal emergency relief was needed. She implored the Congress to avoid the trap of "denial syndrome" and to hear her as the voice for "three hundred or four hundred small friends under the age of five" who were victims of "organized operations of child predators, whose operation is designed to prevent detection, and is well insulated against legal intervention." She presented preschools as part of "larger unthinkable networks of crimes against children," vast conspiracies.

Anyone familiar with the history of prejudice or Prejudice Studies can recognize this kind of statement as obsessional prejudice: there is a conspiracy that has infiltrated agencies meant to protect us and polluted the very bowels of our society (tunnels under preschools . . .); the conspiracy will soon take over if not stopped by emergency measures. Anti-Semites, for example, speak this way, demanding the elimination of the infiltrators, with their invidious controlling network, their cover-ups, their "international Jewish conspiracy," through what the Nazis had called "emergency laws."

Congress responded to the crusader by doubling the federal budget for Child Protective Services, a result that the Reagan administration approved since it was understood that this money was going to protect children against a vast, infiltrating conspiracy; no interference with parental rights or family integrity or "family values" would be involved because the crimes were in schools and daycares. The SRA phenomenon—dubbed by MacFarlane a national emergency—effectively deflected attention away from in-house parental abuse and the question of whether the government was responsible for prosecuting abusing parents or aiding at-risk families. The budget of the National Center for Child Abuse and Neglect (NCCAN), from which MacFarlane had been downsized, was never restored, however, thus limiting the research that could be performed by CAN experts while encouraging protective services to hunt down alleged conspiracies of nonfamilial child predators who had satanized children. The first report put out by NCCAN on the subject, *Characteristics and Sources of Allegations of Ritualistic Child Abuse*, did not appear until 1994, after a great deal of damage had already been done not only to the accused but to the thousands of children around the country who were swept up in the panic. And to the truth.

One reason why Congress failed to recognize a conspiracy theory when they heard it was that though her statement was alarmist, MacFarlane presented it in a professional manner, with statistics and lists, in the manner made famous (or infamous) by Senator Joseph McCarthy. (In 1986 her professional qualifications were further legitimated when she and her colleagues published *Sexual Abuse of Young Children,* in which they had not one word to say about SRA or conspiracies to cover it up, as though the matter she had described at the hearings as a national emergency did not exist two years later.) More important, MacFarlane presented her statement to people who had already been made fearful by the images of serial sexual predators and rampant sexual abuse that were in wide circulation before the SRA phenomenon exploded in 1983. The representatives were no more able to understand what was frightening them than the 70 percent of the American public, who, according to a *Redbook* magazine poll taken ten years later, in 1994, still believed the stories about SRA. Many also said that they believed that there had been a conspiracy (of just the sort MacFarlane alleged) among law enforcement and FBI agents to ignore evidence of SRA and keep it from being discovered. (By 2005, similar polls showed that only 10 percent of the population still believed this; the SRA phenomenon had largely receded by then. Fear of terrorizing infiltrators had a new focus in the post-9/11 world, where President George W. Bush was establishing a new Department of Homeland Security and using a strike-back emergency law, the Patriot Act, in his "war on terror.")

The political context for the satanic ritual abuse hysteria was the entry of a growing rank of Christian fundamentalists into the Republican camp as voters and into the American political process as opinion makers bent on reframing the time-honored "wall of separation" between church and state. The president, helped by this large bloc of voters, actively allied with religious institutions, which were increasingly organized on the model of corporations or private enterprises, with television advertising and image making. Reagan's privatization policies also favored these churches, which launched "faith-based initiatives" to replace public services. Soon the doors of the civil services were also opened to Christian appointees who were not confining their evangelicalism to church. Science was widely politicized, particularly in areas involving medical research, reproduction, sex education, environmental protection, and evolution theory, the last largely through the influence of anti-science curriculum reformers who were gaining new power on school boards. An anti-Enlightenment atmosphere was being created in which evangelical ideas about Christianity's great enemy—Satan, aided by fallen angels and secret agents—circulated freely, although Reagan himself continued to locate the satanic "Evil Empire" in the Soviet Union. Personally, he had more of the Nixonian obsessional in him than the narcissistically tinged grandiosity of his fundamentalist constituents. But his embrace of these voters and their agenda led a country that had once feared Bolshevik spies and secret Communist agents to imagine a new enemy: satanic pedophiles, waging war not just against America's children but against God himself. As Jean LaFontaine, an anthropologist who later studied the SRA phenomenon for the British Department of Health, noted in 1994: "Pedophilia is the most potent representation of evil in modern society." (The pedophile next door has since been succeeded to a large extent by the Muslim terrorist next door. But it is important to note that the Muslim terrorist is held to be obsessed with child or adolescent virgins awaiting him as a reward for his martyrdom in the next life—that is, he is a thoroughly politicized pedophile.)

In this Christian conservative atmosphere, feminism came under attack, and one key target of this backlash was the feminists' focus on the problem of child sexual abuse. Their commitment to prosecuting *parental* pedophiles was viewed by many conservatives as a desire to break up families by defaming fathers, particularly middle-class fathers. But these men had the resources to fight in court those who accused them of incest. A national organization, Victims of Child Abuse Laws (VOCAL), was founded to help fathers accused of incest find lawyers, share information, and proselytize for a key VOCAL claim: that accusations of father-child incest were increasing because they were useful in custody disputes. According to this theory, wives were accusing their husbands of molesting their children in order to win custody suits. And they were using the weapons given them by feminists: the debunking of the incest mother stereotype and the new trend in the courts of favoring maternal custody. State-based branches of VOCAL became the chief lobbyists for a new disease, which of course had an abbreviation, FAS: false accusation syndrome.

The idea behind false accusation syndrome had received some attention from scientific researchers exploring the relation between memory and suggestibility, and important investigations of memory development had come out of this research, which were followed up later by neuroscientists. But FAS as conceived by VOCAL was a weapon against feminists, and it was soon joined by another new "disease" on the domestic-violence front: battered man syndrome. A clear response to battered woman syndrome, battered man syndrome was invoked when battered women "battered" back (and then pled self-defense) or attacked men whom they accused of abusing their children. But even more frequently "battered man syndrome" was invoked to describe men who were metaphorically battered by false accusations of incest or pedophilia, or both. The extremist fringe of the Male Consciousness Movement that gathered momentum in the early 1980s embraced battered man syndrome.

From the moment the SRA phenomenon appeared, organizations with conservative political agendas and CAN experts involved in investigations and trials alike produced hardly a nonpolemical word about the provocatively named false accusation syndrome. FAS identified a real problem: false accusations, particularly about satanic ritual abuse, were filling American courtrooms; the promotion of suggestive interview techniques, particularly by prosecutors and a new generation of police experts, was seeping over into contentious custody cases. But the problem of false accusations was not a *syndrome* and it was not a *condition* of child victims. Like battered child syndrome, FAS was misnamed; it was made into a child's problem when it was in fact an adult's problem: convinced that they were helping children, adults projected their images of children as liars onto children. In its assertion that adults speak the truth while children lie to harm adults, FAS was yet another manifestation of childism.

Among those who were most convinced that they were helping children and adult survivors of sexual abuse were hundreds of therapists who invented a therapeutic technique called recovered memory therapy (RMT). Therapists who practiced in this modality, which, like the medical technique reflex anal dilatation (RAD), has now been almost completely discredited, had no interest in the traditional therapeutic goal of avoiding suggestion. This was the goal that had drawn Freud to the creation of psychoanalysis, which he thought would avoid the danger built into hypnosis. But RMT therapists believed in suggestion as a way to recover repressed memories. In fact, they suggested to their adult clients outright that they had been victims of child abuse at the hands of their parents or strangers or multiple abusers. That these clients might not have repressed memories of abuse was rarely considered. With the use of hypnosis, automatic writing, art and drama therapy, self-help books (which proliferated in the mid-1980s), and abuse-survivor groups in which they shared stories and details of childhood abuse, adult clients of these therapists could come to believe that they had recovered detailed memories of being abused—even at age six months, a year, two years. In *The Courage to Heal,* for example, which became a best seller in 1986, readers could find lists of "symptoms" that would help them diagnose themselves as survivors of childhood sexual abuse. (One such symptom, for example, was the fear of running water over one's face when taking a shower.)

At the height of the RMT craze, in the 1980s, clients went to court by the hundreds, where they often accused their own parents, and this made it difficult for those who had formulated false accusation syndrome largely as a response to the abuses in the SRA and MV/MO trials to insist upon its validity without seeming to blame the victim rather than the therapists. The creators of false accusation syndrome could find themselves giving testimony for the defense of people whom they believed to be genuine abusers uncovered by RMT. Rather than defending victims of sexual abuse, that is, they were defending the system that fostered sexual abuse. It took a number of years for legitimate scientific investigators into the workings of human memory to explore the social problems involving the use and abuse of both science and therapy that permeated what came to be called the memory wars and might as well have been called the truth wars. But their study of the theory and technique of RMT, which rightly appalled them, left many scientists extremely distrustful of psychotherapy in general.

Contending experts and organizations flourished in

the feminist camp, too. Roland Summit (of "children never lie" fame) became the key expert for many feminist organizations. At the same time, however, Summit was promulgating SRA propaganda, operating as one of the celebrity experts who helped export the SRA panic to Britain, Canada, Australia, and New Zealand. His rise to prominence as a defender of both victims of domestic abuse and those claiming involvement in satanic ritual abuse confused the issue for feminists, who ended up committed to a researcher who was rigidly opposed to any charge that children involved in multiple-abuser and SRA cases might have been influenced by their interviewers. Many feminist organizations trying to protect the progress that had been made in the study and prevention of child sexual abuse became contributors to the SRA panic because they were unable to see it for what it was—part of the very backlash they were fighting. (It should have been striking to these feminists that the majority of defendants in satanism trials were women: sexism played a role in the SRA trials of the 1980s as it had in the Salem witch trials of the 1690s.)

A fight against a common enemy, particularly one perceived as the epitome of evil, typically brings about alliances between people whose views would otherwise make them opponents. During the 1980s, many feminists allied with conservative Christian groups to advocate for anti-pornography legislation. Such alliances sprang up despite the opposition of fundamentalist Christians to abortion, which was being branded as a new form of child abuse ("unborn child abuse"), this time perpetrated by pregnant women and their doctors. Most Christian groups also opposed the U.N. Convention on the Rights of Women because the Convention backed a woman's right to chose whether to have an abortion. I see this confusion between conflicting feelings and loyalties as the social version of what happens to abused children when they are caught up in situations in which their abusers are loved family members who demand their loyalty and encourage them to speak the truth—as the abusers have dictated it. Confused children have reasons both to love and to hate their abusers.

While the strategy of naming something a "syndrome" in order to pathologize opponents was preoccupying a new generation of self-appointed experts in domestic controversy, the mental health professions, already corrupted by the rise of RMT, were also confronted with a new disease phenomenon: a tremendous surge in cases of multiple personality disorder (MPD). MPD had been known during the 1970s to correlate highly with childhood abuse, particularly sexual abuse. Most MPD patients had long histories of dissociating or splitting off their unwanted, intolerable memories to such an extent that the memories became, as it were, the property of "selves" (called "alters") within the patient's own fragile self, each alter unknown to the others. MPD sufferers project horrible feelings onto "others" inside themselves, rather than onto external others, as prejudiced people do. While prejudice is ubiquitous, MPD was relatively rare, although well established in the popular imagination by novels and films, especially *Sybil,* which appeared concurrently with the "discovery" of child sexual abuse (the book came out in 1973 and the film in 1976).

Many critics of RMT assumed that it was RMT therapists who were creating the sudden outgrowth of MPD; some argued that the MPD pathology itself was entirely an "iatrogenic effect," that is, a creation of suggestion therapy. As an analyst, I do not agree that MPD is always an iatrogenic effect, but I do think it likely that RMT contributed to the explosion of MPD cases in the 1980s and 1990s. In RMT the patient is simply serving the therapist's need to be a healer and thus has no chance to develop a sense of how to discover the truth of her or his own experience. (This phenomenon can be seen at work in the best seller *Michelle Remembers,* written by a Canadian psychiatrist about "a Multiple" to whom he suggested that she had been satanized.) I would argue that the general narcissistic milieu in which a variety of unqualified people marketed themselves as healers and people who knew best how children should be helped was what turned many abused women, who already had fragile senses of identity, into fragmented people with no identities except the ones dictated to them. (Anna, I think, narrowly avoided multiple personality disorder and becoming an extension of her father's "healing" narcissism by learning how to perform in her healthy theater-studies school—but even then, she had to learn difficult lessons about how not to be just a performer.)

Childist narcissism, I think, lay at the center of the mass hysteria of the 1980s: it sanctioned or legitimated people's making reality be what they thought it was. By the 2000s, this *"make* reality the way you *think* it is" idea was the *goal* of American domestic and foreign policy, as Undersecretary of Defense Douglas Feith explicitly announced on several widely reported occasions. It had come to be the goal in the context of national panic over the terrorist attacks of September 11 and America's retaliatory invasion of Iraq in 2003, but preparation for it had begun in the context of the panic over the satanic ritual abuse. This panic brought into daily and family life an endless confusion over what constituted the truth, as some saw in SRA an epidemic of evil, while others (far fewer) saw in it a hysterical and narcissistic media-propelled contagion. But even the critics and skeptics who were in a position to point out the extremely deleterious effect of the panic not just on the nation's children but on the society's capacity to discuss truth and perception did not do so. They lacked the needed concepts.

The panic over satanic ritual abuse in the United States went on for two decades, from the mid-1980s until the mid-2000s, when it subsided rather abruptly, as panics usually do, whether they are individual or social. They are like an acute anxiety attack—absolutely absorbing while in course and then suddenly gone, leaving in their wake bewilderment, fear of confronting the causes of the panic, and bafflement about what just happened. But it is also the case that much of the anxiety that had developed around childhood sexual abuse and SRA was rechanneled into a panic over terrorism following the attacks of September 11. The attackers struck many commentators as a new kind of satanist—cold-blooded religious fanatics like Osama bin Laden, infidels, or, as I suggested before, politicized pedophiles. The mass trauma of September 11 obscured how much damage had been done to the nation's collective ability to recognize hard truths and speak them aloud. And to its ability to care for its children and the future they represent.

I have been unable to find a single study of the effects the child sexual abuse and SRA panic had on the national consciousness, or, for that matter, on any of the specific communities within which the accusations and trials took place, or the thousands of parents and children directly involved in that panic. But traces of its presence—like traces of a hurricane that has passed through a town and then disappeared—can be found without much difficulty in the Child Abuse and Neglect literature. The panic, and the way CAN personnel had contributed to it, made the field more self-reflective and self-questioning. CAN practitioners had been shocked by the spectacle of their colleagues battling one another in court-rooms, disputing with one another in congressional hearings, unable to halt the media hype and commercialization of the sensation, unable to distinguish between real events of abuse and mass hysteria over alleged satanic abuse.

Personnel in social work, child services agencies, and Child Protective Services departments began writing in the early 2000s about what David Hamburg had called "a genera-tion in crisis," and their work acknowledged that their own field, CAN, was a contributor to that crisis. Dissatisfaction with CPS became widespread: the system was obviously over-whelmed by the rising number of child abuse and neglect reports, and the CPS departments were understaffed, with young, ill-trained, underpaid workers, may of whom burned out quickly. Children were falling through the cracks of bu-reaucratic jurisdiction while many others were being harmed or even disappearing while their cases were being investi-gated. Americans read in their newspapers about a Florida child who simply vanished during an investigation and was never heard from again; about a New York City child who was beaten to death by her lawyer father while her family was under investigation; about a New Jersey teenager the size of a six-year-old who was found frantically trying to feed him-self from a garbage dumpster even as social workers were look-ing into his family. The nation's enormous foster care system appeared to many of those who helped create it like a revolv-ing door in which few children found even a safe and loving temporary home much less a good adoptive family. Duncan Lindsay, a professor at the School of Public Policy and Social Research at UCLA, began his 2004 *The Welfare of Children* with the harsh truth that summed up the country's decades of CAN effort: "The country that pioneered strategies to pre-vent child abuse and now spends more money fighting it than do all other industrialized countries has the highest rate of child abuse in the world. In fact, more children are reported for child abuse and neglect in the United States than in all the other industrialized countries combined."

Things were almost different. While leading researchers in CAN were reviewing what had been learned since the Kempe group "discovered" child abuse, the field almost experienced a paradigm shift, a revolution in thinking that could have redefined child abuse and neglect in a way that might have brought CAN into the purview of Prejudice Studies—and introduced the idea of childism. Two efforts to rethink CAN's basic framework—the scheme of distinct types of abuse (physical, sexual, neglect)—signaled this revolutionary moment. First, in the early 1990s a fourth type of abuse, emotional abuse, was officially added to the existing three. Then, in the late 1990s, many in CAN joined forces with a newly emergent field called Trauma Studies or sometimes Traumatology or, more specifically, Psychotraumatology.

Emotional abuse was not "discovered" in the early 1990s, although that is when books about it began to appear. Among social workers, it was well known, and it too had been richly described in Leontine Young's *Wednesday's Children*. Young described types of emotional abuse combined with physical abuse that became staples in the 1990s CAN literature. She noted, for example:

> Abusive language and verbal expressions of hostility were common with more than 80 percent of the severely [physically] abusing families. Some parents state bluntly that they hated their children and wished they were dead. Some threatened to kill them. Some remarked that they had never wanted them and it was a pity they had ever been born. Some parents yelled at children, calling them derogatory names and threatening them. Others said much the same

thing in quiet tones that were perhaps even more frightening. One father shaved his son's head and then called him "criminal." Others referred to their children as "idiots," "crazy," "monsters." Some emphasized to the child and in the child's presence to other people how ugly he was or how stupid or how hopelessly clumsy. *Whatever the specific expression, they all conveyed the idea that the child was hopelessly inferior, an object of ridicule* [italics added].

Young also pointed out that physical abusers often abused pets and forced their children to watch the torture, just as they would force one sibling to watch the torture or exploitation of another. Many children who had lived within an abusive home would report that what they had witnessed was much more horrific to them than what they suffered physically. "The destruction of loved pets was another torture—not physical, but a torture nonetheless—indulged in by this group of parents. A dog or cat would suddenly disappear only to be discovered killed, or the animal would be killed in the child's presence. One father put his son's dog alive into a hot oven, forcing the boy to watch."

Similarly, Young had described what would in the 1990s be called isolation as a consistent feature of physically abusing families:

Children were consistently denied normal activities, prohibited the usual educational and recreational opportunities open to other children in the community at their economic level. School activities, sports, parties, neighborhood games, the clubs so dear to the hearts of most children were forbidden to the children of many of these [physically abusive] families. One young girl was finally, at the urging of her school teacher, permitted by her mother to attend a school dance. She came home glowing from perhaps the most carefree experience of her life. The next school dance she was promptly denied. In some families even neighborhood play and games were forbidden the children, who had to be home at a specific moment. Any delay—even so slight a one as that occasioned by a bit of casual conversation—was dangerous to them. . . . In effect, the children were withdrawn from the contacts and experiences which might have taught them that not all families were like their own. . . . The isolation of the children in these families could only add to *their frequent conviction that they were outsiders in this world, unable to partake of its warmth and vitality, alien and unwanted intruders* [italics added].

You can observe how close Young came to the concept of childism in the two sentences I italicized in these examples. When she reported the ideas—which had become internalized as convictions of the child's—that children were "outsiders . . . alien and unwanted intruders," and "hopelessly inferior," she was noting the basic childist justification for extruding or eliminating children as intruders or infiltrators, as well as the basic childist justification for manipulating children. Further, she was observing the common feature of all forms of childism, which I have noted came to be known in the 1960s by Steele and Pollack's designation, "role reversal": the expectation placed on children to be parental.

But, as we have seen, the researchers in CAN who came after Young had not followed up on her insights, and when the first International Conference on Psychological Abuse was held in 1983, it was largely given over to definitional questions: What is psychological (or emotional) abuse and how does it relate to the three accepted abuse types? The conference was not set up to allow study of multi-act abuse of the sort suffered by 80 percent of children Young had observed, who were both physically and emotionally abused. Nor was it designed to look into the question of whether there is an emotional and ideational prejudice, childism, behind *all* abuse.

After nearly a decade—the initial SRA decade—of conferences and research projects, what the researchers in CAN were prepared to consider was a new, discrete classification: emotional abuse. Five subcategories of psychological or emotional maltreatment were parsed out and identified in a widely praised, standard-setting, frequently updated work by Marla Brassard, Stuart N. Hart, and Robert Germain (*Psychological Maltreatment of Children and Youth*, 1987); they included:

- spurning (belittling, degrading, shaming a child for showing normal emotions, singling out a child for special criticism or punishment or work, publicly humiliating);
- terrorizing (placing at risk or in danger, threatening loss, harm or danger if unrealistic expectations are not met, threatening violence);
- isolating (placing unreasonable limits on freedom, unreasonably restricting social contacts);
- exploiting/corrupting (modeling, permitting or encouraging antisocial behavior or developmentally inappropriate behavior, not permitting developmentally appropriate autonomy, restricting cognitive development);
- denying emotional responsiveness (being detached and uninvolved through incapacity or lack of motivation, interacting only when necessary, failing to express affection, caring, love).

Researchers continued to see child abuse as consisting of acts that were categorizable into types and subtypes, even their new category, emotional abuse. This is the way the field had developed from the first, and categorizing by acts was as natural to CAN researchers as it is for criminal lawyers to categorize types of crimes by the acts criminals engage in rather than by their motives and belief systems, which come into consideration only in sentencing. Even so, the CAN researchers, once they had formulated the category "emotional abuse," did ask, What relation does emotional abuse have to the physical abuse, neglect, and sexual abuse categories? And while they were asking that question, the satanic ritual abuse phenomenon posed a further challenge. The phenomenon called SRA clearly involved all kinds of abuse at once and was, at the same time, more than the sum of those categories. In addition, the mass hysteria surrounding it raised complicated questions about whether SRA abuse had actually happened or was a kind of collective fantasy spun from one person to the next in an emotional abuse contagion. SRA was an abuse-act typology breaker.

When they formulated the category "emotional abuse" and confronted the challenges of SRA, CAN researchers came close to reexamining the three-story edifice of abuse types in which they had worked for nearly thirty years, and to which they were now adding a fourth story. They almost looked at the structure within which all maltreated children had been classified, all treatments designed, all social policies developed, all reporting statistics generated and gathered, with the idea that it might be fundamentally unsound. Perhaps, rather than adding another story, it was time to tear the structure down and build it up anew on the basis of the truths children had to tell about the reality of their experience (if only those truths could be heard and trusted). But this is not what happened. An emotional abuse floor was added to the top of the building with the justification that the fourth floor could contain everything that was not housed on the lower floors. "Emotional abuse" encompassed the negatives: it was maltreatment that was *not* physical abuse, *not* neglect, and *not* sexual abuse but *somehow* involved with them all.

Before the 1990s CAN researchers did know that what they were calling emotional abuse accompanies the other types of abuse—many studies and statistics had made this clear even before they coined the term. Leontine Young had pointed it out in 1964. So it was not difficult for CAN researchers to agree with the position taken by Brassard and Hart: the emotional consequences for the child are the unifying factor in all types of maltreatment. They also concurred in the idea that regardless of whether a child is physically harmed, at the core of maltreatment is lasting damage to the child's sense of self plus all the damage to social, emotional, and cognitive development and functioning that can follow on the damage to the sense of self. Questions remained about the small percentage of cases in which researchers determined that emotional abuse appeared by itself. But even the claim that there were such cases seemed shaky when it was examined more closely because emotional abuse is seldom reported and almost never constitutes the basis for intervening in a family or starting a legal proceeding. There is no obvious "research population." School and daycare staff, coaches, nannies, and other professionals who have ongoing contact outside of homes with an emotionally maltreated child are the ones most likely to discover and possibly to report emotional abuse.

Why this consensus within CAN about the ubiquity of emotional abuse among maltreated children did not prompt a complete restructuring of CAN categories is a crucial question. And it seems to me that the simple answer is that no one proposed an alternative approach based on study of the motivations and beliefs of the abusers as those are known and internalized by the child. No one compared what is known about child abusers and neglecters with what is known about prejudiced people. Researchers continued to consider children and abusers separately, outside of the abuser-abused, adult-child relationships, and they continued to neglect the way abuse is internalized or what children have to say about it and about their abusers' motivations—information that comes out in therapy contexts, not in statistics-gathering operations.

Consider as evidence one of the best of the many CAN handbooks—distillations of hundreds of books and thousands of articles—that started appearing in the 1990s, while the field was undergoing some self-evaluation. *The Spectrum of Child Abuse* (1994) was written by R. Kim Oates, M.D., a professor (now emeritus) of pediatrics and child health at the University of Sydney. The book is a model of comprehensiveness, clarity, and good judgment about controversial topics like SRA. But Dr. Oates admitted frankly in his opening pages that there is a problem in the whole CAN field that should be clearly acknowledged: maltreatment is dealt with as a matter of different types in CAN, but fewer than 5 percent of abused children are the victims of only one type of abuse; the other 95 percent have been abused in multiple ways. Yet even as he made this important observation, Dr. Oates acknowledged the limitations he was allowing the field to set on his book: "However, for ease of discussion the four areas of abuse will be considered separately."

Having accepted these parameters, Dr. Oates could not then go on to say that considering the four types of abuse separately, even "for ease of discussion," would be futile, misleading, and untrue to what children and adult survivors of maltreatment say about their own experience. He could not say that his discussion format meant that part of the child's experience would be taken for the whole, or that the crucial consideration of internalization would be missed.

Recognition of how constraining the CAN categories were—even with the fourth category added—though certainly present in the second reconsideration by CAN researchers of their field in the 1990s, was once again not potent enough to force a restructuring of the field. But the alliance formed with Trauma Studies or Traumatology did bring an umbrella concept into common usage in CAN: "trauma." Trauma could embrace physical abuse, neglect, sexual abuse, and emotional abuse; it was the overarching act.

The first sign that CAN workers were making use of Trauma Studies insights was the increasing incidence in the 1990s of the diagnosis posttraumatic stress disorder (PTSD) for all traumatized children, no matter what kind of act had traumatized them. It was hoped that PTSD, which had been officially added to the 1980 edition of the *Diagnostic and Statistical Manual* (*DSM*-III), could be a unifying diagnosis. Just as it had become possible to say "emotional abuse is part of all abuse" or "emotional consequences follow from all abuse experiences," it might be possible to say that all traumatized children, no matter what their type of trauma, suffer from PTSD. Among those who argued for the PTSD diagnosis as a unifying diagnosis, one of the best known was Judith Hermann, who had written extensive, pioneering articles and monographs about child sexual abuse, particularly father-daughter incest. Her *Trauma and Recovery: The Aftermath of Violence—from Domestic Abuse to Political Terror* appeared in 1992, reissued with a new afterword in 1997.

But even as the diagnosis PTSD was under consideration within the field of CAN, researchers were coming forward to point out that abused children do not always meet the criteria for that diagnosis. David Finkelhor, for example, noted that not all survivors of child sexual abuse qualified as PTSD sufferers. Nonetheless, considering the PTSD diagnosis as a unifying concept did suggest a more holistic approach to therapists treating traumatized children. The child psychiatrist Lenore Terr, for example, author of the popular *Too Scared to Cry* (1990), summarized the Trauma Studies approach to children in a 1991 article. She brought to her overview her wide experience in assessing and treating children who had been traumatized by what she called "one event" traumas—accidents, natural disasters, kidnappings (including group kidnappings), war-related explosions and evacuations— as well as children who had been repeatedly abused and neglected over time, either in their homes or in various childcare settings. Terr employed the CAN categories physical abuse, neglect, sexual abuse, and emotional abuse in her writings, but her more general categorizing scheme was set up on a different basis.

In the article, "Childhood Trauma: An Outline and Overview," Terr acknowledged that because the consequences of traumatization and the symptoms that refer back to it are so diverse, doctors and psychiatrists had often overlooked it, or, in looking at one consequence or symptom very closely, they had sometimes overlooked its context, its cause. "We must organize our thinking about childhood trauma . . . or we run the risk of never seeing the condition at all. Like the young photographer in . . . Antonioni's film, 'Blow-Up,' we may enlarge the diagnostic fine points of trauma into such prominence that we altogether lose the central point— that external forces created the internal changes in the first place. . . . We must not let ourselves forget childhood trauma just because the problem is so vast."

All children who have been traumatized in any of the multitude of ways share four characteristics, Terr proposed. First, they have strongly visualized or otherwise repeatedly perceived memories, though sometimes these are repressed and only inferable from their drawings or games. Second, they repeat their traumatization in their behavior and in the stories they tell and enact. Third, they have trauma-specific fears or phobias. And finally, their traumatization profoundly changes their attitudes about people (who they feel cannot be trusted or counted on for protection), about aspects of life, and about the future ("a landscape filled with crags, pits, and monsters," in Terr's description).

These four common features can be enormously helpful to therapists, as well as to CPS investigators, because they offer a good general guide to what a child who has been traumatized needs to talk about and what a listener needs to be listening for and helping the child talk about. The talking will help the child abreact (re-create and re-experience) the trauma, but it will also help determine the trauma's context, not just what qualifies the child to be put into the classification box of physical abuse, neglect, sexual abuse, or emotional abuse, or even into the general diagnostic category of PTSD.

This revision, so sensitive to the range of posttraumatic symptomatology, has begun to help contemporary therapists and investigators think more holistically. And it has had the further important result that the large role trauma plays in adult illnesses and adult character disorders of all sorts is now being studied. In the field of preventative medicine, for example, a study titled "The Averse Childhood Experiences (ACE)" appeared in 1998. ACE researchers in several U.S. cities showed conclusively that adults who responded to a questionnaire about their childhoods would usually, if they reported being traumatized, report more than one type of the seven traumas listed on the questionnaire. And the more traumas they had experienced, the more prone they were to ill health and destructive behaviors. There is, in fact, a direct correlation between averse childhood experiences and increased health risks for alcoholism, sexually transmitted diseases, physical inactivity and obesity, smoking-related illnesses, heart disease, and other illnesses. The implication for the prevention of these diseases was obvious: reduce the incidence of averse childhood experiences of all kinds, and the general physical and mental health of the nation would improve dramatically.

More and more frequently, within the CAN literature and within the programs—chiefly social work programs—where Child Protective Services workers are trained, the research and practice that stem from the "trauma" orientation are being connected to the insights about intergenerational transmission of trauma developed scientifically by, for example, those like James Gilligan who study violence and cycles of violence.

Important as it was, the view-broadening brought to CAN by Trauma Studies did not contribute much to the understanding of adults' motivations and beliefs (their childism) or children's internalizations. Nor could it show how and why beliefs aversive to children can intensify and, in a situation like the SRA phenomenon, pervade a society and reinforce a culture that is hostile to children. CAN and other child-advocacy specialists were understanding children better, but they were not consulting children more about the abusive adults in their lives. For this reason, a common characteristic of traumatized children that I think should be added to Terr's list did not show up. Children become internally split when they are traumatized: part of them struggles to overcome the trauma, and part of them, internalizing the childism that comes with the trauma, lapses into self-blame and self-traumatizing, which contributes to later ill health and destructive behavior. When maltreated children or adults who were maltreated as children speak in clinical settings, as I know from my own experience, they talk about the battering acts, the neglecting acts, the sexual acts, or, generally, their "trauma," but this is not where their attention rests; it is where it begins. When they reveal the four experiences that Terr outlined, they are also searching for answers to motivational questions: Why did he do that to me? Why was she like that? Why did they let that happen? Was I a bad kid? Don't they love me? Have I turned out just like them? Do you think I am a bad person now? Children understand that the abuser's motivation has shaped their whole experience, of which the acts they endured are a part. They know that they were in an abusive relationship (and some will go farther, identifying their environment as an abusive culture), and they are bearing it inside themselves. Their bodies and minds bear the burden. And they want to discover and tell the whole story.

While I was considering Anna's story and others that I shall discuss in the next chapter, I developed the definition of childism and the ideas about its forms and political-historical contexts that I now work with as a clinician and a theoretician. The three forms of childism (narcissistic self-erasing, obsessional eliminative, and hysterical role-manipulative) could offer an alternative to CAN's restrictive abuse-act typology, an alternative that was not available when CAN went through its period of reevaluation. It has finally become obvious to CAN researchers themselves as well as to Trauma Studies researchers that physical abuse, neglect, sexual abuse, and emotional abuse seldom appear alone. But that admission would have real significance if it led to the further thought that *each of the abuse types* and *any combination of them* can serve any of the three forms of childism, and they need to be analyzed as such, as weapons of childism. "Trauma" serves well as a general category for all individual and societal *acts* that traumatize children, but the trauma concept does not address the question of motives: What makes parents turn against their children?

A person (or a society of persons) who believes that children are inherently bad and burdensome and who wants to eliminate them—or eliminate a particular child—can use *any* type of act as the means to this end. A person who believes that children are wild and sexual and wants to manipulate them into playing a role inappropriate for a child, especially a sexual role, can use any type of act as a means to that end. A sexual act will be used most frequently, but a child can be tamed with a blow or silenced through isolation in the home or through being deprived of an education that might be a path to freedom. A person who believes that children are owned by their parents and that their identities can be shaped and molded at parental will can use any type of act to bring this about. The acts are weapons in a war between the generations. And it is impossible to understand the war through inventories of the weapons or by counting the number of children who have themselves become weapons. Nor is it possible to work for peace and the prevention of further wars.

Anna's case, as I noted, was particularly illuminating because she had three main abusers and each was childist in a different way; her father, perverse and narcissistic, was out to erase her identity; her stepbrother, an immature, dependent pedophile, wanted her as a child mistress, a sexual toy, like his pornography magazines; her stepmother, depressed but actively and jealously sadistic, was primarily a neglecter, but her general goal was to get rid of, eliminate, her little competitor for attention. Anna grew up in a household that was "like a cult," and the most difficult of her experiences to remember were the ones that involved all the kinds of childism at once. The abuses called SRA also involve all three kinds of childism. Their total—or totalitarian—abusiveness is what makes SRA maximally frightening and terrorizing and thus less likely to be understood or evaluated properly either as acts in reality or as imagined acts.

But I have also worked with patients whose experience was shaped primarily by one form of childism (practiced by one or more adults), and with these patients the dynamics of that one form can be distinguished more clearly. I would like to illustrate each of the three forms of childism now by presenting three children who each experienced one form—although each form was, as always, manifested through more than one type of act. All three young people were born between 1975 and 1985 and were children of Baby Boomers, so their stories will also show the shift toward narcissistic parenting that I have been arguing was widely practiced by the Baby Boom generation. Some grew up in poverty, some in affluence. Some would have qualified for a Child Protective Services intervention, some not.

These children, whom I saw as adults, also taught me something further about childism that I could not see in Anna's case because her family hell was so complicated, full of all three forms of the prejudice. Although it seems to me that there is no such thing as a type of family that correlates to a type of abuse—no physically abusing family type, no sexually abusing type, no single neglecting type—there are family types that are childist in one of the three childism forms. There are families that are predominantly role-manipulating, like many racist families, as studies in prejudice have shown. There are families that specialize in identity-erasing, like sexist families, in which studies have shown both female and male children are erased, though in different ways. There are families that are predominantly eliminative: the children are prejudged to be undermining and burdensome (sometimes as co-conspirators). I believe that CAN needs to turn away not only from its act-oriented typology, but also from its (so far futile) search for the family types practicing a single abuse act. If researchers began to study families where role manipulation dominates, where identity erasure dominates, and where elimination dominates, and where these three forms of childism mix, they would be more able to deal with the whole of the child's trauma—and the adults'.

I would also like to offer these case vignettes (disguised to protect confidentiality) as examples of what a clinician could see and hear and experience when working with a theory of childism. This theory is not intended to replace existing clinical theory; it is rather an extension of it, and one that brings into existing clinical theory Prejudice Studies and its explorations of hysterical, obsessional, and narcissistic prejudices.

CHAPTER SIX

Forms of Childism
in Families

MOST PATIENTS WHO HAVE BEEN VICTIMS OF CHILDISM reveal the form or forms of the prejudice they have suffered at the beginning of treatment. If the patient has suffered more than one form, as Anna did, he or she can describe only a composite in the opening sessions, and a good deal of psychotherapeutic work is needed to reveal the full complexity of the prejudice. In Prejudice Studies, the comparable phenomenon might be, for example, the experience of an African American female who was unwanted because she was homosexual. She knows that she is a victim of racism, sexism, and homophobia all at once, but she is not sure which one made the most difference to her childhood experience or how the prejudices intermingled in her experiences then or now.

In a household where all the forms of childism are present, the dominant form is usually narcissistic childism, with obsessional eliminative childism playing a secondary role. Hysterical role-manipulative childism can take many forms when other childisms are at work in a household—adults move from one kind of role assignment to another and often change their children's role assignments as the children grow older. But those who suffered a single form of childism can reveal a great deal in their first few therapeutic sessions. In this chapter I shall focus on the opening sessions with patients who each experienced only one (or predominantly one) of those forms.

Unwanted Children

I remember vividly how Mary, a young woman of thirty—bright, artistic, well-educated, from a middle-class professional family, bohemian in her dress but tentative, unsure of herself—tried during our first meeting to give me what understanding she had of why her mother "didn't really seem to like me much," why she accused her daughter of being "mean and ungrateful." When I asked, "What makes you think she didn't like you much?" her answer took me by surprise: "She said that I was born very quickly, in a really short delivery time, and to her this meant I wanted to get away from her—that I didn't like her. How could I not like her? I was just a newborn baby!"

Mary's mother had projectively pronounced judgment on her child because she felt that the child had pronounced judgment on her: "She is hateful." Her childism took the form of obsessional elimination: thinking that children hate their parents, that they are ungrateful, neglectful. Mary had seen this prejudice at work, but she could not believe her own insight. If she had believed it, she would have had to believe that her mother was crazy—attributing rejection to a newborn! So Mary preferred to think that her mother was right and she had been born mean and ungrateful, like all children, and had made her mother unhappy from the start. Later in the session, however, she let me know, tentatively, that she thought that her mother might be "a part-time psychotic."

It took a long investigation of why Mary's mother

didn't like her to get to the specific experiences making up the mother's "part-time psychosis," experiences that for the most part stemmed from an abusive maternal grandmother. But Mary had quickly let me know—as do all children who are unwanted—that she herself was a burden, bad, toxic, and that I should be careful or she would burden me. She was depressed, and she would make me depressed (and, indeed, her depression was almost contagious). But she was also, she told me, dedicated in her social work career to rescuing others who are being neglected or abused—even though she considered herself a self-involved, selfish, even mean person. This is a characteristic split in children who have been the victims of an elimination desire and justification, and you can hear it right away.

Karen, a young woman in her twenties, needed only fifteen minutes of our first meeting to give me her version of the "I am burdensome" warning. But the first words out of her mouth when she came through the door foreshadowed it: "I forgot to bring my wallet, so I can't pay you—do you want me to go away?"

"Of course not," I told her, indicating where she should sit. I went slowly to my chair, being careful to convey deliberation, predictability, because I already felt her to be depressed; then I used both my hands to make a sign that, to me, means blessings, welcome. "We can talk about money later. Make yourself comfortable." Karen smiled at this, probably wondering whether I had any idea—or ever would have any idea—that she was incapable of feeling comfortable.

She was skittish and apprehensive, her pale face covered in a fine layer of sweat. Neatly dressed in the skin-tight, all-black uniform of the East Village, with a stripe of bare belly showing a silver navel ring, she sported a bright dyed-white streak through her reddish hair. Tense and upright, she sat forward in the chair but stared at the floor. "I've never done any therapy, and I don't know where to begin. All day I've been thinking like crazy of things to tell you, but it's all so . . . like, jumbled. It's not, like, in a story."

After I encouraged her to give me some of the jumble, starting with whatever was on top of the pile, she smiled nervously and took the plunge. "I know I need help because I am just haunted. Haunted. I mean, like, I can't get away from thinking about my past, and I'm afraid all the time. Things go before my eyes. I think I am depressed, but I have never had any medications for it. Sometimes I think about killing myself."

"What haunts you? Specific memories?"

"All kinds of memories. My whole past. It's, like, overwhelming." She paused for a long time, and then said: " I can tell you, like, . . . maybe . . . some specific things. My mother and her second husband—he's not my father—had a relationship that was all about sex and drugs. Pot. They smoked a lot, a lot of dope. And they were always in debt. Dirt poor. When I was eight or nine, this stepfather dude began hitting my mother. One day I was terrified, and I went after him with a baseball bat. But he took it away from me and tried to hit me. The police came. It was beyond embarrassing. There were other escalations like that, with the police coming, and you know, doing nothing, just going away again. Why didn't they . . . well, I guess there was nothing they could do. And once my stepfather screamed at me, 'Get out! You have ruined my life!' I was, like, always having to protect my mother, and my mother was always coming home drunk and vomiting. I hate talking about this stuff, it's so disgusting. Gross. It's like I make everything dirty."

"Who have you talked to about it? Anyone then? Anyone now?"

"I have a boyfriend now, kind of a boyfriend, and I have told him a little. But I don't want people to know about it, and I don't want people to know I am still so involved in it, depressed by it. And I don't want to burden them either."

There it was: "I am burdened, and I am dirty and a burden to others." Her warning meant both "Watch out, I will hurt you" and "When you know me, you will be disgusted and reject me or go away yourself." I decided to ask for a bit of background, to give her a chance to talk about something that might be a little easier. But nothing was easy.

"Yes, I finished high school, a year early. This was in a kind of rural region, a working-class town. I had a rough time because I was attracted to women, and when I was seen with some girl by the local toughs, there was ridicule and fighting. I went to the nearest city for community college, making money by nannying. But I couldn't concentrate in school, and I got depressed and OD'd on some pain medication that's prescribed for scoliosis. I have scoliosis—do you know what that is? The roommates I had left, they couldn't deal—and why should they have?"

While I was pondering this information about a suicide attempt and her scoliosis (curvature of the spine) and wondering whether she had suffered from malnutrition or anorexia, Karen looked at me intently, scanning my face for any sign that I was appalled by her. She described her troubles with relationships. "I was kind of neglected as a kid, and it means that I want love so badly that I get kind of obsessed. I start to get in too deep with people too soon. Like, I scare them."

"What happens when they get scared?"

"I, like, try to calm down, slow down. So I smoke pot.

When I'm chilled out, I like to paint. My grandmother is an artist, and she taught me about painting, sewing, pottery making. Those were the only happy times, when my mother couldn't take care of us and we were sent to my grandparents for a while—never long enough. I did tell my grandmother some of what went on at home. I told her about the pot smoking, and she said she had always feared my mother would turn out bad. She realized she made a mistake by making my mother marry my father. My mother was pregnant with me when she was eighteen. They were Catholic. So my mother had no education, no nothing, and this lame dude for a husband, who was just poor and a bar fighter. I never knew him, but that's what my mother said, that my father was a son of a bitch. And he left her and had three kids by some other woman, so he didn't do anything for her or for me. I just got his name, which I do like—it's kind of French."

"So there were these pockets of happiness at your grandmother's, but the rest was violent and disgusting?"

"Yes. When I think about it, I feel suicidal. I have suicidal thoughts almost every night, at bedtime. I try to resist taking a bunch of allergy medication in order to sleep."

"What are your thoughts?"

"Oh, I imagine jumping off bridges . . . the Williamsburg Bridge . . . or I see myself taking enough pills to finish me off. But I don't do it because then I imagine my sister's face and my brother's face, how scared they would be . . . I'm all they have . . . They live with my mother . . . I should be there to help them, but I . . . I can't . . . I had to get away, as far as possible . . . There, I really would have died . . ." She fell silent.

"Tell me a little about them."

"My sister is two years younger than me, and my brother is nine years younger. I'm twenty-two. She's severely overweight, and she felt so bad that she dropped out of the community college, so she's home now, and she's smoking pot with our mother. She thinks I am overcritical of our mother, and she is all about bonding with her now, smoking with her. It's bad. And my brother started smoking pot at age eleven. And he got in trouble at school for taking stuff there and trading it for CDs. It's bad."

She paused, then described the form her rescue operation in the family has taken. "I always bought their clothes and things, when there was any money. I wanted them to look attractive. And I tried to keep some food in the house, more than just sodas and cereal, you know, I mean healthy things. I can't even look at a cereal box now, it makes me feel how I was hungry and how . . . It's awful . . . My mom's third husband is a construction worker, and he doesn't make that much—certainly doesn't bring much home after all the alcohol and drugs. Five years ago my mother got it together to earn a paralegal degree, and so the money situation got a bit better. But then she lost her job and now she's just home, smoking. How could she keep a job, she's such a mess?"

We talked a little about Karen's own job, which she likes very much. She is the manager of a small veterinary clinic, where the vet gives her a great deal of responsibility and lets her help with the animals. "It's every kind of cat and dog you can imagine and every kind of owner . . . two zoos! And we get strays, too. People leave animals on our doorstep in boxes. It's awful what people will do to animals, abusing them, you know, throwing them away . . . But I also see my vet do really wonderful things for animals. I think he's a basically good person. But he has a terrible temper, really bad, and I am afraid of him, too, which is a shame, because he can be a good person when he's not so fucking enraged. Why do men have to be like that?"

"Do you have a picture of the kind of person you want to be? Do you have a dream for yourself?" I always ask this question at some point in a first meeting with late adolescents or young adults because their conscious ideals or dreams reveal what it is they are protecting themselves against as well as what they have not found yet. I also think it is important to accept young peoples' wishes as a goal in the treatment, to sign on in the first session for whatever pull they feel in themselves for their own future, whatever hope they have. With an adolescent who has felt eliminated, this is a concrete way to show that you, as the therapist, are not going to be neglectful or exclude them from your presence or from the future.

"I would like to go to school and learn photography, and then I could teach it in, like, a high school. Or maybe I could become a massage therapist and work in spas, or maybe have a private practice. I love children, too." Her dream is also the dream for the therapy; she was giving me my assignment: help me not to be haunted so that I can do these helpful things, which I actually need to have done for me. Each path, I assumed, would be a path away from some act of abuse that she had experienced as eliminative.

After a long pause Karen told me more about what the future might contain, if I could help her stop being depressed and haunted, and if I could be consistently helpful and not become enraged with her. "I had terrible anxiety about coming here today, and talking about me to a stranger. Explaining all this stuff. But I had to make a productive step. Yesterday I went with my boyfriend to his parents' house. We took the train. And I almost collapsed because of envy. That's a terrible thing to admit. I envied him his parents, and their house. They are sort of nice people. Sort of mean, too. Nasty. But at least they try in their way to love him—you can tell. And they want him to have everything he has, all his accomplishments, even though he's not as successful as his older brother. He's an artist." She began to cry, and looked at my Kleenex box for a moment before she allowed herself to take one and dab her eyes with it.

"Is it a romantic relationship?"

"It's a little bit . . . domestic . . . It's been going on for four months, which is longer than anything has ever lasted in my life. He's sort of a good person." She paused. "Being attracted to males is not easy for me. Men scare me. But I tell myself to just take it as it goes, to be attracted by the person's personality. If they are interesting, good . . . I miss being with women . . . But also my grandmother really harshed on me about being a lesbian . . . That Catholic stuff again . . . But with my boyfriend, I get kind of paranoid. That he will be angry with me. You know, guys hit on me all the time. I play the lesbian card with them, you know, I say, 'I'm into women, sorry.' But I get afraid he will leave me, or that he only wants the sex . . . But he phones me all the time, he does try to care. And he's taking me on a vacation this summer, a trip. That will be a first for me, a vacation trip."

"Sometimes you feel happy?"

"I have, like, two sides. There's a happy one that is very attractive to other people. People do like me. But then I do something to let them down, push them away, so they won't be hurt by me in the future. I think this has something to do with the way my mother treated me. I don't know. The other side of me is this miserable person who says, 'Oh, you have no friends, you have no prospects, you won't be able to go to school, you won't make anything of yourself.' My grandmother once said to me, 'You'll be bad, just like your mother!' It's my family's story. My mother has a sister who is a crackhead, and she has a seventeen-year-old-daughter, my cousin, who's somebody I really like. But my cousin is doing crack now, too. She and her mother are bonded. My cousin is going to be destroyed."

"You're very afraid of becoming like your mother?"

"Part of me is already like my mother. That's what I'm so afraid of, that I am already dead. And committing suicide would be, like, you know, just an announcement to the world."

For Karen, the key question about her mother was whether her mother had intended to neglect her and eliminate her from the family because she was her son-of-a-bitch father's daughter and because she would not "bond" as the two younger stepsiblings did. Karen did not know whether to accept her grandmother's judgment that her mother had turned out badly, as the good, helpful, artistic grandmother obviously harbored a "bad child" prejudice herself, which had been very destructive to Karen's mother and to Karen. Generally, Karen spent her life trying to determine which people were good and which bad and why. And to determine whether she herself was good or bad. This was one of the deepest legacies of the abuse and neglect she had suffered: she could not trust her own sense about people's intentions, or trust herself. Maybe she was already dead.

Children Who Play a Part

Children who have been targeted for exclusion from their families or from life generally present themselves as highly anxious and needy, protecting themselves with obsessional defenses against the obsessions they felt being turned against them. Usually they appear to be functionally and emotionally competent, but behind that mask they are intensely self-denigrating or actively suicidal, and their erotic lives tend to be sadomasochistic. Very different are children who have been forced to play a role (or many roles, one after another) that is not appropriate for a child or that no child can play without terrible distortion. These children are actors, and their performance leaves them full of anxious questions about who they really are, or whether they are, really, anybody at all. They are histrionic, but they desperately long not to be in the play they feel has entrapped them. If they must take part in a play, they want it to be one of their own scripting. They are like David Copperfield, who wondered whether he could be the hero of his own story.

Children who play a role or roles come from a family regime that is hysterical or histrionic, in which boundary violations and invasions of privacy are the norm. The atmosphere is highly eroticized or sexualized (sometimes also explosively aggressive), and crises, attention-seeking scenes, and depressive reactions sweep through the ranks like a contagion (a mass hysteria on a small scale). Because the parents seem to be immature and unable to control themselves, a child can easily be pushed into the role of a parent. That is, the role-reversal demand made by the parents is that the child do the parenting in a specific way: that the child does *not* seek attention but gives "parental" attention. In psychoanalysis, much study has been given to the little lover or darling possession or concubine or sexual plaything of the father or mother or an older sibling. A girl becomes a little mistress-wife as "Daddy's girl," and some form of incestuous sexuality may develop. A boy becomes a little boyfriend-husband and provides his mother with the support and attention that his father denies her. Mother-son incestuous relationships are less frequent than father-daughter incest, but they are not uncommon; sometimes, the intergenerational relations are homosexual. The child in this kind of adult role is caught up in a triangular rivalry with the excluded spouse, who may—or may not—actively collude in the role playing.

Since Freud, Oedipal rivalries have continued to be the most commonly observed type of role manipulation. But a child can also be asked to play a specific role, like a character part in a play: the young hero or heroine, the young villain, the redemptive good child, the outlaw or renegade child, the replacement child (for a lost sibling or a parent's deceased sibling), the fantasy idealized or angelic (asexual) child. Or the child could be asked to play the role of family provider, as Dickens was when he was sent out to work at age twelve. A child may be asked to compensate for the disabilities or illness of another child or to become "mother's little helper" to a frail sibling. The family may need a child to be a talisman, protecting everyone from some kind of danger felt to be surrounding the family or from enemies within the extended family. A child may be required as a sacrifice or a martyr (obsessive eliminating parents and narcissistic erasing parents can also sacrifice or martyr their children).

Older children and adolescents may be pushed into the role of family banker, bailing out the others whenever there is a financial crisis, or family psychiatrist, performing the same function for emotional crises. One of my patients, who had become the family problem-solver, in her professional life solved problems on a huge scale for educational institutions, providing schoolchildren with the care and concern she had always lacked herself. She taught me that the basic experience of children who are pushed into becoming financial providers, psychiatrists, or problem-solvers is that the perverse family regime demands that they give this help but at the same time rejects the helper in some way. They shoot the messenger. For instance, a family banker's business solutions will be ignored, and the financial crisis will continue; a family psychiatrist's recommendations will not be followed and the family dysfunctionality will grow worse; a problem-solver's solutions will be sabotaged or turned into new problems. A hysterical family regime needs boundary violations and crises, and its underlying dynamics—its open secrets—must not be openly revealed or owned up to or deprived of their capacity to trigger further crises.

Because children who have been forced to play roles usually come from families where the sexual roles are blurred and often untraditional—the men are often wounded and passive, the women are often assertive and anxiously angry—they have complicated self-identifications, and in their fantasies they often see themselves in a male aspect and a female aspect. In an analysis I conducted with a male hysteric (who had many obsessional features), the bisexual fantasy self made its appearance in the first dream, in which he was both a clever, powerful thief stealing Seiko watches from other men—a symbol for him of sexual prowess—and a girlish flirt behaving seductively with men.

This was the fantasy of a man I will call John, who had described himself in the first session as lost and confused. He was floundering in his graduate program, unsure of himself, ambivalent about continuing his studies, tense all the time with his male professors, critical of his peers, often unable to concentrate, and constantly infatuated with unavailable women. Burdened with a tremendous amount of anxiety, much obsessional thinking, and debilitating self-consciousness, he told me that he could hardly do anything without internal commentary, self-censorship, self-doubt, and self-questioning about whether he had chosen the right word or done the best job possible.

John's description of himself sounded so textbook Freudian that I questioned him about it and learned that he had, in fact, been raised in what might be called a Freudianly hysterical household, with a Freudian script. His father, an artist, whom John presented as both a brilliant superman and a caricature of the egotistical academic eccentric, had read Freud religiously, and constantly quoted him. The mother, also an academic, respected Freud, too, but she felt him to be her enemy in the complicated battles she fought with her husband. John had been assigned the role in his family of being the child onto whom both parents projected their anger at each other in the form of judgments about his development. They did not want to eliminate him, although neither had wanted children; they needed him to be there as the witness, stage after developmental stage, of their painful story. The childist prejudice behind this was the belief that children are blank slates on which their parents must paint, scripting them, keeping them busy on their parents' behalf.

John was able to tell me in the opening sessions of his analysis that his parents' marriage was under a curse from the start and should never have resulted in his birth or those of his even less wanted two younger sisters. The father had left his first marriage precipitously, for which his first wife and their children hated him; John's mother then married the father because she had been accused of being the "other woman," an allegation she denied but that had nonetheless led her own puritanical Christian family to shun her. "Marry only for love!" was the warning John's mother issued to him many times, implying that she had never loved his father but only sought escape from her dilemma. To John it was obvious that he had always been in the parental crossfire, coming between them yet often being their point of contact as well: their reason for being together. They did not want him, but where would they be without him? That he had ended up as a person who "goes up and down like a yo-yo" and was in a permanent state of ambivalence nonetheless struck him as inexplicable.

The ambivalence John felt toward his parents was palpable. He despised his father as a tyrant, a critic; this was the man who sent him to the dictionary every time he misused a word so that he would get it right the next time. John's father also "smacked [him] around." But as soon as John expressed any criticism, he would feel compelled to retract it, saying that he had overstated the case: for his father had many virtues and talents. John also desperately longed for his father's love and admiration, and he sought it from older male mentors, teachers, employers, and authors, to whom he could never be good enough. In the transference, I was Freud before John ever got to my consulting room. But I was also criticism waiting to happen; at any moment, I would cut him down, smack him, beat him to a pulp.

At the same time he admired his mother, especially her elegant artistry, and longed for her love with all the poignancy of a toddler who cannot persuade his mommy to behave warmly toward him or seem to be happy with him. He recognized that her scolding, self-enclosed, insensitive, exploitation of his love was done for her own consolation. In his dreams, she was "the phallic woman"—once she was an Indian maiden who threw a spear straight through his heart. But he felt that he must retract these criticisms by behaving protectively, as he did to me in the transference.

The parents screamed at each other and carried on huge struggles throughout John's childhood. His mother threatened to pack up and leave, marking John with a deep fear that all women would desert him, including his woman analyst. Although women can now sometimes (and sometimes could then) behave as the nurturing and talented mommies he craved, the parents remained unreliable. Nonetheless, in every current crisis of his own he would telephone them immediately, and he had complicated the family dynamic even more over the years by relating to his siblings as extensions of the parents, one female and one female-male.

Both parents hit John, but the main maltreatment he suffered throughout his childhood was emotional abuse, particularly terrorization or threats of abandonment or punishment. His mother, who often threatened to leave, was also given to grabbing the kitchen knives and brandishing them in the face of anyone who provoked her—often John. I learned this when he came to his third session greatly upset because the night before, when he had been cooking in the kitchen with a girlfriend (one of many girlfriends who needed his rescue and could not give him the rescue he needed), he suddenly had the fantasy that he might plunge the knife he was using into her back. He was terrified by this fantasy.

The fantasies John wanted to enjoy did not feature him as a knife-wielder. He wanted to have conventional male sexual power—the ability to charm and dominate women, controlling their time, as it were, with his Seiko watch. But he also had a conscious fantasy (not just a dream image) of himself as a charming girl, which he had sometimes played out in waking life: for example, he had once as a high school student induced some of his buddies to dress up as cheerleaders, with balloons for bosoms, and make a group play for the attention of the football team. This behavior was harmless in and of itself. But he got into trouble when he recreated his family roles in his workplaces, his graduate program, and his love life. His internalization of his parents' childism became his script. He tried to charm and dominate women, but he could only chose women who, like his mother, were bitterly unhappy and had been rejected by their own families. He tried to attract the attention of powerful men, but he could only choose men who were offended by his overtures and thought he was affected, fake, or homosexual.

Children Who Serve Their Parents' Egos

Narcissistic family regimes come in many varieties. There are tyrannies dominated by one narcissistic parent, who treats the other parent—as well as one or more of the children—as nonexistent, a nobody. Sometimes two narcissistic parents vie for power, battling each other on an ongoing basis or tacitly agreeing either to take turns being the tyrant or to divide up the family realm and each rule one part. Children quickly learn the power setup, and they also learn that resistance to self-erasure is a dreadfully difficult matter, as the self that might resist is exactly the self that is being erased. Cordelia made a valiant effort to act with self-possession in the face of a parent who was furiously dictating all the terms of ownership and power, but King Lear could not fathom her silence before his "Obey me!"—and their tragedy was set in train.

Unhealthy narcissism appears in more than one form. The key common characteristic is self-absorption so strong that the narcissist is unable to relate to others or, especially, to empathize with others. Most analysts would agree that there are two basic manifestations or states of unhealthy narcissism and that most narcissists exhibit each in turn. Grandiose narcissism characterizes self-promoters, presenting themselves to the world as a powerful, commanding figure. In depleted narcissism the commander rules by making people pity them as victims and want to help them regain power. The grandiose narcissist makes direct attacks on other people's selves; the depleted narcissist is passive aggressive, like Anna's father.

Both unhealthy types suffer from some kind of "narcissistic wound" or a cluster of wounds that are central to their preoccupation, and which they use to justify their self-righteousness. They are forever licking their wounds (which often are, in fact, dreadful) and seeking compensation for the damage they feel has been done them unfairly, either by particular persons or by circumstances. In their family regimes, their spouses and children—often one child in particular—are drawn into the compensation business. Usually, the family members are required to enhance the narcissist's standing in the world; they are the "trophy spouses" who arouse envy of the narcissist in others or the "trophy children" who bring home praise and glory—as long as they are not too successful and appear better or more accomplished than the narcissist, results that would arouse jealousy and blame. Sometimes, at the other extreme, the narcissist requires a child to fail, feeling enhanced by being so much better than the child or by grandiosely assuming the burden of the child's failure—paying for the child's psychiatric hospitalization, for example, or paying for the child's therapy (as my patient Anna's father paid me).

Since the appearance of George Cukor's 1944 film *Gaslight*, narcissists who make other people ill or who convince others that they are well and the others are ill are described in psychiatric circles as "gaslighting" their victims. A much more histrionic and extreme, even psychotic, version of the gaslighter is the parent with Munchausen by Proxy syndrome. This parent makes a child ill (sometimes by poisoning it) and then drags the child from doctor to doctor seeking attention for the child and demanding appreciation of his or her own suffering and conscientiousness as a parent. If the parent is careful enough to see different doctors, thus avoiding arousing suspicion, the child can be permanently damaged, even killed, by the inappropriate medical treatments solicited, including the prescription of unnecessary, potentially harmful drugs (including psychotropics) and even surgery. Less extreme versions of this narcissism manifest in parents who lobby for better grades or different assignments or enrollment in special classes for their children, presented either as geniuses or troubled. The child acquires a reputation for being "difficult" when the difficulty was created by the parent.

Often in a narcissistic regime one child has the job of having emotions that the narcissist cannot have or does not want to show because they would not reflect well on him or her. Narcissists who are full of anger, for example, might have difficulty presenting themselves publicly as a morally justified commander-in-chief. They may therefore require the child to have that anger and be their hatchet-man or violent accomplice. On a grand scale, dictators use secret intelligence services and even armies—often with youth corps or child soldiers—to carry out the actions they wish to present as in the service of national glory or world-historical progress.

A child can be required to house a narcissist's self-doubt so that the narcissist can go forward without hesitation. When a physical abuser is beating his child, he may be projecting onto the child in the most literal manner all his unacceptable feelings and then destroying them, crushing them and the child who carries them. A sexual abuser may put all of his fear that he is sexually inadequate into a child and then prove his manhood by being powerful in relation to the child, commanding loyalty and silence. (This was the dynamic between Anna and her perverse, depleted narcissist father, who felt himself to be a victim and who needed her— and other young women—to build himself up.)

Children who are maltreated by narcissists know that they are not supposed to have any identity or feelings of their own; they have been taken over, like an occupied or colonized country, by the feelings that their abuser (or abusers) project into them. In narcissistic childism, children are blank pieces of paper on which an adult's story is written. But they do not play a part in the story, as victims of hysterical childism do; their job is to carry the story on or bear it into the world or support it in some way. In my experience, children who have been narcissistically inscribed are among the most knowing and analytical of survivors, but they are often powerless to help themselves get over their own injury or get away from their abuser or build relationships with anyone outside the narcissistic family regime. Their split is that they have insight but no desire, no motivation—these are what has been erased. And they recognize this. They even realize that their own preoccupation with their dilemma makes them appear to be, like their abuser, narcissistic.

One of my patients, a European-born, thirty-year-old graduate student, described at the beginning of our work her amazement the day she started to read a pretty little "Our Baby" book that her mother had kept about her. Ava read about all the usual proud developmental milestones—the first tooth, the first independent steps, the first words—and then came to a halt before a note made next to twenty-two months: "I beat her for the first time today."

Reflecting on this discovery, she went on: "Did you see the film *Good Will Hunting*? Do you remember the part where the boy shows pictures? And the therapist-teacher, the Robin Williams character, says to the boy, very intensely, over and over, 'It was not your fault. It was not your fault.' I watch the movie a lot, and I'm always waiting for that part—so those words can be spoken to me. I once had a teacher who knew something of my story who said those words to me: 'It was not your fault.' I get a release of a knot in my stomach whenever I hear them, or remember them. But even so, I do not really believe that it was not my fault."

Ava has the problem characteristic of children who have grown up with a parent who wanted to erase their self: she cannot believe that the self that was attacked did not deserve the attack. Such children do not believe that they are bad or evil, as children who have been the target of an eliminationist effort usually do; they simply think that they did not (or were not able to) help the attacker—they did not serve well, and thus were, by definition, rebellious. The childist prejudice they experienced and then turned against themselves is the belief that children are inadequate to their job, they always fail the tests set for them. In my work with Ava, her expectation of failing came out in a specific way: she always assumed that I would have trouble understanding her English, which was almost perfect.

The narcissistically attacked child understands the attacker's narcissistic wound, and often sympathizes with his or her pain. My patient went on: "My mother was diagnosed with polio nine years before I was born. But nine years was not enough time for her to reconcile herself to being a cripple. She has never reconciled herself; she is still furiously angry and bitter. She behaves recklessly, doing things a person reconciled to her condition would never try to do, if only not to hurt other people. She drives her specially outfitted car when she is drunk, she goes to bars and tries to dance even though she falls over and crashes into others. When she is drunk and in a great fury, she uses her canes to beat me. I think she resents that I am beautiful, that I can dance, that I am not a cripple." This insight came from Ava's conviction that it was not her fault, but that conviction was not strong enough to prevent her from believing that it was, that she was beaten and erased because she could not alleviate her mother's unhappiness over her condition.

"And your father?"

"He dealt with her by having affairs and being completely interested in himself. Eventually, they divorced and he moved away."

"People used to say to me, 'Oh, you poor girl, you live with two big children.' Everyone knew that my parents had never grown up, that they were not adults. They were so . . . adolescent. My father used to talk to me like he was an adolescent when I was an adolescent. It was about all his girlfriends. And then he makes me swear not to tell my mother. So when she finds out about one of the girlfriends, or two, she also finds out that I knew, and she beats me. She did not beat him."

She paused, thinking about why she was beaten. "My mother used to pretend she was dead, and scare me until I would start frantically crying . . . when I was, like, two, three years old. I don't remember this, but my aunt told me. My aunt used to tell Mama, 'Don't do this, it's terrible for the baby,' and Mama used to say, 'I know, but I just cannot help it, it is so much fun to see her worry about me like this.' You see, I have been programmed from the start. A few days ago my mother was giving me a speech on the telephone: 'I am disabled, old, alone, and out of work. You should assume responsibility, you should take care of me, buy me a plane.' Literally, can you believe this, 'buy me a plane.'"

Ava had always looked for teachers and adults like her aunt to whom she could tell her story, which she understood very well. She had not sought therapy before because she did not have the sense, so clear in patients who have been targeted for exclusion or manipulated, that her experience had left her inhibited. Unlike such children, she did not feel stuck in a conflict between a desire to live normally, love intimately, or work well and an injury—a self-eliminating impulse in herself or an anxious discouragement addressed by a fantasy of running away. Ava simply felt that she had been "programmed from the start," and this meant that she had been totally erased by her mother's injury. She was fatalistic.

Once when I asked her how her doctoral dissertation was coming along, she replied matter-of-factly that it was going well: she was working very hard on it, but she had no motivation. This was her way: she went about her life with great verve, wit, and intelligence but inside she felt hollow, with no reason for being or doing anything. "I have read what Jean-Paul Sartre said in *La nausée* about *ennui,* and I recognized myself. But it is not quite boredom with me, it is more like absence of desire. I only know how to try to minister to others' desires."

Stopping to reflect on what she had just said, Ava offered a further refinement: "I think people experience me as being very concerned about myself, very self-centered. But that is not so. My mother is selfish. My father is selfish. But what I am is very concerned about the fact that I have no self to be centered about. There is a void in me. I cover this up with a lot of activity—mostly to minister to others. Although I cannot succeed in this, really."

I thought about this conversation on the first day that a young woman whom I will call Cherie came to see me, referred by her father's psychoanalyst, a man who was, the father had told me while he and his wife were setting up her initial appointment, "the greatest psychoanalyst in the world, a genius, who saved my life." When she arrived, Cherie began her session by reaching into her capacious leather tote bag and drawing out a worn paperback. I could not see the title as she tapped the cover with a long, lacquered fingernail. Didactically, she told me: "I know what my problem is, because I have read all about it in this book. But I have read the book over and over and I still don't know what to do to help myself. It has sections on helping yourself, exercises you can do. But nothing there works for me." She handed the book over to me: *Children of the Self-Absorbed: A Grown-Up's Guide to Getting over Narcissistic Parents,* by Nina W. Brown, Ed.D., LPC.

Currently, Cherie explained, she was doing nothing, as she did not know what to do. Almost a year earlier she had dropped out of her university. "It was a big drama. My father said I should by all means drop out and take the time I needed to find myself—after all, he had taken years of chaos to find himself and look what a huge success he is. My mother said that I should absolutely stay in school because we all have to learn to tough it out when things get hard—that's what she does when she feels challenged and look how successful she is. Neither of them, of course, could ask what was going on in me. But I shouldn't really blame them for that; I couldn't have told them if they had asked."

"What can you say now about what was going on in you?" I asked her.

"I'll tell you what happened—but, like I said, I do not know what to do with this story any more than I know what to do with that book. I had been taking a music-composition class. My parents thought that this was a waste of time: Why go to a liberal arts school to compose? Music is for music students, in music schools, or for summertime recreation. Anyway, I thought the teacher was great, and he took a big interest in my work. So there was this class during which he listened to my piece when I played it on the piano, then came over and stared for a long time at my score, telling me how great it was. Then he reached out with a heavy red pencil and rewrote several parts of it. 'There, now it's perfect,' he said. I was stunned. I couldn't say anything. But walking out of the class when it was over, I had . . . I don't know what to call it, like a . . . breakdown? All the people and objects around me rushed away from me and I was standing on the steps of the music building like on the moon. Totally alone, completely without anything to hold onto or get oriented by. Totally alone. I wondered if I had died."

"After that, later, what did you feel about the teacher's act? Did you want to say something, or do something?"

"No. Nothing. I was stunned, and then I went blank. And I stayed blank. It was impossible to go back to the class. It was impossible to stay at school."

I suppressed my desire to offer Cherie some possibilities: she might have felt invaded, humiliated; she might even have felt dangerously grateful for the teacher's patronizing "help." But I know that offering to fill in a blank, particularly for someone who has been blanked out, is the route to becoming the next abuser.

"Ever since I dropped out of school and went home, everyone in my family has been all worried about me because I am not doing anything, and I can't seem to get a focus, get going. I am now the problem child. My siblings, who used to look up to me, now worry about me. My father and mother see this psychiatrist for couples counseling, and he is now seeing all of us as a family, and sometimes he asks to see just me, because I am the problem. He thinks I should take medication."

"Why did your parents arrange for you to come see me?"

"Because my father's psychoanalyst said that I needed to have my own therapist and not be seeing someone who sees everybody in my family."

"What do you think about that?"

"I wish my father would really listen, instead of just going on and on about how his psychoanalyst is a genius. I do want to have my own therapist—but I know my parents will expect me to continue to see their couples therapist as well. They swear by him. They do whatever he says, he's their guru.

In my family, there is this idea that we are all so close and so loving, and we all have to help each other. We are the perfect family. But you know, there is not a square inch in my family where I can even draw a breath. I bet you that they will call you up later today and ask you what your impression of me is and what kind of a problem you think I have."

The parents insisted—as she expected they would—that Cherie keep going to their own psychiatrist, who was, as Cherie suspected, violating many rules of good practice and confidentiality by telling the family members one another's stories. She was diagnosed—and everyone accepted this—as suffering from bipolar II disorder, and prescribed a powerful new medication for it. In addition to being the object of her parents' narcissistic childism, that is, she now suffered from the narcissism of the mental health profession—a childism of the sort that is now fueling an epidemic of diagnoses of bipolar II disorder and the prescription of medications to children who are, in effect, being doped into acquiescence. This childism sees children who do not do what narcissistic adults say they should do as a mental health problem.

Ava was required to support her grandiose mother's delusion that she was not a cripple (and to keep her from depletion); Cherie was supposed to be just like her parents, who offered two irreconcilable grandiose conceptions of perfection, and thus two different understandings of why she was a problem child. But neither of these young women had been required to fail, and neither had learned the lesson that corporal punishment, called discipline, could be justified, and the regime it supports also justified, to ensure that a child fail. This was the lesson learned by a third erased patient, Alice. In Alice's world, "spare the rod and spoil the child" meant "spare the rod and the child will succeed—

which would be terrible." Alice is an excellent illustration of why corporal punishment is so often a manifestation of narcissistic childism, and of how narcissistic childists justify corporal punishment.

In our first session, while she was explaining to me that her father beat her and made her feel that she could never do anything right, Alice made a slip that she described, when she realized she had made it, as "my true feelings speaking, insofar as I have any." What she had said about her home life was, "I was always on the edge of terror . . . I mean error. Well, no, I guess I do mean terror."

Alice had an iconic image of herself at age eight, sitting on the back steps alone, staring at the dreary backyards of the dreary working-class row houses that defined her neighborhood. Weeping and wondering what she had done to earn the beating her father had just given her, she suddenly thought, "I have to leave": "I was in such pain, my whole backside stinging and aching. But I couldn't think where to go." When she was ten, in the fourth grade, a ray of hope came into her world: the Mother Superior, the school principal, called her parents in for a conference and told them that Alice was a very gifted girl and should go to college. Her father did not understand exactly what he was being told, but he came away from the conversation with one thought: women with college degrees can be teachers and live at home, bringing their salary home. "Later, when I told him I wanted to be an artist, he couldn't fathom it."

Her father's lack of understanding was not simply the ignorance of a man who had never been to college or the provinciality of an immigrant's son whose own father had been a stable boy in Russia. He reacted as he did because he was a man who had had a dream: he had enlisted in the air force and been trained as a pilot, based in Europe, where he had begun imagining himself returning home and getting into commercial aviation. "But nothing worked out for him, and my mother didn't want him to have a job that would take him away from home," Alice explained. "He became a mechanic, he repaired planes."

Her mother, Alice explained, had held her father back because she had suffered a childhood abandonment trauma, and she did not want to be without her husband's steady presence. At fourteen, Alice's mother had contracted a disease that kept her out of school for a year. Then her parents decided she should not go back to school; she needed to work and bring in money for the family. Alice detailed her mother's story with the awareness that is typical of narcissistically abused children, who never miss a crumb of information that will explain the wounds their parents have sustained: "There were too many mouths to feed for her to live at home, so they hired her out as a nanny, even though she was below the legal employment age. She felt she had been thrown away, and she was always nervous about being arrested. She only came back to our town when she had a fiancé."

While Alice was telling me her family's story, she was clear about its meaning for her. These defeated people, who had settled for a life without ambition or spirit and were filled with anxiety, did not want their daughter to outgrow them; they wanted her to stay close to home and take care of them. Her despairing conclusion, "I have to leave," was exactly their nightmare, and they had produced it in her. Her father had literally beaten her down whenever she showed any sign of independence, any behavior that wasn't at his command. Both parents criticized her constantly.

This much about Alice I learned in two sessions. Several months into our work, when Alice decided to try to go on a diet, we began to see clearly how the family anxiety style and the family depletion had seeped into her character and left her (in her phrase) "without willpower." She suffered through a tense Sunday of successfully fighting off the temptation to overeat, and was very proud of her self-control, which she imagined reporting to me on Monday, as I had begun to represent "the new me" to her. She went to bed and slept well, but woke up "in a terrible anxiety state, cold, clammy, agitated, in a panic." It was all she could do to get herself ready for work and out the door. "On the street, I felt very disconnected from everything, like I was enclosed in my skin, letting nothing touch me, but all the same I felt at every step like something was going to . . . I don't know, it was like I was going to get clobbered."

"Did you expect the blow to come from behind?" I asked her.

"From behind, yes. But also on the top of my head, like I would be a nail, hammered." She was startled when I pointed out that she had revisited the old trauma of being beaten on her backside and also the old emotional maltreatment of being nailed—criticized and rammed down into the hard wood of her home, her town. Trapped.

Three Children of 1980s Narcissistic Divorces

"I have this image of myself as a little guy, full of excitement and running around making contact with people. When we went out as a family, like to restaurants, I visited with everybody—went from table to table, cheery, charming. That was my M.O.: 'He's such a charming little kid.' But after my parents divorced when I was nine, I closed down. I began to have trouble in school, and the school psychologist said I had attention deficit disorder. I was worried all the time."

A tall, handsome, articulate, intelligent young man,

Jason is one of three patients I saw whose parents divorced in the 1980s. The parents were all members of the Baby Boom generation that I have been discussing as densely populated with narcissistic characters, and we can see in their family dynamics the narcissistic form of childism and how their children internalized it.

When I asked Jason what he had worried about, he responded, "I've thought a lot about that, because I think I have exactly the same worries today—and that's why I am paralyzed. I was worried that my mother was not trustworthy and that she would leave me. She had, it turned out, been seeing another guy, as I had suspected, and she brought him to our place not very long after my father got another apartment. I hated the guy; he was a total jerk. Mother did figure out he was a jerk, but it took her months. Later, years later, my mother married a guy who is not a jerk, who is actually quite a good guy and good for her. But by that time, I was already sure she was lost to me, and lost in herself. After their divorce, my father was all hurt and wrapped up in himself even more than usual. He started his career of one girlfriend after another, finding each one unsatisfactory and telling us kids that we should never leave him and be always, you know, on call. Everything revolved around him, like the planets around the sun. He started running my life, telling me what to do and how to do it to the point where I could not make an independent decision. I played into it: I thought I had to do what he said, and consult him about everything, or he would reject me, or maybe he would die. He gave me advice that I know has bent me totally out of shape, like 'Don't ever trust a woman.' But you know, I cannot trust women! It's pathetic. I am not myself. I chose my profession because it is sort of like his profession and he told me it was right for me. Really pathetic. That happy, free kid really got lost. I am so anxious that my dentist says what I have done to my teeth grinding them should be on exhibit at the dental school."

"Lost" was this young man's theme in our first session: both of his parents were lost in themselves, and he had lost himself trying to hang onto them, please them, not dissolve in worry that everything was lost. By the second session, it was clear that Jason had accepted an assignment, a role, in his broken family: he was the family psychiatrist, charging himself with helping them be less self-absorbed and more attentive to others (his motive was that they would then be more attentive to him). He was attracted to women who had abusive, narcissistic fathers (often sexually abusive, alcoholic fathers), and he played the role for the women of the good, rescuing father until it turned out that they were not reliable and had other men or other commitments that kept them from committing to him. One of the girlfriends was a born-again Christian who told him how sorry she was that he, like all Jews, would end up in Hell. Jason's mother liked this girl very much.

Jason understood himself quite well after all his practice as psychiatrist to his family, but, like other "children of the self-absorbed," he could do nothing to help himself. He procrastinated at work and could not assert himself; he put off any conversation with a woman that might be difficult or demand honesty and self-revelation. Slowly, he was able to tell me intimate details about his life and his fantasies. "It's so childish that I have this fantasy that when my father dies I will buy a motorcycle and just tool around town, free, and some gorgeous girl will say 'you are like way cool, I like you just the way you are.'"

When I was listening to a young woman I'll call Jenna, Jason's story came into my mind. It reminded me of the subtitles at the bottom of a film—the same plot in another language. Like Jason's parents, Jenna's had divorced when she was nine, after her mother ran off with another man. The departure scene was staged in Jenna's memory like a tableau: her mother had left three envelopes on the kitchen table, each containing a letter—one for her father, one for her, and one for her younger brother. The letters announced that the mother had left. No details from her letter remained in Jenna's memory, but there was a second scene in the tableau: her father, his forehead resting on the kitchen table, weeping into his letter, and herself trying desperately to comfort him.

After her mother left, Jenna's parents launched an eight-year custody battle, which defined her adolescence. She and her brother lived with their father until the mother returned to their town several years later with her second husband; then the children went back and forth between the houses while the custody battle continued (following a course that could not have been farther from the recommendations of *In the Best Interests of the Child*). The court allowed the battle to drag on, and it engulfed her entire adolescence. Finally, Jenna was able to do what she had dreamed of doing for years: leave. She was accepted at an excellent college—as she was a superior student—that was as far from her home as she could find. But she barely made her escape: she attempted suicide after her high school graduation and was still in a precarious emotional state when she left home. To leave her father, who needed her to comfort him, was to be a deserter like her mother; to leave her mother, who needed her to affirm that she was a good mother, was to be like her father, who was accusing his ex-wife in court of being a bad mother.

During her first high school year, Jenna had learned a horrible lesson about what can happen if you do not hand yourself over to other people's needs and wishes: one night at a party a boy in her class tried to get her to have sex with him, and she refused. The next day, he killed himself, and she held herself responsible. For the rest of her high school career she was in a kind of self-imposed solitary confinement: she never told anyone what had happened at the party or revealed that she was bearing the guilt of it. Her own suicide attempt was a form of self-punishment, although it was also an expression of anger.

Both parents remained frozen in their break-up positions. The mother thought she was communicating with her children and being a good mother because she had written them a letter when she left. She always righteously did what she thought was right, and needed to be praised for it; but what she did was consistently wrong for her children and out of touch with any reality other than her own. When she wanted affirmation of her decisions, she would consult her tarot cards or a psychic. The father continued to need solacing, and he made Jenna into his chief comforter and his parent, as she had been in the mother's desertion tableau. She felt that his attention to her was, as she told me, "sexually inappropriate." Like many Baby Boomers at this time, he believed that nakedness in front of children and adolescents or sharing beds and intimacies with them short of molestation was healthy. But she was even more affected by his need to be, generally, the center of solicitude and the recipient of praise that affirmed his correctness in everything. "He is so confusing because he does things like write me a letter from his vacation place in which he goes on and on showing his sensitivity and concern for the local people—his Christian concern, as he was, after all, the son of Christian missionaries—but it is so obvious that he is really only concerned about the impression he is making. He seems to be so emotional, but I am coming to understand that he . . . it's like he is only emotional about his own emotions; he's all turned in on himself and inaccessible to other people." Then, with that wisdom of the erased, she added: "His Christian missionary mother left him alone a lot when he was little so she could be good to the needy children, and he must have felt abandoned again when my mother left him, and so I absolutely cannot leave."

Elaine's parents broke up when she was eight, after years of screaming fights that were much more frightening for her than the fights Jason or Jenna had witnessed. They did not fear physical violence. But Elaine always had to be afraid of violence, and she had needed an immediate, daily refuge from her fear; she could not fantasize about leaving home in the future. Her answer was lying in the kitchen freezer, where her parents kept a stash of marijuana. She discovered that if she stole a small, undetectable amount, she could go out to the back garden, roll up—she prided herself on being better at rolling joints than they were—and be "far, far away" by the time they got home from work. Soon she was addicted, and she continued to be a daily multi-joint user until she came into therapy with me at the age of thirty-five. Her parents never noticed that anything was going on.

Elaine told me about her pot addiction during our first session, but she focused on a particular episode in her childhood that she thought "says it all." When her mother left her father, she took her two children and moved to another state. "Looking back on it, I think she was, like, psychotic or something. She's not like that now, her better qualities are available now, but then she was furious, just furious. And she turned that anger on us all the time. Us, our father's children. That's when she began to hit me—and once she threw me across the room. I remember on that day when she threw me that I said to myself: you can't fight this, you have to take it. It was like a decision I made. After that, pot became a means to pretend I was not there and also a means to just take what came. There was a certain pleasure in the passivity."

There was hardly anything in Elaine's life that she could not form an addiction to that would help her not be present, enable her to sink into a self-erasing masochism. She collected—and drank—fine wines. She learned foreign languages. She spent hours on the Internet. She wrote and read blogs. She took up fasting and Vegan dieting and exotic cooking—all food rituals. Her relationships, too, had an addictive quality: after she was able to leave home for boarding school, she always had boyfriends, sometimes one after another, sometimes simultaneous. She was "addicted" for years to a female friend at school who treated her sadistically. After college, the boyfriends tended to be older men, each with some kind of grandiosity about him—this one a great scientist, that one a great musician, the other a great wine connoisseur—to whom she could submit herself and be the perfect appreciator, knowledgeable in the man's area of achievement and hungry for his appreciation of her talents as well as her submissiveness. In these relationships, which could become overtly sadomasochistic, she showed no judgment and often no ability to protect herself. She once went on a date with a larger-than-life stranger who drugged her drink and then raped her.

Elaine's father was grandiose, too. He thought of himself as quite a superior being, but he was unable, after he and her mother were divorced, to do anything with his life. He gave up working and lived on money that came from "investments" (unspecified), while the women he lived with worked to earn money. Marijuana remained the organizing principle of his life, although he presented himself as an artist. "He is kind of a hippie," his daughter explained, "one of those hippies who can complain about all the bourgeois materialists, but who is a major bourgeois materialist." Elaine always hoped that he would in some way come forward to help her or protect her, but he remained remote and complained when she asked him for money, as she often did—punishing him with her own bourgeois materialism. She had a great deal of trouble making any money herself—to the consternation of both parents—because she wanted to upset them, but even more because she had such a strong fantasy that a provider-knight would ride up one day and rescue her so she would never need to earn a living. With her great self-knowledge, she had said to me the first day we met, "I have to, like, get real." And slowly she did.

All three of these children of 1980s divorces were astute social critics. Each could have written a version of Christopher Lasch's *Culture of Narcissism*, which came out in 1979, about the same time they were being ignored in divorce proceedings and custody battles, despite the fact that courts were recognizing that they needed to be more attentive to children's needs. Their wishes were not heard—although Jenna, because her parents' battle was so protracted, was consulted toward the end, when she was a teenager and the damage had already been done. All three grew up to be politically liberal, supportive of social-liberation movements, and eager to vote for candidates who backed social welfare and help for families. Their parents, by contrast, avoided social and political issues and focused only on themselves. The dynamics in their families and the dynamics in America during the 1970s and 1980s when they passed their childhoods were one and the same for these young people.

The national discussion about divorce—about whether the 50-percent divorce rate is the root of the nation's social malaise and can be fixed by an infusion of "family values"— seemed to all three hopelessly abstract and polemical. They are simply afraid of divorce, afraid that they cannot have relationships that will last because they are too much like their parents; they are, they fear, the self-absorbed children of the self-absorbed. Fortunately, they are not. But the childism they have internalized makes it hard for them to liberate themselves from their fears.

CHAPTER SEVEN

Education and the End of Childism

THROUGHOUT THIS BOOK, I HAVE BEEN ARGUING THAT there will always be people and societies that act against the principle Aristotle articulated in his *Nicomachean Ethics:* "The parent gives the child the greatest gifts, its existence, but also cherishment and education; . . . and because the child receives, it owes the parent honor and helpfulness." Adults who do relate to children according to the natural principle, provisioning them for healthy growth and development, protecting them, preparing them for participation in family and community life, will never be able completely to change those who behave immaturely and harmfully toward children. But they can influence the conditions that provoke, permit, and even encourage such behavior. And they can work to identify and address the prejudice, childism, that legitimates it.

To have an influence that is more than episodic—more, that is, than the identification of an abused child and the incarceration of the abuser—child advocates of all sorts must address not only the conditions of the specific abuse but the conscious or unconscious justifications for it: the childism of the abusers and the childism within American society. They need to legislate and enforce a national comprehensive child development program, drawing on the best Child Development science, that articulates a minimum standard of attention to each child's needs. And they must articulate a platform of children's rights like the U.N. Declaration and Convention on the Rights of the Child, and find ways to monitor and enforce them. But crucial to achieving these political aims is the education of both adults and children about prejudice against children and how it is manifested within individuals, within families, and within American culture. Only then can parenting practices, state programs, and children's-rights advocacy be directed toward supporting children's growth and development on principles free of childism. Ongoing studies of childism—the forms it takes, the ways in which it manifests, and the conditions that cause it to intensify—should guide ongoing efforts to reform child-rearing practices, societal programs, and children's-rights advocacy.

The histories of people of color, women, and homosexuals in overcoming the prejudices against them have demonstrated that social change is achieved in stages. It requires, first, understanding gained by the victims of the ideas and institutions that say to them, "You are naturally inferior." For people of color and women, for example, that understanding began to be expressed in the eighteenth century first as arguments for a minimal protection (emancipation, the franchise) from harms that even racists and sexists might regard as evil. The concepts of racism and (later) sexism guided the next stage, in which blacks and women demanded not just minimal protection but full and equal civil and political rights.

And these stages of action required, and still require, the third stage: education about the causes and meanings of these prejudices, and the harms they have done and continue to do. And with education comes the creation of programs to repair the damage, secure the progress that has been made, and continue to work to eradicate the prejudice.

For children, all these stages have to be led by adults— the very group from which prejudice against children comes. And progress has been made in achieving the first two stages. In the nineteenth and early twentieth centuries adults led and largely won in some places the fight to abolish child labor, while in the nineteenth century, reformers like Charles Dickens wrote not only about child labor but also about philanthropists who called themselves child-savers but were really childists (though he did not use that word), like Mrs. Pardiggle in *Bleak House*, whose idea of helping the poor was to read them the Bible and lecture them about being good, and who forced her own neglected children to give up their weekly allowance to charity.

These first two liberation stages are still in progress for children, while the third stage, education, lies ahead. Because children are not actors, as adults are, there is more overlap among the stages, and the movement to combat childism has been intertwined with the movements struggling against racism, sexism, and other prejudices. Signs that we are reaching the education stage are relatively new, but some can be seen in the youth movements of the 1960s and cultural changes that have occurred since then. Today organizations are springing up in which young people are preparing to be actors. And these organizations are especially effective when the adults and children involved in them can reach beyond local and national contexts.

I am thinking, for just one example, of an organization that originated in the United States in the 1990s but is now worldwide, PeaceJam and The Global Call to Action. The mission of the PeaceJam Foundation is "to create young leaders committed to positive change in themselves, their communities and the world through the inspiration of Nobel Peace Laureates who pass on the spirit, skills, and wisdom they embody." A 2010 documentary film, *PeaceJam*, presents the work of this organization and the life stories of the Nobel peace laureates who mentor in it.

Throughout *Childism*, I have been implying that each dimension of adult-supported freedom for children needs a more fully developed analysis of the prejudice against children. We need to hear *their* experience of the ideas and institutions that oppress them; we need to offer clearer guidance to the civil and political rights movement that has grown up to support their growth and development; and we need to develop better efforts to educate—or re-educate—and build programs to repair damage, secure progress, and move forward. "Childism" is the unifying concept needed to organize and guide the movement.

How can we use analysis of childism and attention to children's experience to reform our understanding of child maltreatment and, specifically, to reform the approach to combating child abuse and neglect that has been taken in America? Can the postwar field of Child Development help guide legislation and policy, beyond the goal of child Protection to encompass Provision and Participation—the 3 Ps articulated in the U.N. Convention on the Rights of the Child? And finally, can we coordinate Americans' concern for the healthy growth and development of their children with the international attention to children represented in the Convention and the initiatives that have emerged from it? These are the questions that can guide us in the third stage of combating childism: education.

The historical "case study" I have been presenting of the development of childism in America since the 1970s might be taken to imply that we could and should simply go back to the crucial juncture forty years ago, when the field of Child Abuse and Neglect was founded, and take the road not taken. Certainly, if the missed opportunities of that time could be seized and adapted to today's world, such action would go a long way toward helping our children and repairing the damage to our national life. But more needs to be done than that.

We need to recognize that the narrow focus on protecting children, to the exclusion of providing for their developmental needs and making them participants in decisions affecting them, produced a huge distortion in this country. We were relying on concepts that ultimately could not even serve the purpose of protection, because children whose development is not being supported cannot be protected. The proposed Comprehensive Child Development Act would have linked protection to the ongoing, broadly conceived War on Poverty, but it was vetoed before it had a chance to work. The time has come for a new Comprehensive Child Development Act.

As the histories of other prejudices—racism and sexism, particularly—have shown, at historical moments when a prejudice is on the rise (as childism is in the United States today), it can be combated only by acknowledging the prejudice and being willing to reconsider the behaviors and beliefs that legitimate it. Prejudices allow those who classify another group of people prejudicially to feel that it is all right to do so. Ultimately, a therapy or an education directed at the prejudice's self-legitimating process is required. That kind of therapy and education appeared in postwar Western Europe as a way to deal with the devastating collective trauma of the war and the Holocaust, and one of the areas of concern was children.

Americans offered financial help in this effort, but they did not have the same understanding of what had happened as those who had lived through it. There was no defining moment after World War II and before "the discovery of child abuse" in which, faced with the horrific effects of racism and anti-Semitism, Americans recognized, as Europeans did, that those prejudices targeted children, too. During the eight months of the London Blitz, for example, more than five thousand British and refugee children were killed in Britain by German bombs, along with more than thirty-five thousand adult men and women. Children in the cities had to be evacuated to the countryside and housed there, receiving support and treatment from teams of pediatricians and social workers. It is not a coincidence that after the Blitz the British wartime government announced a plan for a National Health Service or that after the war a huge majority of British citizens voted for the social-democratic Labor government that instituted it. (There is still broad public support for the NHS in Britain, despite political efforts in the 1980s and again currently to scale it back and partially privatize it.)

Most Americans did not experience the devastating effects that the war had on children, for their children remained relatively safe throughout it. Although they joined in the goal of trying to prevent future wars by supporting the United Nations and the 1948 Universal Declaration of Human Rights, most postwar Americans did not focus specifically on the plight of children, for the huge population of orphans and stateless children was largely located elsewhere. Americans with a larger vision, like Eleanor Roosevelt, who developed and taught in an educational program for schoolchildren about the Universal Declaration, which she had helped to draft, were few.

When Americans finally realized, in the 1960s, that children in America were at risk, they focused on a subgroup of children who were not safe: the physically abused or battered children. That narrow focus still prevailed in 1983, the year the satanic ritual abuse panic began, when Ronald Reagan simultaneously cut the budget for the National Center for Child Abuse and Neglect research programs, increased budgets for prosecutors and police to root out SRA, and established April as Child Abuse Prevention Month.

Nothing in the way Child Abuse Prevention Month was legislated, set up, advertised, or reconsidered each year by the Office of Child Abuse and Neglect in the Department of Health and Human Services connected it to policy concerning the broader range of children's needs or to the Children's Rights Movement. Protection from physical abuse was the sole focus, and the rhetoric of the month focused more on the need to "strengthen families" as the years went by.

Child Abuse Prevention Month could stand as an example of what needs to be done educationally to reform our approach to helping children—all children. It needs to include protection, provision, and participation in its goals, and it needs to be connected to an understanding of childism. In fact, as it now stands Child Abuse Prevention Month does not resemble other, better-known group observances and educational efforts in the United States: Negro History Week (inaugurated in 1926), since 1976 Black History Month (February); and Women's History Week (1981), since 1987 Women's History Month (March). In these months, the achievements of women and people of color are celebrated in schools and through public education programs and cultural events.

Histories of how women and people of color have been discriminated against—the histories of sexism and racism—are the contexts for celebrating their achievements. These two months are part of a national educational effort to overcome the prejudices of racism and sexism. By contrast, Child Abuse Prevention Month acknowledges only one group of children, the abused, and these abused children are not seen as members of a larger, politically oppressed group, children. Child abuse is not described as connected to the general condition of children or as a manifestation of prejudice against children, comparable to sexism and racism. Similarly, this month does not celebrate anything: the achievements of children in themselves or as participators in community life are ignored. The narrow focus obscures the bigger picture that child abuse stems from a prejudice and that until our society supports child development comprehensively, we will never be able to combat that prejudice. Rather than a Child Abuse Prevention Month, we need a Children's History Month, complete with recommended reading lists, in which the whole story could be given.

Indeed, in considering any program or policy concerning children, we have to train ourselves to ask: Is it guided by the whole story?

It was not because they lacked a science of child development that Americans concerned with the plight of children narrowed their approach to children's needs to a focus on protecting abused children. A broad developmental framework in which to understand children's basic needs and rights exists. The challenge is to help parents and policy makers understand this framework better.

Although Americans had no visceral understanding of the plight of children after the war, they did begin to appreciate the tradition of developmental thinking about children that became part of the British National Health Service owing to the efforts of psychoanalysts, both émigrés like Anna Freud and Britishers like D.W. Winnicott, to include Freudian child therapy. But in the United States that thinking was largely disseminated by one book published in 1946: Dr. Benjamin Spock's *The Common Sense Book of Baby and Child Care.* It is no exaggeration to say that this best seller, read by millions and now in its eighth edition, prepared the way for the controversies over "family values" that eventually grew into the American cultural wars after the 1970s. Dr. Spock was a major figure in those wars, but his role was blurred for many because of his politics: he opposed the Vietnam War, was arrested during an antiwar demonstration, and figured in a controversial court case. The debate that grew up around him and his book was between those who subscribed to his developmental views of parenting and those who felt that he had corrupted an entire generation—the Baby Boomers, the student rebels. His baleful influence, so these critics contended, could be seen on the streets of America in 1968. He had prepared the way for a conflict of the generations.

But what Dr. Spock had actually done was inspire a generation of Child Developmentalists to educate parents about the growing reliability of their science. This has been a slow process, and it had not advanced enough to affect the outcome of the 1971 Comprehensive Child Development Act. Later, when the "No Child Left Behind" legislation was being developed in the first years of George W. Bush's administration, the science had grown even more reliable and the educational efforts more effective, but they were not strong enough to defeat the legislation, which, by focusing on test scores and other statistical indicators, ignored the developmental needs of the child. Today this science will help adults say "This is childism" to combat policies that are not in the best interests of children.

Along with *The Common Sense Book of Baby and Child Care*, a good book to put on the national recommended reading list if we had a Children's History Month would be *The Irreducible Needs of Children: What Every Child Must Have to Grow, Learn, and Flourish* (2000). The co-authors are the neonatologist and child psychiatrist T. Berry Brazelton of Harvard University, America's best-known writer on child-rearing since Dr. Spock, and Stanley I. Greenspan, a psychoanalytic clinician and founding president of the Zero to Three Foundation, which (as its mission statement says) "informs, trains, and supports professionals, policymakers and parents in their efforts to improve the lives of infants and toddlers." For thirty years these clinicians had worked in the psychoanalytic developmentalist tradition that had been so influential in shaping the Comprehensive Child Development Act as well as the U.N. Convention on the Rights of the Child.

In *The Irreducible Needs of Children*, Brazelton and Greenspan tried to be as comprehensive as possible in their definition of "every child." Formulating seven needs of "every child" that should be met by family and community, they ranged like anthropologists across childrearing practices worldwide, considering the diverse circumstances under which children live. Although many of their specific recommendations were aimed at American middle-class families, their framework draws on their own wide-ranging experience as researchers and clinicians as well as on a huge store of data from reports by others. Their goal was to formulate, taking cultural differences and national histories into account, the range of practices and attitudes that have been good for children by meeting their developmental needs. With that reference they considered how to prevent the whole range of practices that are not good for children (including child abuse as a part of the whole).

The book offers a framework of seven "irreducible needs." The first is loving, attentive interaction between the child and its caretakers, which Anna Freud's *In the Best Interests of the Child* had described as "unbroken continuity of affectionate and stimulating relationships with at least one adult." The second need is for physical protection, safety, and regulation. Protection from child abuse and neglect is a specific need under this broad rubric. Regulation includes protection against all kinds of things that can constitute "chaos" in a child's environment, ranging from too much television viewing to too many environmental toxins and too much exposure to domestic violence or war (or street war). Like "trauma," "chaos" is a helpful general term that has the advantage of implying both quantities and qualities: it points to degrees on a continuum from too little to too much stimulation, while it questions which stimulations are appropriate and which not. Chaos is not a type of act.

In their chapter on the third need, "Experiences Tailored to Individual Differences," the authors make a case for avoiding standardized or over-ritualized childrearing or education. They make a strong, politically important objection to the standardized testing and standardized education that have been the norm in American schools through the twentieth century, supported recently by the No Child Left Behind educational policy. "Simply doing more of what has not been working will not prove helpful, nor can you teach a child simply by testing him."

Raising the crucial question "Is testing in the best interests of children?" the authors note that testing is about failing and being tracked according to failure. Children are shamed by such an approach, not encouraged. As violence-prevention theorists have also stressed, shaming harms children; it produces anger and resentment. Standardized testing does not aim at what the authors call mastery, which would point a child in the direction of improvement and indicate what *individualized* help the child might need to improve. Brazelton and Greenspan thus urge schools, teachers, and parents to meet each child's individual way of actively relating to the world, encouraging the child to learn through their own calm guidance and modeling.

In their chapter on the fourth need, "Developmentally Appropriate Experiences," the authors argue that adults should provide each child with an emotional and intellectual environment that is appropriate to the child's developmental stage. They offer specific examples: for healthy development of their brains, children under three should not be allowed to watch television for more than half an hour a day; school-children should not be asked to spend so much time on homework that they are not able to enjoy family activities, play with their peers, or become involved in sports. Specific recommendations can certainly be debated, but the principle articulated would not strike any child developmentalist as wrong: children should not confine themselves to only one kind of activity, especially one inappropriate to their developmental stage, one that isolates them from others, and or one that promotes passivity. This is the basic developmental reason why child labor, particularly in single-task sweatshops, is so bad for children. Countries must not abolish child financial labor only to replace it with child school labor.

Describing the fifth need, for "limit setting, structure, and expectations," the authors take a strong stand against corporal punishment. "Physical discipline, such as hitting or spanking a child, is no longer an acceptable alternative to discipline. Discipline means teaching, not punishment." Parents need to offer good modeling, not blows, and good modeling can be offered only by parents who are child-oriented and calm, not harassed or exhausted—much less ill, addicted, or desperately poor. So Dr. Brazelton recommends, for example, that working parents maintain a daily routine of spending time with their children as soon as they get home. "I feel strongly about recommending to working parents that they set up a homecoming ritual in which everybody gets close all over again. Then they are ready to play a disciplinary role. But not until then." Children should be encouraged to participate in family limit- and rule-setting to the degree that they are developmentally able to. As Dr. Greenspan explains, "When families brainstorm together on what the consequences are going to be for not doing what you are supposed to do, then everyone becomes a participant in setting down the rules. An atmosphere where there are expectations, structure, and limits appropriate to a child's age and level is necessary for . . . basic security."

The chapter "Stable Communities and Cultural Continuity," on the sixth need, asks parents to take a larger part in school and community governance, but it also acknowledges that parents themselves need the support of communities (including income support, safety nets, and parental leaves at the birth of a child). The authors are clear that children should not be asked to parent their parents, which goes against the natural order of caretaking. Parents' needs for support must be met within the community by other adults. Parents, teachers, and child services workers—all of whom care for children—must cooperate with one another, and neither compete nor shift blame onto one another for problems that arise as a child grows up and moves into the arenas that the various adults oversee.

These six needs are set in the context of the seventh (and most generally orienting) need articulated in *The Irreducible Needs of Children:* "protecting the future." Adults must keep in mind not just their own children, or their community's children, or American children, but all children—the "every child" of the book's subtitle. "Throughout the world future generations of children and families will be much more interrelated. In order to protect the future for one child, we must protect it for all." The authors do not explicitly articulate the Aristotelian principle (freed of Aristotle's own childist framework) that adults must prioritize or make paramount the needs of their children over their own needs—the needs of the future adults over the needs of the present adults—but the principle is implicit in what they do say.

With the kind of broad cross-cultural developmental framework offered in *The Irreducible Needs of Children,* the child's best interest can be defined as "meeting these developmental needs as well as possible." Parenting practices as well as policy proposals and specific legislation can be evaluated in terms of whether they meet these developmental needs. Both in terms of political and legislative processes and in terms of preventive public health policy, the positive focus is clear. Though the word never appears, education about childism is built into the guidance Child Development offers.

Connecting efforts to go beyond CAN to comprehensive development with efforts to draw effectively on the guidance Child Development has to offer, educators need to become historians. They need to write a new version of the history of childhood in America to show clearly how childism can be built into "child-saving," to aim a critique at the self-legitimating function of prejudice. Such a history should expand to include the education programs being created around the world that are based on the recognition that prejudice has to be recognized in order to be overcome.

The key historical-educational theme should flow from the principle built into *The Irreducible Needs of Children* but not fully articulated there: children must come first. Childist adults are those who do not assume that their obligation or responsibility to cherish and educate their children takes precedence over any obligation their children as adults will have to them. At its basis, childism is a legitimation of an adult's or a society's failure to prioritize or make paramount the needs of children over those of adults, the needs of the future adults over the needs of the present adults. It is role reversal at the level of a principle.

A new version of the history of childhood in America could show when this prioritizing principle has governed policy and parenting and when it has not. The history of the past forty years is crucial for the present—the policies that need immediate remediation arose during this period. But for the future, we have to look farther into the past, like analysts going into the parental histories that their present clients know but may not have raised to consciousness. As an illustration of the history I am imagining, let me offer a short case study of the fathers and mothers of the late-nineteenth-century crusade against cruelty to children.

The founders of the American Society for the Prevention of Cruelty to Children (SPCC) were middle- and upper-class philanthropists, members of the group often described as white Anglo-Saxon Protestants, and beneficiaries of the surge of wealth available through the expansionary capitalism of the Gilded Age. In almost all U.S. history books and social work texts published to this day, they have been celebrated as "the child-savers." But their guiding principle could more aptly be described as "Adults first," as can be seen in the three basic strategies and institutions they developed for their work. To me, these strategies are evidence for the three basic forms of childism that I have been describing, for the philanthropists spontaneously developed one strategy for each form—eliminative (obsessional), role-manipulative (hysterical), and erasing (narcissistic). Finding these three strategies at the originary moment of American "child-saving" also seems to me evidence that the three forms, which have been with us for more than a century, will be with us in the future, and that we must be continually alert to them and continue our efforts at education and legislation to address them.

Few among the three types of childist philanthropists realized that when they looked upon children who obviously needed saving, they saw those children as a threat to their own needs, or to their position, their authority, their way of life, their moral order. The needy children they saw were undermining, wild, or rebellious. The philanthropists were full of self-righteousness and self-legitimation. Unlike the scientific "discoverers" of child abuse in the 1960s, who focused on types of acts children had endured, the child-savers of the 1870s classified children in terms of the kinds of threats they posed to "good" society. Concentrating on one particular subgroup of children—the poor who lived in the metropolitan centers of the East Coast, particularly New York, the immigrant capital of America—the child-savers came up with the categories "destitute," "delinquent," and "neglected."

Specific adults, usually their impoverished parents, were said to have harmed these children, and a word was invented for them: *cruelists*. Such adults were perpetrators of "cruelty to children." But beyond labeling them, the child-savers had no interest in the parents: they cared nothing for the parents' motivations or their experiences—or their poverty. They did not ask, "Why do people sometimes turn cruelly against their own children?" On the contrary, the poor were widely understood to be people who carried a physical disease, pauperism, which manifested itself as a hereditary inferiority and even a hereditary proclivity toward criminality. Like their parents, poor children were assumed to be bad, sexually wild, or rebellious. The child-savers thought that the solution to the social problem the poor children represented was to protect good people and good society *from them*. The strategies they came up with were to further eliminate the destitute, to further manipulate the delinquent, and to further erase the neglected.

American philanthropists founded private societies like the Society for the Prevention of Cruelty to Children in the 1870s. As protecting good society and its moral standards with private institutions was their goal, they were—like contemporary "limited government" advocates—hostile to any governmental solutions to social problems. They considered idleness and moral corruption virtually synonymous, so they thought that the children of the poor had a natural need to work. Child labor was crucial to the nation's health: "If a child is not trained to useful work before the age of eighteen, we shall have a nation of paupers and thieves" was a representative claim. The "moral benefit" of lower-class child labor was taken for granted by philanthropists who imagined the consequences of increasing numbers of useless poor children going unsupervised and being tempted into crime and vagrancy. "Idle hands do the Devil's work" was the motto— the shared ground of all their forms of childism.

Writing in 1872, Charles Loring Brace, a theologian trained at Yale Divinity School and the head of the Children's Aid Society in New York, was unusually conscious of his own motivations. He explicitly summarized the prejudice un-

knowingly shared by those private citizens who placed themselves in charge of children's issues: "The class of a large city
most dangerous to its property, its morals and its political life,
are the ignorant, destitute, untrained and abandoned youth:
the outcast street children grown up to be voters, to be the
implements of demagogues, the 'feeders' of the criminals, and
the sources of domestic outbreaks and violations of the law."

Brace, a man of clear obsessional traits, as his autobiographical writings show, was one of the foremost proponents of the obsessional childist strategy called "placing out"
for dealing with destitute children who had already been cast
out of or abandoned by their families. On a local scale, he
organized residences in New York, like the Newsboys Home,
where young boys could pay a portion of their tiny salaries to
live while they labored, and thus avoided becoming dirty
"gutter snipes" on the streets. But Brace's most ambitious
scheme was a national "children's train" for removing children from East Coast cities to settlements in the West, where
they were placed with Christian foster families for whom
they labored without pay. "Placing out" was particularly favored in 1865, after the U.S. Congress considered—and fortunately rejected—exempting children from the Fourteenth
Amendment, which had made indenturing and slavery unconstitutional for adults. But "placing out" was child inden-
ture by another name.

A child classified as delinquent was one who had
found a "home" of sorts in an immoral or illegal adult activity: as a gang member, a thief (freelance or in a "den of
thieves"), a prostitute or a hustler, an all-purpose laborer in
the "white slave" trade. A special category of "defective delinquents" was created for adolescent male delinquents accused
of being child sexual abusers. The first 1890s laws designed
for adult sex criminals (called "sex psychopaths" and said to

be congenitally depraved) were applied to these youths. Because crimes were involved, delinquents could not be dealt with directly by private philanthropic organizations and institutions, so a state criminal-justice system was needed, and in 1899 the first juvenile court opened in Illinois. (This was the type of court that was reined in somewhat by the 1967 Supreme Court decision *In re Gault.*) Control of sexual activity, however, remained a philanthropic not a government or legal concern, and the private children's organizations were assiduous—and hysterical—in their campaigns against masturbation, which was assumed to lead directly to insanity and adult sex psychopathy. A system of reform schools and prisonlike facilities was developed for delinquents, as were residences for girls who became pregnant out of wedlock. We have this system still—it is called juvie.

The juvenile-court system, once established with child-saving intentions, became a major reinforcer of hysterical role-manipulative childism. Alternative approaches to delinquency appeared only later, and only in countries that had never tried delinquents in courts. (The Scots, for example, who have never had a juvenile-court tradition, created the Children's Hearings in the 1960s, on the assumption that a court-based system of justice is inappropriate for children and inimical to their developmental needs. Following the recommendations of the Kilbrandon Committee [1964], it was decided that court proceedings interfere with open discussion of and assessment of the needs of children who have committed offenses. Therefore assessments should be made by child development professionals trained to make them, not by judges, who are trained only in the law. The principle followed in this non-prejudicial approach was that delinquency is symptomatic of a child's unmet need; it is not a manifestation of the inborn aggression or wildness or insubordination that childists—

particularly hysterical ones—presume exists in children and youths. If U.S. states adopted the Scottish approach, the United States would no longer have the highest child-incarceration rate of any nation in the world.)

A child was classified as neglected who was known to be the victim of a family that could not or would not see to its proper training and education at home, thus making the child "wayward." "Neglect" included physical neglect, but its main reference was to isolation or lack of socialization and educational neglect. Pediatricians developed a diagnostic category, "psychosocial dwarfism," for children who failed to grow normally because of all types of neglect.

For the neglected, the strategy of creating institutions known as Houses of Refuge emerged. At the New York City House of Refuge, located on the isolated Randall's Island, children labored at least six hours a day. They were not allowed to talk at work, at mealtimes, or in the brief periods of rudimentary schooling; the regime was Prussian, almost military, and obviously designed—in the narcissistic manner—to erase any waywardness or rebelliousness these children might have been born with or developed.

The child-savers held sway for about twenty years (1870–1890) before other reformers entered the arena. Homer Folks, secretary of New York State's Charities Aid Association, reviewing the history of New York's House of Refuge in his 1890 *The Care of Destitute, Neglected and Delinquent Children,* criticized its philanthropic managers as retrograde for their support of child labor, their "cell system" (solitary confinement meted out as a punishment), their use of severe corporal punishment, and generally for being far less progressive in their institutions than the New York State authorities were in theirs. Folks's attack marks the slow ascendancy in America of public officials with less punitive, more progressive views toward the destitute, the delinquent, and the neglected. It is no accident that these reformers all belonged to the generation born after the Civil War and the Emancipation Proclamation—they understood that children should not be treated like African slaves or indentured workers. These officials were similar to the European social democrats after World War II who had learned from a collective trauma, a civil war among European nations.

The entire staff of the federal Children's Bureau in Washington, D.C., from the director to the social workers, had been born after the Civil War; in addition, it was composed entirely of women and infused with the vision of the suffragists. Grace Abbott, the most famous director, had been raised by a suffragist mother, and in 1921 she oversaw the drafting and implementation of the Sheppard-Towner Act, which provided federal and state aid for mothers and children. In 1938, after a remarkable career, she wrote the classic interwar progressive text, *The Child and the State*, which would make another excellent text for a Children's History Month recommended reading list.

The progressives in municipal, state, and national politics, in combination with the progressive educators and social workers who ran settlement houses and community centers—like the Henry Street Settlement in New York, or Jane Addams's Hull House in Chicago—were advocates of social change. They saw in children a better future and new beginnings, not the dangerous damaged goods of the industrializing world. For these reformers, it seemed obvious that political institutions—municipal, state, and federal—should take responsibility for damaged and at-risk children, particularly to give them or guarantee them what neither their families nor the child-savers would or could: freedom *from* labor, and freedom *for* public education. In short, freedom for childhood as a developmental, preparatory stage that would result in good citizens. Some of the child advocates were socialists, followers of the great Swedish feminist and reformer Ellen Key, who in 1900 had confidently proclaimed the advent of "the Century of the Child," in which children's needs and rights—she spoke the language of *rights*—would be paramount in social planning and efforts to end poverty.

Those Americans who opposed child labor and generated laws against it recognized that it was a political problem, an injustice, a form of slavery, a form of childism (although they did not have that word). Rather than adding to the problem by isolating poor or abused children they looked at these children as part of a whole: *all* children have a right to a childhood in which they can be healthy and educated for their future as citizens, and that right must be guaranteed. At the same time, they saw the great, prejudice-based weakness of the philanthropic child-saving organizations: the child-savers approached children's issues singly and on what came to be known among social workers as the "deficit" or "residual" model. The philanthropists dealt with children whom a childist social system had already classified as destitute, delinquent, or neglected, and then dealt with them in a punitive, childist fashion. Their childist outlook legitimated their childist actions.

After legislation outlawing child labor had finally made its way through the Congress in 1916 and was beginning to be enforced in cities and, more slowly, farms and ranches of the West and South, the conflict between the progressives and the child-savers shifted almost completely to the question of how to organize public education. Working with the Children's Bureau and through the White House Conferences on Children, which took place every ten years until 1970, the progressives continued to dismantle the House of

Refuge system, develop settlement houses, and replace the "children's train" scheme with a foster care system, with the eventual goal of creating a system of social security for children and their families. Their work finally resulted in the Social Security Act of 1935, passed at the height of the Depression (though the act was designed to eliminate poverty first among the elderly and only afterward to focus on children, which it never did).

In addition to social security, one of the progressives' main goals was to retain the public education system and keep it focused on character-building and preparation for citizenship. After World War I, however, they faced a far more formidable and powerful group of childist philanthropists than the late-nineteenth-century child-savers. Their opponents were among the wealthiest and most influential industrialists and bankers in the country, each of whom had a philanthropic educational foundation in his family's name: the Rockefeller Educational Trust, the Ford Foundation, and the Carnegie Foundation. These foundations were dedicated to taking over the newly established public school system—literally, by financing it—and creating instead a system of vocational schools that would turn out workers for their industries and commercial enterprises. To this end they also took over teacher-training programs at most of the country's major universities, with Columbia Teachers College as their model creation.

Teachers in training at Columbia Teachers College and the other foundation-sponsored universities were frequently sent to Germany for their Ph.D. work because psychologists there were pioneering methods for using schools to train workers. About 90 percent of German children went to Volkschulen—worker training (vocational) schools—while much of the remaining 10 percent were prepared in Realschulen to be managers for business enterprises. A tiny portion were enrolled in super-elite Akademischensschulen to become university researchers, teachers, and national leaders. A psychologist, Wilhelm Wundt, at the University of Leipzig was the chief architect of the three-tier school system, and his laboratories supplied the descriptions of developmental capacities that justified the tracking system and the standardized testing system required for the tracking. The German educational philosophy tied in with pseudo-scientific theories about hereditary racial inferiority, inborn intellectual defects, and eugenics, all of which the Nazis later drew upon.

Historians critical of American schools and schooling have described how the nineteenth-century common schools—which began as one-room schools without any age differentiation, much less tracking of abilities—turned into huge factorylike institutions that directed students toward their future occupations on the basis of their class, sex, and race. Progressive educators reacted against the privatizing vision from the start, emphasizing its authoritarian and utilitarian purposes: the majority of children were being schooled to fulfill adult needs and to fulfill particular low-level positions in adult enterprises, not to develop their potentialities and their characters. The teaching methods were producing generations of role-reversal children, eliminated from opportunities, manipulated into preset roles in workforces, and deprived of encouragement to independent thought. The schools practiced all kinds of childism at once—eliminative, manipulative, and erasing—under the rubric of "tracking."

Because they were well financed, American post–World War II public schools were, despite their basically childist organization, consistently ranked higher than schools elsewhere in the developed world. That ranking lasted until the late 1970s, when a decline began that has not been remedied since. Without corporate funding, the inherent inequality of the tracked schools grew worse, at the same time that inequalities within American society were growing. When parents and legislators woke up to the crisis in the school system, they once again turned to standardized testing and tracking as the solution—though this time students were tracked into different types of schools at both the elementary and high school levels. The U.S. educational system now consists of public schools, some well-endowed and some with almost no funding; private schools; and, recently, the hybrid "charter schools," which are corporately owned but funded with a mix of public and private money. In recent years, reformers like Jonathan Kozol have been leading a movement against what Kozol calls the "savage inequalities" in American schools. They use the Cambridge Institute for Public Education, which Kozol founded, as a model for mobilizing research into child development and to criticize standardized testing, the privatizing of public education, and the racial resegregation that has come with increasing child poverty.

Through a reassessment of the original child-saving project, we need to educate Americans to reject policies and programs that "rescue" children by segregating them into the current equivalents of the child-savers' categories. At the same time we need to reassess the history of American schooling. Good research exists showing the harmful effects of programs in which children are placed out or indentured into prisonlike institutions, in which those deemed wild are categorized as delinquents or juvenile offenders, or in which "education" means standardization and identity erasure. But these assessments need to be grounded in an analysis of characterologically based forms of childism. The history of American childism needs to be studied in terms of motivation and character types, and it needs to be disseminated more effectively and broadly via the science of Child Development to the American public.

As I noted at the beginning of this book, America lags behind the rest of the international community in its care for children. U.S. laws and policies do not meet children's developmental needs or defend their rights, and the United States has yet to support the 1959 Declaration of the Rights of the Child or ratify the U.N. Convention on the Rights of the Child. But political and social progress is unlikely unless Americans acquire a better understanding of their own progressive history, as well as of the difference the Convention has made for children worldwide.

We have American examples of the kind of understanding that is needed. For T. Berry Brazelton, for example, *The Irreducible Needs of Children* was a natural continuation of work he had done since the early 1970s, when he and his Boston colleagues published *The Neonatal Behavioral Assessment Scale*, outlining a development theory that is now used around the world, in diverse cultures, by trainees of the Brazelton Institute. The assumption behind the scale is that all newborns, whatever their culture, have basic developmental tasks that they need to be able to fulfill to succeed on what Anna Freud called "developmental lines." To help children, mature adult caretakers must communicate with the baby using the first language the baby speaks, which is bodily. Each newborn is a unique individual who has already been developing for nine months and can already make choices and communicate needs, so it is crucial that adults be able to recognize and attend to each baby's unique way of fulfilling the universal maturational and developmental program. The children described by Brazelton are not lumps of clay to be shaped or blank slates to be written on or helpless beings to be trained into robotic conformity. Not property, not servants, they are also not the empty, bad, wild, or originally sinful beings that childist projections and stereotypes have made them out to be.

But many of the important examples we need are not American. In the homeland of Ellen Key, the Swedish reformer who hoped that the twentieth century would be the Century of the Child, a history has unfolded that could provide a model for America as well as other nations—a history that, if we had a Children's History Month, could be offered as an example of a successful struggle against childism. In one generation, the Swedes brought about a huge change in their attitudes toward children.

It began with a program that targeted corporal punishment of children. The program did not, that is, focus on a particular abused group, as happened in the United States, where the target was children diagnosed with "battered child syndrome," but on a practice and an attitude that effected almost every child in Sweden in the 1960s, when the majority of the population approved of corporal punishment (as did the majority of adults throughout the world). The childist legitimation was the time-worn admonition "Spare the rod and spoil the child."

A group of Swedish child developmentalists, who rejected this rationalization (as child developmentalists like Brazelton and Greenspan did in America), started an educational campaign. Unusually for the time, the Swedish researchers asked children for their stories and thoughts. When enough data had been collected to show that corporal punishment—even a relatively mild spanking—shames and humiliates children, leaving them deeply alienated from those who hit them, the developmentalists drafted a law banning corporal punishment in schools or in public for consideration by the Swedish Parliament.

In 1969, after the Parliament passed the law, a second research and education program followed. Through the public health service, brochures and pamphlets prepared by developmental psychologists and children's-rights advocates were made available to all parents, and *free* state-sponsored parenting education *and free therapy* were guaranteed to those who admitted that they had a problem refraining from "punishing" their children. At the same time, the researchers measured the effects of the ban on corporal punishment (which was extended in 1979 to include punishment by parents in the home). Children, parents and parenting practices, the healthcare system, and the mental healthcare system were all studied, and the researchers discovered that all had improved; there were many fewer demands on children's physical and mental health services. The whole program was, in effect, a public health prevention program, and the researchers were functioning as epidemiologists as well as developmentalists.

What happened in Sweden is important for many reasons. In societies where corporal punishment is tolerated, very high percentages of parents (94 percent in America currently) say that they punish their children with a smacking or a spanking and that they think such punishments are reasonable and appropriate. Many educators agree. Meanwhile, child battering and physical abuse, which most parents reject, is thought to be something utterly apart from corporal punishment. One effect of the Swedish legislation banning corporal punishment was to make it clear that smacking and beating and battering are on a continuum of maltreatment, and that in a context where one is sanctioned, so will the other be. There should be no "reasonable chastisement" or "lawful correction" that can be part of an abuser's defense: "I only meant to smack him, to discipline him, and physical discipline is good for children." In the childism analysis I am proposing, this is adult narcissism claiming, "What I think is good for you is good for you, and what you think doesn't matter." (The extreme version of narcissism takes the form "This will hurt me more than it hurts you.") Or it is adult hysteria claiming, "Your role is to be broken and tamed." Or adult obsessionality claiming, "Good children are orderly children who are seen and not heard." Most adults who punish their children have experienced such defenses as children themselves, and, remaining in character, they repeat them when they punish their children.

Out of the pioneering Swedish legislation, the Global Initiative to End All Corporal Punishment of Children has emerged, overseen by the U.N. Committee on Children's Rights. The U.N. committee receives communications from organizations around the world that are working to formulate a legal framework for extending the Swedish initiative, and the framework has already been adopted in twenty nations. In 1998, the European Network of Ombudsman for Children issued a statement:

> *As spokespeople for the children of Europe* [italics added], we believe that eliminating violent and humiliating forms of discipline is a vital strategy for improving children's status as people, and reducing child abuse *and all other forms of violence* [italics added] in European societies. This is a long overdue reform, with huge potential for improving the quality of lives and family relationships. Hitting children is disrespectful and dangerous. Children deserve at least the same protection from violence that we as adults take for granted for ourselves.

The U.N. committee has also encouraged research into children's understanding of violence and its effects on themselves, as well as into children's ideas about how to prevent it. In its recommendations following a Day of General Discussion (September 28, 2001) on "violence against children within the family and in schools," the committee noted: "In conceptualizing violence . . . the critical starting point and frame of reference [should] be the experience of children themselves."

The Global Initiative to End All Corporal Punishment is a model anti-childist effort because it combines a developmental approach to children's needs, a public health approach, and a children's-rights approach, and it is, further, universal: it is for all children in all nations. It encourages children's participation. It recognizes that to achieve its goal we must all confront social and cultural norms that sanction corporal punishment, and educate ourselves to reject those norms. But it is crucially a model initiative because it is connected to international efforts for children that are grounded in developmental and nonviolent principles.

The American Pediatric Association as well as other American children's advocacy groups support the Global Initiative to End All Corporal Punishment. The APA, at whose convention Dr. Kempe had read his path-breaking paper "The Battered Child Syndrome" in 1961, issues educational brochures for parents, teachers, and police about "positive discipline" (not involving hitting) that is appropriate for children at different developmental stages. But there has been no step toward creating legislation in favor of the initiative, nor is there any mention of it in the informational material from the relevant federal organizations—for example, the federal government's Web site for Child Abuse Prevention Month.

The child-development research that guided the Global

Initiative to End All Corporal Punishment now stands behind most of the international initiatives to prevent violence
generally, at all developmental stages, adult and child. It has
been used in the creation of an international public health
program by the World Health Organization, which has pri-
oritized the health of women and children. The WHO recognizes that children who get off to a healthy, developmentally
supported start are at far less risk of future disease, future
developmental failure, future mental health problems, or future inability to establish their own healthy families. Well-
supported child development is the conditio sine qua non of
all people's well-being.

On this basis, in the 1990s the WHO developed a program, "Preventing Violence," that includes child abuse and
neglect but does not take child abuse and neglect out of the
context of other types of violence—especially domestic violence, economic violence, and wars without borders involving civilian populations—or out of the context of overall child
health and development needs. Preventing Violence does categorize child abuse and neglect with the usual four types—
physical abuse, neglect, sexual abuse, and emotional abuse—
but the program is broad enough that this classification does
not shape the program itself or splinter it into four separate
ways of addressing the problem. And because the program
connects violence involving children with violence involving
women, and sexism is recognized as a prejudice that is involved in domestic violence, childism is at least implicitly
recognized as well (although childism needs, as I have said,
to be recognized as distinct from sexism as well).

I have been describing a widening circle of prevention-
oriented programs that have been gaining international momentum. In 1997 the U.N. General Assembly proclaimed that
the millennial year 2000 would be the "Year of the Culture of

Peace" and then, in November 1998, it declared that the first decade of the new millennium would be the "International Decade for the Promotion of a Culture of Peace and Non-Violence for the Children of the World." In the intervening year, "nonviolence" had clearly entered the conceptualization as the positive premise of "the culture of peace." The phrase "for the Children of the World" was added to underline the international community's realization that this initiative was an obligation on the part of adults to all children.

The U.N. delegates were obviously not thinking of peace as simply a negative, the absence of war. The word *nonviolence,* with its roots in Gandhi's political movement and philosophy, had come to signal something richly constructive: ecological nonviolence, social nonviolence, and political nonviolence—a broad, Gandhian program of recovering the natural world and natural ways of living "for the children of the world." By 2005, so many nongovernmental organizations around the world had agreed to the U.N. intention, and were educating so many millions of people in techniques for establishing a culture of peace and nonviolence in their countries, that one NGO report referred to this worldwide educational community as, collectively, "the other superpower."

It is as citizens of this "other superpower" that the citizens of America should, for their own children and "for the children of the world," seek a new beginning.

Bibliographic Essay

Introduction

Much of the general theory of prejudices in *Childism* derives from and updates or revises my earlier work *The Anatomy of Prejudices* (Harvard University Press, 1996). The earlier book set out a framework for a field of Comparative Prejudice Studies based on analyses of sexism, racism, anti-Semitism, homophobia, and other prejudices that are usually studied separately. I discussed prejudice against senior and adolescent age groups briefly, but *Childism* extends that discussion to all children under age eighteen. See also my "Childism" in *Contemporary Psychoanalysis* 45 (2009): 251–265.

Two psychiatrists proposed the word *childism* in the early 1970s. One was Chester Pierce, a clinician and researcher based at Harvard University, who modeled his understanding of childism on racism, which he knew from his own experience as an African American: C. M. Pierce and G. B. Allen, "Childism," *Psychiatric Annals* 5 (1975): 266–270. The second was Jack C. Westman, a professor at the University of Wisconsin, who used the term in essays and in his *Child Advocacy* (Free Press, 1979), explaining it as "juvenile ageism," following the introduction of the term *ageism* by Robert N. Butler in "Age-

Ism: Another Form of Bigotry," *Gerontologist* 9 (1969): 243–246. The term *childism* did not catch on, although a third psychiatrist, Michael B. Rothenberg, alluded to it in a provocatively titled article, "Is There an Unconscious National Conspiracy Against Children in the United States?" *Clinical Pediatrics* 19 (1980): 15–24. (A version of Rothenberg's thesis had been raised in the popular press in a collection of articles under the title "Do Americans Suddenly Hate Kids?" *Esquire*, March 1974.)

For a representative recent collection of essays on prejudice by psychiatrists and psychoanalysts, see *The Future of Prejudice*, ed. H. Parens et al. (Aronson, 2007), which also contains a useful current bibliography. But these essays, like a representative current handbook by J. H. Ponterotto, S. O. Utsey, and P. B. Pedersen, *Preventing Prejudice: A Guide for Counselors, Educators, and Parents* (Sage, 2006), which contains a comprehensive bibliography, are directed at prejudice in the singular. In the handbook, *prejudice* refers only to racism or ethnic prejudice and "ethnoviolence."

Neither of the fields History of Childhood or Children's Studies has been studied historically, although *The History of Childhood Quarterly* and numerous other similar journals provide fruitful material for launching such inquiries. A step in the direction of a historical periodization that distinguishes a current period of childhood in the West is J. Kincheloe and S. Steinberg, eds., *Kinderculture: The Corporate Construction of Childhood*, 2d ed. (Westview, 2004). See also J. Cleverlex and D. C. Phillips, *Visions of Childhood: Influential Models from Locke to Spock* (Teachers College, 1986), and P. Stearns, *Childhood in World History* (Routledge, 2006).

There is a great deal of debate (known as the Ariès debate) about the founding text of the History of Childhood field, Philippe Ariès's *Centuries of Childhood* (1961; English trans., Random House, 1962). Ariès had advanced the claim that "childhood" was a concept known to the Greeks, whose word for "education" *paideia,* also meant "childrearing," but that the idea then disappeared until it was resurrected in the late Renaissance. Linda Pollock, in *Forgotten Children* (1983; Cambridge University Press, 1996), reviewed Ariès's historical claim and rejected it, appealing to evidence from private diaries and letters rather than public cultural objects and treatises. But like most historians, Pollock also rejected the thesis of Ariès's most prolific critic, the psychoanalytic historian Lloyd deMause, who has edited the *Journal of Psychohistory* since the early 1970s and directs Psychohistory Press. De-Mause had argued that the history of child abuse belonged front and center in the History of Childhood field because infanticide had been pervasive in the ancient Western world (whose *paideia* Ariès had praised). But, deMause continued, through six stages of development that reflect six different modes of relating to children, adults have grown progressively less violent and deadly, more understanding and helping, although it was not until the late twentieth century that the primitive impulse to abuse or murder children was curbed by rationality. Indeed, deMause claimed that it was his own generation of "mature" parents who could, finally, be considered good "sixth-stage" parents of "the helping mode": see Lloyd deMause, "The Evolution of Childhood," in *The History of Childhood* (Psychohistory Press, 1974). The helping mode, noted deMause, results in "a child who is gentle, sincere, never depressed, never imitative or group-oriented, strong-willed, and unintimidated by authority" (54). I have not found any evidence for this linear, Hegelian scheme in which perfectly parented children—the admirable Baby Boomer generation—finally emerge. Rather, childism seems to flourish in some times and cultures and decrease in others, and it takes different forms under different historical conditions, which would need to be studied in their particularity before a general pattern through time could be discerned (if there is one). In my opinion deMause's work constitutes what Freud called "wild analysis" (in a narcissistic, self-aggrandizing mode) and should be read with great caution; it has had more influence among psychoanalysts than it deserves and has inhibited the development of a psychoanalytic history of childhood to this day.

At the Web site of the institution where Children's Studies was born in 1991, Brooklyn College (www.brooklyn. cuny.edu) there is material on the field, as there is on the Web site of the one university now offering a full B.A. to Ph.D. program in Children's Studies, Rutgers, home of the Center for Children and Childhood Studies (http://children.camden .rutgers.edu) and of Rutgers University Press, publisher of the Series in Childhood Studies. See also J. Qvortrup, W. A. Corsaro, and M.-S. Honig, eds., *The Palgrave Handbook of Childhood Studies* (Palgrave Macmillan, 2009), for articles and bibliographies on the key topics in the field. A good place to begin ranging over the field of Children's Studies is the thousand-page *The Child: An Encyclopedic Companion*, ed. R. A. Schweder (Chicago University Press, 2009). It is noteworthy that the encyclopedia has an article on children's prejudices but none on prejudice against children.

Among the standard texts in the field of Child Development, which by now has many subfields and approaches, is the three-volume *Encyclopedia of Childhood and Adolescence* (Gale, 1997). The early history of the field in America is well told in A. B. Smuts, *Science in the Service of Children, 1893–1935* (Yale University Press, 2006). Since the end of World War II, the volumes of *The Psychoanalytic Study of the Child* have tracked the major psychoanalytic contributions; see particularly S. Abrams, "Development," *Psychoana-*

lytic Study of the Child 38 (1983): 113–139. I think that the moment in which the Child Development field became fully interdisciplinary can be flagged with the publication of Urie Bronfenbrenner's *The Ecology of Human Development: Experiments by Nature and Design* (Harvard University Press, 1979).

Historical study of the U.N. Declaration on the Rights of the Child and the Convention on the Rights of the Child can be found in S. Detrick, *A Commentary on the UN Convention on the Rights of the Child* (Nijhoff, 1999). Important work on children's rights in the context of the Convention can be found in P. Veerman, *The Rights of the Child and the Changing Image of Childhood* (Nijhoff, 1992), and M. Freeman and P. Veerman, *The Ideologies of Children's Rights* (Nijhoff, 1992). For an overview, see former secretary general Kofi Annan's *We the Children* (UNICEF, 2001). In terms of America's relation to the Declaration and Convention see M. Mason, "The U.S. and the International Children's Rights Crusade: Leader or Laggard?" *Journal of Social History* 38(2005): 955–963.

The Children's Defense Fund has its own Web site (with archives), and much of its founding history is compassed in the various autobiographical writings of its main founder, Marian Wright Edelman. There is as yet no good general history of U.S. social policy toward children in the postwar period, but there are studies of specific facets of this history, among them E. H. Pleck, *Domestic Tyranny: The Making of American Social Policy Against Family Violence from Colonial Times to the Present* (University of Illinois Press, 1993), which illuminates how idealizations of the family and biases toward parents' rights have stood in the way of policies supportive of children and children's rights.

The literature in the field called Child Abuse and Neglect (CAN) is now enormous, although little of it concerns what children know about abuse and their abuser's motivations. I refer to specific studies later in this bibliographic essay but for a good introduction to the field's history read the volumes of the journal *Child Abuse and Neglect* chronologically; note that the field widened its scope internationally when the journal became the official organ of the International Society for the Prevention of Child Abuse and Neglect. (ISPCAN, founded in 1977, has its own Web site: www.ispcan .org). Also useful is Leroy Ashby's *Dependency, Neglect, and Abuse in American History* (Twayne, 1997). J. Briere and colleagues gathered many helpful articles for the *APSAC Handbook of Child Maltreatment* (Sage, 1996); and in 2001, Facts on File published a second edition of *The Encyclopedia of Child Abuse,* ed. R. and J. Clark. A little dated, but still helpful is the summary volume by Thomas Nazario, *In Defense of Children: Understanding the Rights, Needs, and Interests of the Child* (Scribner, 1988). David Bakan's lectures for the CBC, *Slaughter of the Innocents* (Jossey-Bass, 1971), are valuable general historical and philosophical reflections composed early in the period of "the discovery of child abuse."

Chapter 1: Anatomy of a Prejudice

The question of why parents turn against their children, neglecting, abusing, even murdering them, has occupied Western civilization for millennia. From Sophocles to Shakespeare, Rousseau to Ariès, Dickens to Freud, the attitudes that I am defining as childist have engaged the attention of some of the most significant thinkers and artists, and have underpinned not only revolutionary theories of children and of human motivation but also some of the greatest dramas and novels of all time.

The psychoanalytic scholar who made the most thorough study of Greek tragedy as a genre that centered on attacks against children is Bennett Simon, first in *Mind and Madness in Ancient Greece: The Classic Roots of Modern Psychiatry* (1978; Cornell University Press, 1980) and then in *Tragic Drama and the Family: Psychoanalytic Studies from Aeschylus to Beckett* (Yale University Press, 1993). The key text for considering King Laius's actions against his son as the origin of Oedipus's Oedipus Complex is George Devereux's "Why Oedipus Killed Laius," *International Journal of Psychoanalysis* 34 (1953): 132–141. The existing collections of the Hungarian-born (and Sándor Ferenczi trained) Devereux's anthropological and ethnographic essays are unusual in their psychoanalytically informed attention to customs and rites hostile to children, particularly among various North American native peoples with whom he worked psychoanalytically. See especially "The Voices of Children," *American Journal of Psychotherapy* 19 (1965): 4–19.

The tragic theme of conflict between generations as it was manifested in Greek comedy has been studied by Dana F. Sutton in *Ancient Comedy: The War of the Generations* (Twayne, 1993). Particularly instructive are his chapters on Aristophanes, who mocked the hard-headed, misanthropic Athenian men who turned away from their proper positions in the world to focus on their families, which they ruled tyrannically—and made fools of themselves in the process. Aristophanes also stood up for sons, presented as fun-loving and joyful followers of Dionysus, hedonists, young men who are at home in the world of wine, women, and song, but mocked their imperial enterprises in his antiwar comedy *Lysistrata*, in which women took center stage. The one surviving comedy by Menander, *Dyscolus* (The Grouch), presents a tyrannical father who is a misanthrope and a cheapskate, and who gets his comeuppance after he has, literally, fallen into a well, representing how narrow-minded and circumscribed his life has become. This kind of narrow-mindedness is explored psychoanalytically by Eric Brenman in "Cruelty and Narrow-Mindedness," *International Journal of Psychoanalysis* 66 (1985): 273–281.

In the Greek epics from before the Age of Tyrants, parents do not attack their children as they do in the tragedies. Homer's poems are full of portraits of loving, companionate marriages like those of Odysseus and Penelope and Hector and Andromache, and loving parent-child relationships such as those between Odysseus and his father, Laertes, and his son, Telemachus: see the article I co-wrote with Joseph Russo, *"Amae* in Ancient Greece," in *Where Do We Fall When We Fall in Love?* (Other Books, 2003).

I would argue that the three most famous Greek tragedians, Aeschylus, Sophocles, and Euripides, presented three different forms of childism: Aeschylus dramatized narcissistic childism, in which children are seen as vehicles for or obstacles to parental ambition; Sophocles presented obsessional elimination of children viewed as pollutants or infiltrators; and Euripides focused on the hysterical exploitation of children in sexual rivalries (*Medea*) and erotic rites (*The Bacchae*).

The Greek "conflict of generation" themes were, of course, presented by Shakespeare in both tragedies and comedies. For thinking about Shakespeare's awareness of childism, I am particularly indebted to a recent book by my friend Fred Tromly, *Fathers and Sons in Shakespeare* (University of Toronto Press, 2010), which has a bibliography oriented toward this theme. Literary awareness of childism shifted when nineteenth-century novelists, particularly Dickens, began to write about it autobiographically, as adult survivors of child abuse and neglect. In recent years, pediatricians and child psychiatrists have examined *Oliver Twist* as a case study in child abuse: see P. O. Brennan, *"Oliver Twist,* Textbook of

Child Abuse," *British Archives of Diseases of Childhood* 85 (2001): 504–505.

In the twenty-first century, psychoanalysts have begun to explore literary, art historical, operatic, and folkloric works (e.g., Grimm's fairy tales) as representations of child abuse. See D. L. Rosenblitt, "Where Do You Want the Killing Done? An Exploration of Hatred of Children," *Annual of Psychoanalysis* 36 (2008): 203–215. They ground their studies in various notions of projection and externalization, and reference the pioneering work by the analysts Bruno Bettelheim and Leonard Shengold. See Shengold's *Soul Murder* (Yale University Press, 1991), *Soul Murder Revisited* (Yale University Press, 1999), and *Haunted by Parents* (Yale University Press, 2007). See also D. W. Winnicott, "Hate in the Countertransference," in his *Collected Writings* (Basic, 1958), although Winnicott wrote more about the neglected children of depressed mothers than children who had been physically or sexually abused.

Many works on prejudice were published in the social science fields before World War II, but the field of Prejudice Studies did not appear until after the war, most notably with the psychoanalytically informed series Studies in Prejudice, of which T. Adorno et al., *The Authoritarian Personality* (Norton, 1951) was the best known. See also *Antisemitism: A Social Disease*, ed. Ernst Simmel (International Universities Press, 1948). In 1954, Gordon Allport surveyed the developing field in *The Nature of Prejudice*, a book that had tremendous influence. For historical overviews, see my *Anatomy of Prejudices* and "A Brief History of Prejudice Studies," in *The Future of Prejudice*, ed. Parens et al. (noted above). Scholars from various victim groups began to compare different prejudices in the early 1970s, soon after the word *sexism* came into use on the model of *racism*, but there is still no field of Comparative Prejudice Studies, so all prejudices continue to be treated as similar or variants on a single type. For a recent example, see the Norwegian anthropologist Marianne Gullestad's *Plausible Prejudice* (Universitetsforlaget, 2006), on the normalization of prejudice.

For an excellent history of theories of sex (including Aristotle's) that underlie sexism, see T. Lacquer, *Making Sex* (Harvard University Press, 1990). Sexism, racism, and anti-Semitism are extensively analyzed as narcissistic, hysterical, and obsessional prejudices in my *The Anatomy of Prejudices*. Mike Males coined the term "Scapegoat Generation" in *The Scapegoat Generation* (Common Courage Press, 1996).

The psychoanalytic literature on projection begins with Freud's 1911 work on paranoid delusions in his Schreber Case; see *The Standard Edition of the Complete Psychological Works of Sigmund Freud*, gen. ed. James Strachey (Hogarth, 1953–1974), vol. 12. Anna Freud, in her 1936 *The Ego and the Mechanisms of Defense*, coined the term *externalization* for—to take an example—a self-critical analysand's attribution of criticism to his or her analyst. Two helpful survey articles by J. and K. K. Novick, "Projection and Externalization" and "Externalization as a Pathological Form of Relating: The Dynamic Underpinnings of Abuse," appeared during the early 1970s and are collected in their *Fearful Symmetry: The Development and Treatment of Sadomasochism* (Aronson, 1996).

Characterology was an important part of psychoanalytic theory before World War II, particularly in Freud's social-theoretical writings of the 1930s and in the work of his Marxian-oriented younger followers such as Wilhelm Reich (*Character Analysis*, 1933; 3rd ed., Simon and Schuster, 1972) and Otto Fenichel, who wanted to link character study with the study of social characters. After the war this line of thought was central to the so-called Culture and Personality school at Columbia University and to "cultural Freudians" like Erich Fromm and Karen Horney. Since then, character study has been mostly confined to the realm of pathology and what are now known as character disorders (or personality disorders). See *Essential Papers on Character Disorders and Treatment*, ed. R. Lax (New York University Press, 1989). In my *Creative Characters* (Routledge, 1989), I sketched the history of psychoanalytic character study and also offered descriptions of the three Freudian character types in relation to types of creative expression. The only analyst that I know of who works with a threefold Freud-based characterology and uses it for social theory is Takeo Doi, in *The Anatomy of Dependence* (Kodansha, 1973), a book that had great influence in postwar Japan.

Chapter 2: Three Forms of Childism

A huge case-study and treatment literature exists about adults who were neglected and/or abused as children. Most of these works fall into one of the four categories defined in CAN: physical abuse, neglect, sexual abuse, and emotional abuse. When the study does not fit neatly into one of these categories the word *trauma* is often used to cover maltreatment generally. In 1990 Leonore Terr, in her very important *Too Scared to Cry* (Harper and Row, 1990), noted that in psychiatry up to that time, "childhood psychic trauma was assumed to be understood while simultaneously being ignored" (10). (I discuss this book further in Chapter 5.) Since 1990, however, the situation has changed.

Some recent trauma studies that I have found particularly valuable while treating Anna and other trauma survivors with extensive physical symptomatology are J. A. Chu,

Rebuilding Shattered Lives (Wiley, 1998), and R. C. Scaer, *The Body Bears the Burden: Trauma, Dissociation, and Disease* (Harvard Medical Press and Haworth, 2001). Also valuable is the survey collection by R. Lanius, E. Vermetten, and C. Pain, eds., *The Impact of Early Life Trauma on Health and Disease* (Cambridge University Press, 2010). Some recent work also considers traumatizers: see, for example, "The Aggressors" in S. Butler, *Conspiracy of Silence: The Trauma of Incest,* 2d ed. (Volcano, 1985).

The literature focused specifically on treating adult survivors of childhood sexual abuse includes many valuable studies, although most of them do not link sexual abuse with other abuse act types. Sexual abuse alone is addressed in the best-known psychoanalytic work in English: J. M. Davies and M. G. Frawley, *Treating Adult Survivors of Childhood Sexual Abuse* (Basic, 1994). *Lasting Effects of Child Sexual Abuse* (Sage, 1988), ed. G. Wyatt and G. Powell, offers important empirical essays. *Home Truths About Child Sexual Abuse: Influencing Policy and Practice—A Reader,* ed. C. Itzin (Routledge, 2000), offers a survey collection.

Memoir literature by adult survivors of childhood sexual abuse is illuminating for developing theories about how abuse experiences affect children. In 1992 the actress Suzanne Somers collected short memoirs by Hollywood stars who had been victims as children of various kinds of abuse in *Wednesday's Children* (Putnam); her own memoir *Keeping Secrets* (Warner, 1978) describes her experience as the daughter of a physically abusive alcoholic father. A study of incest memoirs (with a bibliography) is available in J. Doane and D. Hodges, *Telling Incest: Narratives of Dangerous Remembering from Stein to Sapphire* (University of Michigan Press, 2001); this takes up many topics and is especially thorough on writings by African American women. Louise Armstrong, whose incest memoir *Kiss Daddy Goodnight* (Pocket, 1978), was a pioneer in the genre, later published *Rocking the Cradle of Sexual Politics: What Happened When Women Said Incest* (Addison-Wesley, 1994).

In describing Anna's treatment, I allude to clinical concepts that are explored in my essays "Developmental Dreaming," *Canadian Journal of Psychoanalysis* 13 (2005):158–182, and "The Wise Baby as the Voice of the True Self," in *Where Do We Fall When We Fall In Love?* (Other Books, 2003).

Chapter 3: Child Abuse and Neglect

There is no comprehensive history of the scientific "discovery" of child abuse since Kempe's 1962 article on the battered child syndrome, which was republished in *The Battered Child* (Chicago, 1968; four later editions contained additional articles). Pollack and Steele's early work on abusing parents is in *The Battered Child*. Among the many informative short studies of the "discovery" are S. Pfoll, "The Discovery of Child Abuse," *Social Problems* 24 (1977): 310, J. Best, *Threatened Children: Rhetoric and Concern About Child-Victims* (Chicago University Press, 1993), which offers a good survey, and B. Nelson, *Making an Issue of Child Abuse: Political Agenda Setting for Social Problems* (Chicago University Press, 1984), which looks at the way child maltreatment came onto political and legislative agendas after 1962. J. E. B. Myers, *Child Protection in America: Past, Present, and Future* (Oxford University Press, 2006), is a good history of child protection, but does not extend to child policy generally.

Ruth and Henry Kempe summarized their pioneering work in *Child Abuse* (Harvard University Press, 1978). After Henry Kempe published "Sexual Abuse, Another Hidden Pediatric Problem" in *Pediatrics* 62 (1978): 382–389, the Kempes together wrote *The Common Secret* (Freeman, 1984), which deals specifically with child and adolescent sexual abuse. The Kempe Center for Prevention of Child Abuse and Neglect in Denver (www.kempe.org) continues their research tradition and now offers training courses for clinicians, lawyers, and children's-rights activists, as well as studies to establish criteria for identifying parents of newborns at risk of becoming abusers and to develop prevention programs. Steele and Pollack's emphasis on "role reversal" was indebted to a very influential brief article: M. Morris and R. Gould, "Role Reversal: A Necessary Conception Dealing with the Battered Child Syndrome," *American Journal of Orthopsychiatry* (March, 1963): 298–299. Among psychoanalytic journals in America, the *Journal of Orthopsychiatry* was (and still is) one of the most attentive to child abuse, as well as to psychoanalytic social theory.

The 1968 edition of *The Battered Child* contained a brief article by Samuel X. Radbill, "A History of Child Abuse and Infanticide," and since then numerous short histories (including another article by Radbill in the 1980 edition of *The Battered Child*) have studied child abuse in different periods and places. For the background of child abuse in America see P. Greven, *The American Temperament: Child-Rearing, Religious Experience and the Self in Early America* (Knopf, 1977), and C. Degler, *At Odds: Women and the Family in America from the Revolution to the Present* (Oxford University Press, 1980). In 1973, Richard Light published a survey, "Abused and Neglected Children in America," *Harvard Educational Review* 43. From the 1970s I have found only one effort to study child abuse and neglect cross-culturally, the interesting (and subsequently neglected) work of Ronald Rodner: *They Love Me, They Love Me Not: A Worldwide Study of the Effects of Parental Acceptance and Rejection* (Human Relations Area Files Press, 1975). Later, more cross-cultural work appeared, including J. Korbin, *Child Abuse and Neglect: Cross Cultural Perspectives* (University of California Press, 1983), and N. Scheper-Hughes, ed., *Child Survival: Anthropological Perspectives on the Treatment and Maltreatment of Children* (Springer, 1987). Beatrice and John Whiting's *Children of Six Cultures* (Harvard University Press, 1975) was standard-setting for the next decade of anthropological study.

In the clinical social work literature available before Kempe's "battered child" theory became well known, I think that the finest study is the one I refer to here and will return to several times: Leontine Young's *Wednesday's Children: A Study of Child Neglect and Abuse* (McGraw-Hill, 1964). Edgar Merrill's typology appears in a thirty-page pamphlet put out by the American Humane Association in 1962, "Protecting the Battered Child," which was published soon after Kempe delivered his paper to the American Medical Association. The pamphlet marks a shift away from the sort of work the Children's Division of the American Humane Association had sponsored during the 1950s, when the Association had emphasized social casework with parents who could not or would not care properly for their children. The AHA director, Vincent De Francis, whose *Fundamentals of Child Protection* came out in 1955 from the Association, believed that bad parents produced bad children, who spread their corruption as relentlessly as a bacillus. Social workers needed to be trained to spot parental "moral and spiritual neglect," which would be manifested in such symptoms as "disrespect for authority, disregard for the property rights of others, immorality, licentiousness, obscenity, profanity, and possibly sexual deviations." Moral and spiritual neglect were "highly contagious and communicable parental patterns which too readily and

too often contaminate children exposed to them at home."
Again and again, De Francis stressed "the deleterious effect
of a home climate polluted by a smog of crime, immorality, or
irreligion." In effect, De Francis harbored what I call an obsessional childist prejudice, viewing the parents as people
who should be rounded up and punished and seeing their
children as carbon copies of them.

This kind of prejudice, which De Francis had great
influence in promoting, had also been common at the end of
the nineteenth century, when children who needed help were
classified as destitute, delinquent, or neglected (see Chapter
7 and notes below). After World War I, there had been a national panic over child sexual abuse, committed not by such
bad parents but by strangers or psychopaths. A similar upheaval after World War II was even more intense, and it was
fed by ominous articles from J. Edgar Hoover, director of the
FBI. His "How Safe Is Your Daughter?" (*American Magazine*,
July 1947) trumpeted frightening statistics on child rape—
committed, again, by strangers, but this time strangers who
infiltrated the homes. The strangers he conjured up resembled the Communist strangers from the Soviet Union that
Senator Joseph McCarthy was soon afterward describing
(also in an obsessional, paranoid manner) as an organized
conspiracy infiltrating the State Department. Like the panic
McCarthy instigated, Hoover's panic mobilized legislators
and prosecutors, who were attracted by Vincent De Francis's
moral cleansing, family punishing approach.

In the early 1960s, progressives like Edgar Merrill
abandoned the De Francis mode. They had been trained
when Freudian social psychology and characterology were
dominant, and the Oedipus complex, both normal and pathological, was an important model. They were familiar with
the earlier psychoanalytic literature, which contained occa-

sional pieces on why parents abuse their children, such as Gregory Zilborg's "Depressive Reactions Related to Parenthood," *American Journal of Psychiatry* (1931): 10. As parenthood became a greater focus among analysts, the number of studies of parental maltreatment increased. E. J. Anthony and T. Benedek, eds., *Parenthood: Its Psychology and Psychopathology* (Little, Brown, 1970), offers a survey of much of this work, including a Steele and Pollack paper on parents who physically abuse their children. In America, the most important leader in parenthood studies was Selma Fraiberg, an associate of Anna Freud's, whose work on intergenerational transmission of trauma (for which she coined the phrase "ghosts in the nursery") can be sampled in *Selected Writings of Selma Fraiberg* (Ohio State University Press, 1987). Most of her key essays from the 1970s were first collected in *Clinical Studies in Infant Mental Health* (Basic, 1980).

Progressive social workers in the 1960s tried to use the work done by Merrill and others on abusing parents to create typologies that would help in assessment and in decisions about how to treat parents and keep families together. The best survey that I know was a two-part article, "The Abused Child," in the October 1966 and January 1967 issues of *Social Work*, in which Serapio Richard Zalba offered a typology of abusing parents (and cited the other social work in this area). Zalba also identified the terminological problem in Kempe's "battered child syndrome" work: "A more appropriate label would be 'families with child-battering adults'—without the term 'syndrome,' since there is no clearly defined entity that can be identified."

In the 1970s, there was little empirical work besides that of Kempe's group that was specifically focused on parental motivations to abuse. Among the few studies were J. Spinetta and D. Rigler, "The Child-Abusing Parent: A Psychological

Review," *Psychological Bulletin* 77 (1972): 296–304; W. Friedrich and K. Wheeler, "The Abusing Parent Revisited: A Decade of Psychological Research," *Journal of Nervous and Mental Disease* 10 (1982): 577–587; and D. Wolfe, "Child-Abusive Parents: An Empirical Review and Analysis," *Psychological Bulletin* 97 (1985): 462–482. Wolfe's article replaced the Steele and Pollack "psychiatric model" of a single abusing parental type displaying a character defect—inability to control aggression—with a focus on "situational events" and stressors in parents' lives, including poverty. Following Wolfe, the literature on abusers put more emphasis on social conditions, "risk factors" in the environment, and other outside problems than on motivations (conscious or unconscious) or character types. A psychoanalyst, Marvin Blumberg, in his "Psychopathology of the Abusing Parent" (*American Journal of Psychotherapy* 28 [1974]: 21–29), applauded the disappearance of Merrill's "typology" of abusers, although he gave no explanation for his rejection of it.

In "Child Abuse: An Emerging Social Priority" in the January 1978 issue of *Social Work,* Stephen Antler reviewed the problems raised by the medical and psychiatric approaches to child abuse of the Kempes and others. He noted diminished attention to parental motivation as well as to helping families and parents through social work. By the late 1970s and early 1980s, it was widely recognized that the child protection effort in America had become disorganized: see the discussion in B. Markham, "Child Abuse Intervention: Conflicts in Current Practice and Legal Theory," *Pediatrics* 65 (1980): 180–185.

Social workers have discussed the legislative history of CAN in such works as L. Costin, H. Karger, and D. Stoesz, *The Politics of Child Abuse in America* (Oxford University Press, 1996), and, more recently, Duncan Lindsey, *The Wel-*

fare of Children (Oxford University Press, 2004). For Jolly K.'s story, see J. Barthel, "A Cruel Inheritance," *Life*, June 1974, 73–82. I know of no history of the Child Abuse Treatment and Prevention Act of 1974 and its many revisions, which reflect the growing conservatism and "family values" orientation of the Congress. But the evolving legislation illustrates how crucial the concept of the "battered child syndrome" and the 1970s sociological literature, which dealt only with physical abuse, were to the revisions. Among the important studies influencing this legislation is D. G. Gil, *Violence Against Children: Physical Abuse in the United States* (Harvard University Press, 1970). Nonetheless, "the battered child syndrome" never found a place in the public health services guides, such as the International Classification of Diseases (ICD) issued by the World Health Organization or the comparable ICD published by the U.S. Public Health Service since 1959. The "syndrome" was so narrowly conceived, without consideration of causes or wider social and cultural references, that epidemiologists found it impracticable for classifying the problem. Further, the syndrome was never connected to evolving ideas about children's developmental needs and the diversity of childrearing practice across America and around the world. (Similarly, Child Protective Services departments were often bureaucratically unrelated to child welfare and education services.) In America, child battering became the phenomenon to which all other ways of harming children were compared by analogy as they were "discovered," lessening the likelihood that a viable, cohesive public health approach to maltreatment would be found. For a survey, see J. Leventhal, "Epidemiology of Child Sexual Abuse," in R. K. Oates, ed., *Understanding and Managing Child Sexual Abuse* (Saunders, 1990). Eli Newberger of the Harvard Medical School was one of the most persistent critics of the narrow medicalization of child abuse, and consistently called for an "ecological" approach; see, for example, E. H. Newberger et al., "Pediatric Social Illness: Toward an Etiologic Classification," *Pediatrics* 60 (August 1977): 178–85.

In the early 1970s, some social workers recognized that progressive policies aimed at promoting child welfare were being abandoned, and that this trend was connected to the way concern for children was narrowing down to concern for child abuse. Government programs began to focus on parents' rights rather than children's developmental needs. President Nixon was changing the focus of all previous White House Conferences on Children to a conservative, "family values" agenda that stressed noninterference from government agencies. June Axinn and Herman Levin assessed the trend in their introduction to *The Century of the Child: Progress and Retreat* (University of Pennsylvania School of Social Work, 1973): "The years 1900 to 1970 were marked by a shift from mass care [like orphanages] to individualization of services to children, a shift from the obligations of children and the rights of parents to a concern for children's rights and parental duties. Simultaneously, the shift resulted in growing governmental responsibility for children, an acknowledgement of a responsibility for the protection of all children, black and white, rich and poor alike, in all circumstances that touch upon their ability to use their physical, mental, and social potentialities to their own fullest advantage. . . . The view now appears to be that societal stability [and full employment] rather than the development of a child's individual potential is of prime importance. There is a fiscal and ideological retreat from what might have been a century centered on children." On this history see also C. R. Margolin,

"The Movement for Children's Rights in Historical Context," *Social Problems* 25, no. 4 (1978): 441.

Chapter 4: The Politicization of Child Abuse

Vance Packard's *Our Endangered Children: Growing Up in a Changing World* (Little Brown, 1983) was received respectfully, but at the same time often dismissed as exaggerated or naive. Anatole Broyard, for example, writing in the *New York Times Book Review* (August 19, 1983) noted: "When we are told that parents' narcissism is a serious threat to children, we may ask ourselves whether it was ever different. Isn't it true that before we knew the word narcissism many parents simply and traditionally put their own concerns before those of their children? Were people, even parents, ever preponderantly unselfish?" Christopher Lasch, on whose *The Culture of Narcissism* (Norton, 1979) Packard drew for his study, had earlier published *Haven in a Heartless World: The Family Besieged* (Basic, 1977), discussing the problems besetting children and their parents. A former Marxist, Lasch had criticized the left's ideological belief in progress, which he considered narcissistic and to which he attributed both the left's failure to thrive in the 1970s and its own contribution to the endangerment of children: see *The True and Only Heaven: Progress and Its Critics* (Norton, 1991).

Others who raised questions about the "anti-child culture" (though they did not always identify it as such) include N. Postman, *The Disappearance of Childhood* (Laurel, 1982); M. Winn, *Children Without Childhood* (Pantheon, 1983); and L. C. Pogrebin, "Do Americans Hate Children?" *Ms.*, November 1983. See also the work of the psychologist David Elkind, such as *The Hurried Child* (Addison-Wesley, 1980).

The chief inspiration of the Children's Liberation writers in the United States was Paul Goodman's *Growing Up Absurd* (Random House, 1960; Basic, 1970), but they also looked to the English progressive educationalist A. S. Neill's *The Free Child* (1952; available online at www.thebluecrane. com) and *Summerhill* (1960, with a foreword by Erich Fromm; St. Martin's 1996). On the English "radical pedagogy" movement see also Jonathan Croall, ed., *All the Best, Neill: Letters from Summerhill* (Deutsch, 1983). John Holt's *Escape from Childhood* (Ballantine, 1974) was one of the leading educational Children's Liberation texts; among psychologists, the leader was Richard Farson, author of *Birthrights* (Macmillan, 1974). A 2005 retrospective on the Children's Liberation writers and their argument that children should be accorded adult rights such as the franchise can be found in Jane Fontin's excellent *Children's Rights and the Developing Law*, 2d ed. (Cambridge University Press). See also M. Freedman, *The Rights and Wrongs of Children* (Pinter, 1983).

I discuss the genesis and background of Anna Freud, Albert Solnit, and Joseph Goldstein's three-volume *In the Best Interests of the Child* in my biography *Anna Freud* (2d ed., Yale University Press, 2008). Their work is often criticized for privileging "family preservation," but that criticism misrepresents the book, which is organized rather around understanding children's needs at different developmental stages and finding ways to be sure those needs are met by "psychological parents" (that is, adults—not necessarily biological parents—who have caring and empathetic relationships with the child).

Since 1977, David Finkelhor, now director of the Crimes Against Children Research Center and co-director of the Family Research Laboratory at the University of New Hampshire, has been the most prolific sociologist writing on child sexual abuse. His first decade of work was summarized in *Sourcebook on Child Sexual Abuse* (Sage, 1986). More recently, in *Child Victimization* (Oxford University Press, 2008), he has tried to unify and integrate knowledge about the diverse forms of child victimization in a field he has termed Developmental Victimology. Although this approach does not focus on the motivations of children's abusers, it does encourage consultation with children of different developmental stages about their abuse experience and is far more integrative than approaches that isolate one type of victimizing act. (I discuss this issue further in Chapter 5.)

The first American feminist who linked concern with women's liberation to concern with children's liberation was Shulamith Firestone in *The Dialectics of Sex* (Morrow, 1970), but her goal was the "abolition of the family," and her claim that "racism is sexism extended," part of the common concern to identify a single root prejudice from which all others derive, drew objections from critics that it was "white solipsism." Florence Rush's *The Best Kept Secret: Sexual Abuse of Children* (McGraw-Hill, 1980) was very thorough, offering historical background, legal commentary, and case studies, and stressing throughout the tendency of societies to blame the child victims; she was identifying, in my terminology, the childism of child sexual abuse. Since then, there have been hundreds of volumes on sexual abuse, therapy with children and adults, and the legal and criminal aspects of the problem. For an early historian's account, see L. Gordon, "The Politics of Child Sexual Abuse," *Feminist Review* 28 (1988): 56–64.

The topic of Freud's (or psychoanalysis') avoidance of child sexual abuse or of trauma in general in favor of emphasis on unconscious fantasies, particularly Oedipal fantasies, is complex, and the literature on it is often polemical. Although

Florence Rush was a pioneer in the criticism of Freudian psychoanalysis, Jeffrey Masson's *The Assault on Truth* (1984; Penguin, 1985) and his edition of Freud's 1890s letters to Wilhelm Fliess (Harvard University Press, 1985), in which Freud reconsidered his "seduction hypothesis" (the idea that actual seductions in childhood are the origin of later obsessional and hysterical symptoms), were widely influential on later feminist critiques of Freud. Masson's accusations—for example, that Freud "suppressed" the truth because he was concerned about his reputation in the Viennese psychiatric community—were widely accepted in the 1980s, often overshadowing the more general (and often correct) claims that Freud's ideas about female development were inadequate. Many have protested Masson's conclusions, but many have also elaborated on them, including Alice Miller (among psychoanalysts) and various academic cultural critics (for a sampling, see F. C. Crews, *The Memory Wars: Freud's Legacy in Dispute* [New York Review of Books, 1995] and Crews, ed., *Unauthorized Freud: Doubters Confront a Legend* [Viking, 1998]). Psychoanalysts did, indeed, underemphasize trauma, but they did not usually ignore it or suppress it: see for example S. Furst, ed., *Psychic Trauma* (Basic, 1967), which long preceded the Freud controversy. In 1981, Kempe co-edited with P. Mrazek a volume titled *Sexually Abused Children and Their Families* (Pergamon), to which Anna Freud contributed "A Psychoanalyst's View of Sexual Abuse by Parents." She concluded: "Far from existing only as a phantasy, incest is thus also a fact, more widespread among the population in certain periods than others. Where the chances of harming a child's normal developmental growth are concerned, it ranks higher than abandonment, neglect, physical maltreatment or any other form of abuse. It would be a fatal mistake to underrate either the importance or the frequency of its actual occurrence." Now that the Freud controversy has died down, the intermixtures in children's abuse experiences of real traumas and their fantasies and *reactive* fantasies are being studied.

By the 1990s, there were some studies of sexual offenders that went beyond the classifications of them used by Kempe and others in the 1970s. See S. Ingersoll and S. Patton, *Treating Perpetrators of Sexual Abuse* (Lexington, 1990). The authors consider typologies of pedophiles developed by A. Nicholas Groth (*Sexual Assault of Children and Adolescents* [Lexington, 1978]) and Ray Helfer's "WAR (World of Abnormal Rearing) Cycle," which was one of the first detailed studies of intergenerational transmission of abuse; see his *The Diagnostic Process and Treatment Programs* (Department of Health, Education and Welfare Publication # OHDS 77 30069, 1977).

Criminology is generally not given to single-type constructions like Anna C. Salter's "predator"; see, for example, J. Holfgott, *Criminal Behavior: Theories, Typologies, and Criminal Justice* (Sage, 2008). Sampling the criminology-typology literature, I found one book that strikes me as remarkably free of authorial prejudices and corresponding research prejudices: *Inside the Mind of Sexual Offenders: Predatory Rapists, Pedophiles, and Criminal Profiles* (Universal, 2001) by Dennis J. Stevens of the University of Massachusetts, Boston. An unpretentious researcher with no national reputation, Stevens built up his general typology—his criminal profiles— carefully, keeping an open mind and explicitly avoiding the construction of a single predator sex-criminal type. Stevens assigned students in his prison classes to tape open-ended interviews with their cellmates, thus avoiding much of the remoteness from reality that troubles academic research. He could also compare the unfiltered confessions that sex offenders made to their fellow prisoners with those he got by the same interview means from other kinds of criminals. The three criminal profiles (character studies) he arrived at are similar to the ones identified in 1962 through similarly low-key inductive empirical methods by Edgar Merrill and his Massachusetts social work team.

The character type Merrill identifies as the angry narcissistically wounded abuser who rights wrongs that he or she has suffered by hurting others is what Stevens calls a Righteous Criminal. Righteous Criminals see themselves as upholding justice in the community, operating as "morality police" by, for example, asserting that sex with children is good for the children, either because it is God's will or because it prepares them for life. This moralistic type views him- or herself as battling with prudes who try to deny children—and women—natural sexual activity. The Righteous Criminal's world is one of competing moral identities in which he or she must win by any means necessary. Where Merrill saw a second, obsessional type, dedicated to asserting control and disciplining children in extreme ways, Stevens saw a Control Criminal, moved by intense, unbearable feelings of inferiority and insecurity, trying to gain power (including economic) over others. Motivated by a compelling need to make the world predictable, the Control Criminal develops rituals of order (or calculated disorder). The Control Criminal needs to be the center of this world of scarce resources, warding off anxiety, making the rules that exclude or eradicate others. This type might commit aggravated assault, armed robbery, and various kinds of torture—including the physical or sexual torture of children. Merrill's third type, described as passive and dependent, immature, suffering from a lack of identity, and lashing out at or seducing children in the hope of receiving care, attention, or parenting from them, is Stevens's Hedonist Criminal. This is a thrill-seeking, pleasure-oriented character, given to establishing scenarios of pleasure, often with child victims who are incapable of defending themselves or resisting the Hedonist's manipulations. Part of the Hedonist's pleasure lies in shocking the victim (a pleasure common among sexual exhibitionists). In Stevens's interviews, the Hedonists were distinguished by their limited attention span and their concreteness: they related to their environments by touch, always moving their bodies, exploring with their hands, manipulating circumstances in every way possible.

Chapter 5: Mass Hysteria and Child Sexual Abuse

Lester Adelson had written on child abuse in "Slaughter of the Innocents" (*New England Journal of Medicine* 264 [1961]) before he published "Homicide by Starvation: The Nutritional Variant of the 'Battered Child'" (*Journal of the American Medical Association* 186 [1963]: 458–460). Following *Damaged Parents: An Anatomy of Child Neglect* (Chicago University Press, 1981), by Norman Polansky and colleagues, the term "apathy-futility syndrome" became central to discussions of neglectful parents, particularly mothers. This concept connected Polansky's work with psychoanalytic work, especially that influenced by D. W. Winnicott, on the children of depressed mothers. Child analysts do not as often use the word *neglectful* as social workers do; they speak of unavailability, unrelatedness, and depression. Sometimes, following Andre Green, they speak of "the dead mother."

If there was one book that could be said to have precipitated the SRA panic, it was *Michelle Remembers*, which presents a woman diagnosed as having Multiple Personality Disorder but whose MPD appears to have been the creation of suggestions made by her psychiatrist (and later husband), Lawrence Pazder, who had a background in Catholic missionary work in Africa, where he had studied the Church of Satan. Dr. Pazder suggested to Michelle that what she was describing sounded like the African Church of Satan rituals; he later, as an expert in SRA and MPD, testified in the Mc-Martin Preschool trial, as well as—by his own count—a thousand other trials. Pazder later became a celebrity, appearing throughout the Anglophone world on talk shows, where he argued that whether "recovered memories" of SRA are true or false *does not matter* to a patient talking about abuse in therapy. What matters is what the child or the adult survivor *thinks* happened. Healing can begin when the child or the adult survivor can reveal what she or he, with a therapist's help, thinks happened, regardless of what these thoughts mean for the patient's sense of reality, or for those accused of crimes. This, in my judgment, is a profoundly and perversely abusive narcissistic childist attitude: it says that statements that serve the therapist's idea of what is good and healing for the patient are what matter to the patient, rather than the truth, or the patient's actual experience, or the effect these "memories" might have on the lives of other people.

As the satanic ritual abuse panic subsided, researchers tried to assess what had happened. David Finkelhor's early assessment, *Nursery Crimes: Sexual Abuse in Day Care* (Sage, 1988), relied on a faulty methodology and offered no firsthand investigation, but better assessments appeared later, including P. and S. Eberle, *The Abuse of Innocence: The McMartin Preschool Trial* (Prometheus, 1993); K. Faller, *Understanding and Assessing Child Sexual Maltreatment* (Sage, 2003); and R. McNally, *Remembering Trauma* (Harvard University Press, 2005). Jean LaFontaine's report for the British Department of Health, *Speak of the Devil: Allegations of Satanic Abuse in Britain* (Cambridge University Press), was published in 1998. And from the psychoanalytic community came *Recovered Memories of Abuse: True or False?* edited by J. Sandler and P. Fonagy of the Anna Freud Centre (Karnac, 1997).

Carol Tavris and Eliot Aronson's recent *Mistakes Were Made (But Not by Me)* (Harvest, 2007) is an important general reflection on the threat to truth in this decade (1983–1993) of moral panic. Among other topics, the authors consider the "confirmation bias" among people who believed the stories of SRA: for these people, lack of evidence that children have been harmed is taken as proof of "how clever and evil the cult leaders were: they were eating those babies bones and all."

As noted, the SRA panic and the rethinking it generated among clinicians and social workers helped break down the rigid four types of abuse classification because the phenomenon compelled investigations of accusations of multiple abuses, not just single types. This questioning coincided with the virtual breakdown of the Child Protective Services and the foster care system. Debates began about whether and how CPS was intruding into family life and threatening "family preservation," which was the goal of most conservative policy makers but also of some liberals who thought more needed to be done to treat abusers and offer therapy to abusing families.

But the process of questioning CAN categories had begun in the 1980s, when there were some who had seen child abuse as a relationship between an abuser and a child; see, for example, A. Kadushin and J. Martin, *Child Abuse—An Interactional Event* (Columbia University Press, 1981). A few researchers had also begun to assume that the distinct types of abuse acts had common effects on children (cognitive deficits, dissociation, PTSD, disturbed affective states, relationship problems or "intimacy issues," a tendency to suicide, substance abuse, and so on); see, for example, J. Briere, *Child Abuse Trauma: Theory and Treatment of the Lasting Effects* (Sage, 1992). These approaches informed work on emotional abuse, which was eventually conceptualized as involving multiple types of acts. But at first emotional abuse was analogized to the battered child syndrome: see J. Garbarino et al., *The Psychologically Battered Child* (Jossey-Bass, 1986), following up on Gabarino's influential study "The Abusive Crime of Emotional Abuse," *Child Abuse and Neglect* 3 (1979). Later it was outlined more distinctly, as in M. Brassard, R. Germain, and S. Hart, *Psychological Maltreatment of Children and Youth* (Pergamon, 1987), and J. Belsky, "Psychological Maltreatment: Definitional Limitations and Unstated Assumptions" (*Development and Psychopathology* 3 [1991]:31–36), which raised questions about abuse-type classifications but failed to pursue them.

Traumatology was originally a field of medicine focused on the study of traumatic physical injury and surgical trauma, but in the 1980s Traumatology and Psychotraumatology developed out of it. This process was related to the growing use of the term "domestic violence" (dating from the late 1970s) for all kinds of trauma to women and children in households; estimates began to emerge from the Centers for Disease Control and Prevention in the early 1980s that 10 percent of American children were involved in or witnesses to domestic violence. The subfields of Traumatology are explored in K. Tal, *Worlds of Hurt: Reading the Literatures of Trauma* (Cambridge University Press, 1995). The Lenore Terr article I discuss is "Childhood Trauma: An Outline and Overview," *American Journal of Psychiatry* 148 (January 1991): 10–20. Judith Herman's *Trauma and Recovery: The Aftermath of Violence—from Domestic Abuse to Political Terror* (Basic, 1992) is the most important work on PTSD as a general concept covering all kinds of trauma. A diversity of approaches are gathered in D. Cicchetti and S. Toth, eds., *Developmental Perspectives on Trauma: Theory, Research, and Intervention* (University of Rochester Press, 1998). "The Adverse Childhood Experiences (ACE)" appeared in *The American Journal of Preventative Medicine* 14, no. 4 (1998), and a newsletter for it began in 2003; the ongoing research project can be accessed at www.acestudy.org.

Chapter 6: Forms of Childism in Families

The literature on treating abused children (and their families) psychoanalytically is very rich, although until recently it continued to be divided into abuse types. A good example in the subfield of sexual abuse is W. Friedrich, *Psychotherapy of Sexually Abused Children and Their Families* (Norton, 1990), which has a comprehensive bibliography. The literature on abusers is extensive but often misconceived, and there is little attempt to construct a typology on grounds other than the types of act committed. The state of the research into child abuse is well summarized by a British social worker, Christopher Bagley, using British, Canadian, and American studies in *Child Abusers: Research and Treatment* (Universal, 2003). Bagley had himself participated in a Canadian study that showed the frequency with which abused children are abused in multiple ways and the significance of the emotional abuse—specifically the betrayal of the child's trust in his or her parents—that is ubiquitous in the abused population. This survey is not psychoanalytically oriented and makes little use of children's testimony or revelations in therapy.

The literature on divorce is huge and diverse. Within psychoanalysis, the work of Judith Wallerstein, which she summarized in *The Unexpected Legacy of Divorce: A 25-Year*

Landmark Study (Hyperion, 2000), has most influenced the increasing appreciation of the traumatizing effects of divorce on children, as well as of the different kinds of divorces and traumas involved.

Psychoanalytic efforts to understand the internalization of prejudice began with Freud's concept of "identification with the aggressor," which Anna Freud elaborated in *The Ego and the Mechanisms of Defense* (1936; International Universities Press, 1956). There is, by this time, a good deal of confusion in the psychoanalytic literature about terms like internalization, identification, incorporation, introjection. For understanding internalized racism, works, whether autobiographical or fictional, by victims of prejudice are often more informative—as, for example, Ralph Ellison's *The Invisible Man* (Random House, 1952) or the novels or essays of James Baldwin. The effect of internalizing prejudice that I am stressing—psychic splitting into an internalized oppressor and an internalized oppressed—seems to me the effect that is common to all forms of childism.

Chapter 7: Education and the End of Childism

In the decade from 2000 to 2010, two words were coined for the individuals and movements that were anti-child, privileging "family values" and parental rights: *familialism* and *adultism*. But unlike *childism*, these little-known words do not express what is happening from the perspective and experience of children. The target of the prejudice is missing.

Most of the current books dealing with the worsening situation for American children are about adolescents, but what they say can be applied to younger children. Henry Giroux's *Youth in a Suspect Society: Beyond the Politics of Dis-*

posability (Palgrave, 2009) builds on Males's *The Scapegoat Generation* and his *Framing Youth* (Common Courage, 1999).

On a global scale, UNICEF most consistently sees the situation of children in terms of public health; among its many reports on the condition of the world's children is "Childhood Under Threat," which was analyzed in the *New York Times* (Dec. 10, 2004): "More than a billion children—over half the children in the world—suffer extreme deprivation because of war, H.I.V./AIDS or poverty. . . . While there have been gains in reducing death rates of young children and in increasing the number of children in school, the report said that some of the progress made over the last decade and a half had been off-set by the toll taken by AIDS and H.I.V. and wars, particularly the 55 civil wars since 1990. . . . Nearly half the 3.6 million people killed in wars since 1990 were children, reflecting the fact that civilians increasingly have become the victims in contemporary conflicts. . . . The report said that global military spending was about $956 billion, while the cost of effectively combating poverty would be about $40 to $70 billion." On violence-prevention work done through the United Nations and the World Health Organization, see later in this chapter.

Around 2000, researchers within the field of CAN began to assess the field's programmatic successes and failures and link them to public health policy. See J. Macleod and G. Nelson, "Programs for the Promotion of Family Wellness and the Prevention of Child Maltreatment: A Meta-Analytic Review," *Child Abuse and Neglect* 24 (2000): 1127–1149. In "The Prevention of Child Abuse and Neglect: Successfully out of the Blocks," *Child Abuse and Neglect* 25 (2001): 431–439, John Leventhal notes the establishment of Healthy Families programs throughout the United States in which a trained social worker or a nurse operates as a home-visitor to promote the healthy development of mothers and their infants.

There are many theories and stage frameworks within the field of Child Development, but there is also much agreement about what children need for healthy development. For a survey see L. Berk, *Infants, Children, and Adolescents* (Allyn and Bacon, 2005). An overview from the point of view of psychoanalysis is P. Fonagy and M. Target, *Psychoanalytic Theories: Perspectives from Developmental Psychopathology* (Whurr, 2002). And an example of current psychoanalytic infant research comes from Tessa Baradon and colleagues of the Anna Freud Centre: *The Practice of Psychoanalytic Parent-Infant Psychotherapy* (Routledge, 2005).

Histories of the nineteenth-century child-savers sometimes focus on a single category of children, as, for example, A. M. Platt, *The Child-Savers: The Invention of Delinquency* (2d ed., Chicago, 1977), which discusses the delinquent. But there are also good general histories, such as Viviana Zelizer's important *Pricing the Priceless Child: The Changing Social Value of Children* (Basic, 1985), from which (p. 67) the quotation about "a nation of paupers and thieves" is taken. Charles Loring Brace's main statement of his (childist) view is *The Dangerous Classes of New York, and Twenty Years of Work Among Them* (1872; Echo Library, 2010). Homer Folks, a progressive Harvard-trained sociologist, published *The Care of Destitute, Neglected, and Delinquent Children* (Macmillan, 1902).

Jane Addams, the head of Hull House settlement in Chicago, was among those most aware that a way of thinking—a prejudice—had determined how the philanthropic child-savers viewed children, and specifically child labor. Writing in 1899, Addams examined the philanthropists' "industrial view." (This was the name she gave to the view that what is good for industry and the adults running and profiting from industries is good for everybody.) Addams was arguing that a philanthropic child-saver, intent on the mission of making a family nonproblematic (and satisfying the charitable conscience), would be inclined to advise a young boy to work for his family's upkeep and get the family off the dole. But this philanthropist would fail to see that "the boy who attempts prematurely to support his widowed mother may lower wages, add an illiterate member to the community, and arrest the development of a capable workman." When children do not develop in a healthy way, because they are pushed into taking care of their parents in a role reversal, they and the whole society suffer (see the collection of Addams's reflections, *Democracy and Social Ethics* [Macmillan, 1902]).

The progressives were also inspired by the work of, among others, Robert Spargo, an English-born coalminer and labor-union organizer who became a lay Methodist minister and socialist reformer. In 1906, he published a "scientific scrutiny," *The Bitter Cry of the Children* (Macmillan), which quickly became the classic of the progressive child-welfare movement. With his files of statistics and reports, interviews with school principals and pediatricians, photographs of diseased children, and descriptions of child laborers *based on interviews with children*—particularly with boys working ten-hour days in coalmines as he had done when he was a boy—Spargo was one of the first child-welfare writers to see all facets of children's suffering as stemming from one problem: failure to guarantee "equality of opportunity as the child's birthright." His unifying concept was not the prejudice childism, but his idea of a "birthright" was a step in the direction of supplying the future Children's Rights Movement with the concept that human rights are indivisible and an emphasis on adults' obligation toward child development.

Much of the childist prejudice dressed up as science

used in early-twentieth-century American schools originated in Germany, but a good deal of it came from England and had been produced by men who misunderstood Darwin, such as Francis Galton, the author of *Hereditary Genius* (1869). Galton was obsessed with the idea that child geniuses could be bred and nongeniuses trained into submission and enjoined not to become parents, so that their inferior stock would eventually disappear. America produced its own eugenics theorists, too, and a cast of these characters can be found in the historian Daniel Kevles's *In the Name of Eugenics* (Knopf, 1985). The most influential U.S. exponent of the school as factory was H. H. Goddard of the Princeton University Psychology Department, whose *Human Efficiency* (Princeton University Press, 1920) offered psychometric advice to the corporate-sponsored schools about how to use testing to organize worker-bee students into "the perfect hive."

There are many histories of the Children's Rights Movement. For the U.S. story, I recommend J. M. Hawes, *The Children's Rights Movement: A History of Advocacy and Protection* (Twayne, 1991), and for the global situation, M. Ensalaco and K. Majka, *Children's Human Rights: Progress and Challenges for Children World-Wide* (Rowman and Littlefield, 2005), and T. O'Neill and D. Zinga, eds., *Children's Rights* (University of Toronto Press, 2008). The Children's Rights Information Network Web site is located at www.crin.org/resources.

On the Swedish initiative against corporal punishment see L. F. Sanders, "Sweden's Unique Approach to Child Protection," in the journal *Child Abuse and Neglect* Reports, 104 (March 1979). For two later assessments, see J. E. Durrant, "The Swedish Ban on Corporal Punishment: Its History and Effects," and A. W. Edefelt, "The Swedish 1979 Aga Ban Plus Fifteen," both in *Family Violence Against Children: A*

Challenge for Society, ed. D. Frehsee, W. Horn, K.-D. Buss-
mann (de Gruyter, 1996).

The International Decade for the Promotion of a Culture of Peace and Non-Violence for the Children of the World
has a Web site at http://www.decade-culture-of-peace.org/.

Index

An asterisk beside a person's name indicates a pseudonym.

Elaine*, 262–264
emotional abuse
  added to CAN classification, 214,
    217–219
  difficulty of identifying in isolation,
    219
  in early child-abuse studies, 119
  link with all types of abuse, 178,
    215–216, 219
  not covered during CAPTA
    hearings, 137
  recognized in social work, 214–216
envy, as part of prejudices, 54–55
ephebophobia, 8, 34
Euripides, 38
Europe
  child development studies and
    legislation, 126–127
  effect of World War II on children,
    271
European Network of Ombudsmen
  for Children, 294
Evil Incarnate (Frankfurter), 197
expectations, as developmental need,
  277–278

false accusation syndrome, 206–208
Faludi, Susan, 151
family
  with all three forms of childism,
    229–230
  and development of hysterical
    character, 49–50
  and development of male narcis-
    sism, 52
  and development of obsessional
    character, 50–51
  feminist revolt against common
    structure, 114
  hysterical childism case studies,
    241–244
  hysterical childism characteristics,
    239–241
  lack of support from CPS, 124–125
  legislative preservation of, 136

multiple abusers in, 198
  narcissistic childism case studies,
    248–257
  narcissistic childism characteris-
    tics, 245–248
  narcissistic divorce case studies,
    257–265
  neglectful, 71–72
  obsessional childism case studies,
    230–238
  as owner of children, 57
  sexual abuse in, 163–167, 168–169
  sexual abuse policies about,
    177–178
  U.N. commitment toward, 10
Family Rights Association, 130
"family values" argument
  challenged by sexual abuse in
    families, 186
  to oppose child advocates, 56, 142,
    152
  to oppose Child Development Act,
    125–131
  to oppose daycares, 196, 203
  to oppose government interference
    through CPS, 124, 139
  to promote "workfare" program, 185
  Reagan's campaign, 140
  Spock's role in, 274
fathers. *See also* men
  in Confucian family system, 52
  neglect through failure to provide
    child support, 160
  ownership of children, 25, 174
  sexual abuse charges and custody
    battles, 206
  as sexual abusers, 171–174
feelings about children. *See* attitudes
  toward children; childism
Feith, Douglas, 211
feminist movement
  alliance with Christian conserva-
    tives on anti-pornography, 209
  clash with Christian conservatism
    over child sexual abuse, 205–206